BOOTS TO LOAFE...
FINDING YOUR NEW TRUE NORTH

TRANSITION, TRANSFORMATION, INTEGRATION

JOHN W. PHILLIPS
Lieutenant Colonel
U.S. Army (Ret)
with Paul Falcone

BOOTS TO LOAFERS

Edited by Karen Pickell

Copyright © 2014 by John W. Phillips

www.bootstoloafers.com
www.linkedin.com/in/ltcphillips

ISBN: 978-1-4960950-5-3

For Melissa, the love of my life;
for her parents, Catherine and Gordon Smith;
and for my parents, Colonel Steve F. Phillips Jr. and
Eileen Phillips.

What Constitutes Success?

He has achieved success who has lived well, laughed often and loved much; who has gained the respect of intelligent men and the love of little children; who has filled his niche and accomplished his task; who has left the world better than he found it, whether by an improved poppy, a perfect poem, or a rescued soul; who has never lacked appreciation of earth's beauty or failed to express it; who has always looked for the best in others and given the best he had; whose life was an inspiration; whose memory a benediction.

—Bessie A. Stanley,
Emporia Gazette, *1905*

It is not necessary to change. Survival is not mandatory.

—W. Edwards Deming

v

ACKNOWLEDGEMENTS

I have had *Boots to Loafers, Finding Your New True North* in my mind for over a decade. As I have observed and experienced the world of business and industry, it has become evident to me that I must share my knowledge and the lessons I have learned to ensure that the next generation is better prepared for life after boots or "outside the gate." It has been a hard fight and I am constantly reminded that the military trained me very well for what I have faced outside the gate. For those who walk in my boot prints, I dedicate this book to you as my effort to help you when the time comes to take that next step and transition out of the military. In my opinion, you are the next Greatest Generation—a generation of young men and women engaged in today's fight for freedom and our American way of life; a generation that has displayed the same determination and drive as all those warriors who have come before them. Many of this generation will return home, hang their uniforms in a closet and put on new uniforms—suits or sport coats and loafers. This book is for them. I will detail how our veterans who have fought the good fight can now find a new "true north" to help guide them through the journey toward their second life, or new normal, outside the gate.

Over the course of the last few years, I have been working during the day and writing at night and on weekends. It has been a true labor of love. As I started to gather my thoughts, I immediately turned to my dear friend Dawn Halfaker. Dawn epitomizes what *Boots* is all about. Her personal sacrifice, dedication to duty, and love of country, along with the hard work she had to go through to get where she is today, make her a truly amazing woman. Also along this journey, I have reconnected with a long lost cousin of mine, Reid Baker, who encouraged me from the beginning of this project.

Although pulling together this manuscript has been one of the toughest things I have done, I could not have completed it without the help of my friend Paul Falcone. Paul is *the* consummate human resources professional and is the subject-matter expert on those topics. Without Paul and his keen attention to detail, I'm not sure this book would have been published. Thank you, Paul.

Special thanks to my editor, Karen Pickell. Her professionalism, enthusiasm, and dedication to this book were second to none. She pulled things out of me that I never knew were there and made this book tell a story while educating the reader along the way. She is a woman with a keen eye and a true gift for words and the knowledge of how to write.

To Peter Overton, thanks for your advice and counsel and strong words on faith. To Jason Falla, thank you for the philosophy of Redback One and explaining the crossroads a transitioning soldier will confront in his or her journey outside the gate.

A special thank you to the folks at ImageMark and specifically Walter Payne who made *Boots* sparkle and really look great.

To my best friends Steve F. Phillips III, Jim G. Lilly, Jerry W. Boyette, and Brent Owens: your enthusiasm, constant encouragement, and always being relentless—just like our many camping trips over the last almost four decades—was appreciated.

To all the soldiers in my life, thank you for molding me into the leader I have become and, more importantly, allowing me to lead you.

To my loving wife, Melissa, thank you for your love, faith, patience, and understanding of this old soldier through the journey of pulling together *Boots*.

To my dad, the Colonel, for teaching me values and always choosing the harder right. And to my mom, for her personal encouragement and love. I miss you both so dearly.

Many have asked me about the source of my drive. Why am I so persistent in a cause or for a particular initiative? The only possible explanation is where I come from. I descend from a long line of soldiers and sailors who served this country dating back to its beginnings. I suspect my military ancestry reaches back to Ireland or Scotland, though I have no proof of that (yet). My heritage comes from William A. Harper, a Scotch Irishman, who traveled from Belfast, Ireland, to Charleston, South Carolina, on the ship Earl of Donegal in the mid-1700s. He and his family settled on land in Lancaster County, South Carolina, given to them by the King of England. To this day, there are still descendants of William living on the same plots of land in and around Lancaster. Since that time, many of his descendants have fought in battles including the Indian Wars, the Revolutionary War, the War of 1812, the Mexican War, the Civil War, World Wars I and II, and, in the present day, wars in Iraq and Afghanistan. Two such descendants of note were Richard Hilton, who fought in the Indian Wars, and General James Blair, a general in the South Carolina militia who was later elected to the United States Congress. My most recent relatives who served our country include David Phillips, my uncle, who served in the US Navy during World War II; Marion Phillips Scherer, my aunt, who served as a US Navy nurse and was stationed at Walter Reed Hospital and Panama during World War II; Charles Phillips, another uncle, who served in the US Air Force; and Steve F. Phillips Jr., my father, who served as an officer in the US Army Infantry for thirty years and who fought in World War II and the Vietnam War. The tradition lives on with the newest addition, my nephew Steve F. Phillips IV, who currently serves in the US Naval Reserve. My family has established a proud history of service and love of liberty, which is now simply a part of our DNA. I am deeply grateful for my family's love of our country and continue to be inspired to pay it forward to all those who love this country as we do!

Today, I stand ready, willing, and able to talk to any military member or veteran about transitioning, transforming, and integrating into the private sector, where the quest for a new true north begins.

Table of Contents

FOREWORD BY DAWN HALFAKER xiii

INTRODUCTION xviii

The BTL Dirty Dozen xxii

   Boots to Loafers® Rules to Live By xxii

Faith—My Own xxiii

TRANSITION 1

  1. SETTING EXPECTATIONS 3

    Military Transition Assistance 4

    Education 6

  2. PREPARING FOR YOUR NEXT MISSION: THE JOB SEARCH 7

    Doing Your Homework 8

     Identifying the Dominant and Growth-Oriented Industries 8

     Tapping into the Hidden Job Market 12

     Discovering Company Culture 18

    Constructing Your Resume 20

     Skills and Abilities 21

     Translating Military Jargon and Terminology

       into Private Sector Equivalencies 22

     What to Include and Exclude 24

     Format and Content 25

     Successful Military Resume Samples 35

    Cover Letters 39

     Cover Letter Sample 40

    The New Millennium Job Search 45

     Job Boards 46

     Social Media 47

    Putting It All Together 50

  3. YOU GOT THE INTERVIEW! NOW WHAT? 52

    Prep Work: Do Your Research 53

     Publicly Traded Company Research Websites 55

     Privately Held, Small Company Research Websites 55

     Nonprofit Research Websites 56

     Company-Culture Websites 56

Phone Screens 57

Courtesy and Exploratory Interviews 60

Dress for Success 62

   Men's Standard Dress 62

   Women's Standard Dress 64

   Tattoos, Piercings, and Other Forms of Body Art 65

What to Take with You 66

   The Two-Minute Drill 67

Understand Your Interviewer 68

   What Interviewers Are Looking For 69

   Typical Interview Questions 72

   Speech, Language, and Appropriate Use of Vocabulary 75

   Behavioral Style Interviews 76

   Targeted Selection and Competencies 78

   What Questions Should You Ask? 87

Post-Interview Follow-Up 91

TRANSFORMATION **95**

4. WHAT IS REBRANDING? 97

Rebranding Defined 99

Communication: From Military Language to Civilian Equivalent 101

Status and Position 108

Stereotypes and Diversity 111

5. ADJUSTMENTS IN WORK AND HOME LIFE 114

Private-Sector Work Life 114

   Attention to Detail 114

   Managing Employees 115

   Social Events 116

   Soft Skills 116

   Job Duties 117

   Availability 117

   Conduct 118

   Personal Life 118

Home Life 119

Work and Home Life Balance 122

Finishing Touches 124

INTEGRATION. **125**

6. LIFE OUTSIDE THE GATE. 127

7. NEGOTIATING YOUR JOB OFFER 127

   Exempt vs. Nonexempt 134

   Market Base Pay and Incentive Pay. 135

8. BENEFITS 137

   Medical Plan Options 137

   Defined-Benefit, or Traditional, Pension Plans 143

   Defined-Contribution, or 401(k), Plans 144

     Traditional vs. Roth 401(k) Plans and IRAs. 146

     The Company Match: Your Key Incentive for Investing. 147

     Calculating Your 401(k) Contribution 148

   Individual Retirement Plans for the Self-Employed 151

     SEP-IRAs 151

     SIMPLE IRAs and Keogh Plans 152

   Personal Time Off (PTO) 154

     Holidays 154

     Vacation 155

     Sick Leave. 155

   Disability Insurance 156

     Short-Term Disability (STD) 156

     Long-Term Disability (LTD) 157

   Life Insurance. 157

     Basic Life Insurance 157

     Supplemental Life and AD&D Insurance 158

   The Value of Fringe Benefits. 158

9. SETTING THE CONDITIONS FOR SUCCESS 159

   Training 161

   Employee Handbooks, Policy and

     Procedure Manuals, and Codes of Business Conduct. 163

10. LEADING IN LOAFERS 165

   Defensive Strategy: Employment Law in the Private Sector 165

     Employment at Will vs. Discharge for Just Cause 165

     Enlisting the Services and Support of HR 167

BOOTS TO LOAFERS

Performance vs. Conduct: A Critical Distinction 167
Conducting Performance Reviews and Managing Office Politics 170
Effective Leadership: Your Best Offense 175
People—the Greatest Asset 176
Redefining Leadership 177
JP's Rules of Engagement 183
Motivation and Employee Engagement 186
Ethics 193
11. THE FINAL TURN: TAKE THE HARDER RIGHT 195
APPENDIX 1: BUSINESS TERMINOLOGY
AND ACRONYMS 199
APPENDIX 2: SAMPLE DOCUMENTS 203
Cover Letter 203
Resume: US Army Officer 204
Resume: US Navy Officer 205
Resume: Junior-Career Level 206
Thank You Note 207
APPENDIX 3: HELPFUL WEBSITES 208
Business Publications and Resources 208
Corporate Culture 208
Education and Training 208
Job Search—Specialty 209
Job Search—Veteran Specific 209
Resume Writing (including Cover Letters and Thank You Letters) 210
Specialty Recruiters 210
Veterans Services 210
NOTES 211
AUTHOR BIOGRAPHIES 214

FOREWORD

by Dawn Halfaker
President and CEO, Halfaker and Associates, LLC

Wounded warriors are all too familiar with the hard fact that we must react to life events that are unplanned and unwanted. For me, the death of my dream as an army officer ultimately led me to realize my destiny in the business world. Regaining my sense of purpose by finding meaningful employment has been paramount throughout my healing process. It is my goal here to share some insights learned during my personal journey from combat to the boardroom so that I may help remove some of the barriers that prevent my fellow veterans from finding employment along their path to recovery and reintegration.

My unexpected journey began in the early morning hours of June 19, 2004, when my dreams of a career as a US Army military police officer ended after I suffered life-threatening injuries in Baquba, Iraq, during a combat patrol. A rocket-propelled grenade pierced the front of my vehicle, drilled through my right shoulder, and exploded next to my head. I can still vividly remember being blinded by the flash, deafened by the sound, choked up by the smoke and smells, and incapacitated by the pain. This was just the beginning—my real journey and fight began in earnest roughly two weeks after my injury, when I awoke from a medically induced coma at Walter Reed Army Medical Center in Washington, DC.

Like many wounded warriors, I was extremely lucky to be alive. However, waking up to the reality of having lost my entire dominant, right arm, amongst other critical injuries, was only the first in a succession of losses. My whole life had changed. I was devastated and I struggled to accept and come to terms with my new reality. Reaffirming the strength of the military community, the turning point of my recovery came after I witnessed the positive attitude and indestructible will of my fellow wounded warriors at Walter Reed. They quickly reassured me that a successful recovery took time, courage, and determination.

Embraced by my family, friends, and support network at Walter Reed, I slowly accepted my new reality by focusing on what I could still do, and I began to forge a new path for myself. Like many transitioning veterans, I had joined the military right after high school and now I struggled to find my identity outside of the military. I was giving up my career, my sense of purpose, and my military community of support. Just sitting down to craft my resume was difficult, as the military jargon that was so ingrained in my speech would not make sense to most human resources (HR) professionals. Furthermore, how would I communicate the relevancy of the specialized training I received in the military or the leadership skills I developed during combat to someone who was only familiar with civilian education credentials? It became increasingly obvious that, with only 1% of Americans serving in the military, communicating what I could offer to the 99% that I was about to join would be a challenge.

Despite the progress I had made since I awoke from my medically induced coma, my future was riddled with uncertainties and self-doubt. Since I had obvious wounds from the war, would employers simply view me as damaged goods? The media highlighted stories of veterans coming back from war with serious post-traumatic stress disorder (PTSD) and anger issues. Would employers view me as a dangerous liability? Would I be able to perform to the level expected while I was still struggling to adapt to new ways of accomplishing basic tasks with my left arm? Furthermore, if I left the Washington, DC, area, would I be able to receive the supportive care I was accustomed to at Walter Reed?

At times, the uncertainties clouding my future were overwhelming. However, I was determined to find the right opportunity to stay a part of the fight. I liked the opportunities, community, and familiarity of DC, so I decided to stay. I found mentors who helped me draft a powerful resume, but as I began interviewing for jobs, nothing seemed to be the right fit. I could not relate to the corporate culture; I perceived a lack of urgency and purpose. Although I was only twenty-six years old at the time, I previously held a job in which I was responsible for the lives of almost thirty soldiers and had the opportunity to make a difference by training Iraq's future police force. It was more than just a job; it was a lifestyle and network of support. Furthermore, the supportiveness of the military community had become my way of life and recently had propelled my recovery. I struggled deeply with the thought of leaving my military family. I was determined to use my recent experience, find a way to feel like I was continuing my service, and surround myself with colleagues who felt the same way. I wanted to continue to serve.

They say necessity breeds innovation. Due to my need and desire to continue to be part of the fight, I decided to forge my own path and start my own company. Today, after seven years in business, Halfaker and Associates, LLC employs over 170 people, 45% of whom are veterans. My proudest moments continue to be the opportunities I have to hire veterans to join my team. Most importantly, my business has served as a vehicle for me to promote issues that I am passionate about, such as helping wounded warriors and transitioning veterans.

Today, I am lucky to be a part of many organizations that work to promote veteran employment and entrepreneurship and that advocate on behalf of wounded warriors. Reflecting on my journey and hearing the struggles of fellow veterans have reaffirmed my belief that finding meaningful employment is a powerful aspect of a transitioning veteran's journey. Many transitioning veterans struggle in finding fulfilling employment and would benefit from the guidance of support organizations, outreach, and a supportive company culture.

After nearly a decade of war, many organizations have been created to ensure veterans and wounded warriors coming out of the military are equipped to find jobs and develop skills to transition their careers. The government has established several programs, including the Post-9/11 GI Bill and the Vocational Rehabilitation and Employment (VR&E) Program, that help veterans and wounded warriors find employment by funding advanced training and education. Some additional resources available include the Warriors to Work, Transition Training Academy, and TRACK programs, offered by the Wounded Warrior Project; and America's Heroes at Work, offered by the US Department of Labor. These programs are vital in reassuring veterans that they are not alone on this journey and helping them navigate the vast number of resources available. Many support organizations such as the Wounded Warrior Project rely on the generosity of sponsors to continue their services and always welcome tax-deductible donations.

Additionally, outreach to veterans at the corporate level is an important aspect of helping them find gainful and meaningful employment. Most civilians cannot comprehend following a career path that is paved for them; military members similarly struggle with the unstructured options of the civilian sector. After previously having little input into which jobs they were assigned, military members can become overwhelmed by the options presented in the civilian sector and have little experience understanding how their skills transfer or where to look for jobs they would be successful in. It is helpful to have recruiters on board who are familiar with military jargon and can assist transitioning veterans in matching their expertise with the right employment opportunity. Furthermore, there are many military-specific online resume databases available, such as Military.com/veteran-jobs, HireVeterans.com, and MilitaryHire. com. It is also useful to partner with specialty recruitment companies such as Bradley-Morris, Lucas Group, and Orion International. HR departments could consider maximizing established employee networks through various mediums including online social media tools. Finally, there are many military specific career fairs, several of which offer onsite counseling services to help veterans sort through career options. Recently, the US Chamber of Commerce launched a robust initiative to host four hundred job fairs in 2012 to help match veterans with employers.

Lastly, the military is built for support, and many veterans feel lost in the typical corporate structure with its nine-to-five civilian mentality. Their jobs in the military were much more than an occupation; their jobs defined them. Their coworkers were teammates and friends with whom they shared the unique bond of having gone to combat together. This bond is obviously difficult to recreate, however corporations can strive to maintain a culture akin to the military's support network by uniting their employees through meaningful work and community service. Mike Bradley, a program manager at Halfaker, did a great job defining this need when interviewed about his transition: "I am an example of a transitioning service member who was given the opportunity to work for a small business. I don't feel like I'm just a number; my company knows who I am—what I can accomplish—and makes me feel important. As a transitioning wounded warrior, I wanted to find a company that closely mirrored that of the military. In the army, the army values were ingrained in me daily, and I wanted to find a company that held itself to those same core values."

During the past seven years, I have found at times that business is another form of combat; the uniforms are just a bit different. Veterans bring with them invaluable and transferable skills they developed on the battlefield: doing more with less, turning adversity into opportunity, and letting nothing stop them or stand in their way—traits that will help corporations succeed in today's challenging economy. Many wounded warriors have sustained severe physical injuries—amputations, burns, spinal cord injuries, loss of vision, and more—but many more suffer from invisible wounds that have taken a very real toll. Having a meaningful job in a supportive work environment is so important for the well-being of our wounded warriors and veterans. I encourage my fellow business partners to establish systems and policies to remove some of the barriers that all too often prevent veterans from finding employment during their path to recovery and reintegration. Let's all take the next step and contribute either time or money to nonprofits that support transitioning service members; establish protocol for HR teams to provide outreach to veterans; and create supportive company cultures. I can't think of a better way to strengthen your corporate team and pay it forward to those who have given so much for our nation.

Boots to Loafers, Finding Your New True North is the perfect tool for any soldier transitioning from a role in the military to one in the private sector. My friend, John Phillips, wore the boots for over twenty years and successfully navigated his way outside the gate, taking note of his experiences along the way and applying them. He has written a well-researched guide with many resources to help those stepping out of their boots and into their loafers.

INTRODUCTION

From the first day you set foot into boot camp, no matter what service you have been in, until the final days of predeployment training exercises or redeployment, you are taught to always pay attention to every detail in every situation. Our military knows how to turn you on and get you fired up for a mission. Transitioning out of boots will require the same focus on details and the energy to get fired up for your next mission—finding a job.

Every service member will experience three phases as he moves from a military career to a life outside the gate: transition, transformation, and integration. The Merriam-Webster Online Dictionary defines these three words as follows:

> **transition:** *Passage from one state, stage, subject, or place to another.*

> **transformation:** *A complete or major change in someone's or something's appearance, form, etc.*

> **integration:** *The process of making (a person or group) part of a larger group or organization.*

The foundation of *Boots to Loafers* is built upon these three concepts. They provide the structure for the advice and guidelines I want to convey to you. You may experience each of these to different degrees depending on your wishes, circumstances, goals, and surrounding environment. These three stages will vary from individual to individual, and they will be shaped by one's attitude and inner strength as well as his ability to manage the hurdles of life.

Each word embraces ideas such as passing from one state to another, evolving from one form to another, and making a part of something. *Boots* considers the changes that occur in a service member's life as she leaves the service. The stages outlined in the book are three unique processes that encompass the journey in transitioning from the military to the private sector, or what I like to call "outside the gate." A process by definition is a series of steps or actions taken to reach a goal and is often continuous until that goal is achieved. The three processes discussed in *Boots* overlap each other. There is no clean break between them.

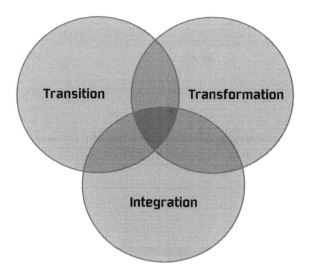

Fig. 1

Let me explain the journey in the simplest terms: At some point you decide it is time to leave the military—the *Transition* process. Leaving the service of your country requires you to reinvent or rebrand yourself in many ways—the *Transformation* process. Lastly, you have to assimilate back into the civilian world, or private sector—the *Integration* process. The journey does not magically begin on the day that a soldier leaves the military. It begins sometime prior to leaving the service as you prepare for life outside the gate. Ideally, at least a year of preparation is recommended to consider all the appropriate next steps. You will learn why through the pages ahead. It has been my experience that the three processes of this journey never end. You will find yourself continuing to transition and transform as you grow your career in the private sector. Every new opportunity in your career, every change in your personal life may require you to reboot these processes in order to reach a new goal. Speaking from experience, this especially holds true for veterans who have retired after a long military career. Do yourself a favor and accept the fact that you have to change as the world around you continues to change.

Boots was written primarily for two distinct groups: those still on active duty who will leave the military through discharge or retirement, and veterans who are actively pursuing employment and need some structure in their job search. To help me compile all the necessary content in *Boots* related to the human resources (HR) aspect of what you will need to do during your transition and integration, I have enlisted Paul Falcone, a HR executive in Los Angeles who has held senior-level positions with Nickelodeon, Paramount Pictures, and Time Warner. He is the author of nine books, four of which were ranked on the prestigious "Great 8 of 2011" and "Great 8 of 2012" bestseller listings by the Society for Human Resource Management (SHRM). A long-term contributor to HR Magazine, Paul is an instructor in the UCLA Extension School of Business and Management as well as a top-rated presenter at the SHRM national conference. As you use this guide to help you find your new true north, Paul will walk you through the job search preparation you will need to complete and speak to you about resume building, interviewing techniques, and one of the most important things you need to understand about your civilian job—benefits. Although Paul never served in the military, he brings a level of knowledge and expertise that will better prepare you when the time comes to interview, negotiate an offer, and then wade your way through the list of benefit options that more than likely are very foreign to you. Through the combination of Paul and myself weighing in with our respective expertise, you will be provided with all the tools you will need to be better prepared for this next mission.

To settle your anxiety a bit, let me level with you. All the training, the deployments, and the difficult days when life just sucked at God-knows-where you were deployed in the world will pay dividends when you use this fairly simple approach to transition, transform, and integrate into your next phase of life after the military. Most of you reading *Boots* have dealt with more complex and life-threatening crises, whether in training or under hostile fire, than you will encounter in the next phase of your life outside the gate. Many times in my civilian career, I have come across a crisis, or what others perceived as a crisis, that did not compare to the catastrophes I experienced while in uniform. I suspect that will not be different for any of you. For example, no one has yelled at me, shot at me, or tried to blow me up since I left the military. Instead, someone has simply spent too much money and is over budget, or someone has not been served the kind of soup he expected in the company cafeteria—an instant crisis for some in the private sector. In the private sector, veterans will take in stride these perceived "crises" and often offer a solution to mitigate a situation long before it truly becomes anything more than an inconvenience.

The same training and experience that helped you to thrive in the military world of ambiguity will bring success outside the gate. This book provides the support you need to rise to the occasion and leverage what you've learned in uniform. Remember, you know more than you think you do.

Boots is largely based on my experience in a multinational consumer-goods company. My company certainly did not select and hire me because of my vast experience and skills as a field artillery officer, but rather as a result of my knowledge, skills, and ability to help grow the profits of the company as a financial controller. All the projectiles my units sent downrange, the number of deployments I made, the number of ribbons and medals on my chest, or the rank I attained were not the focus nor the determining factor in my landing a job. A prospective employer will hire a veteran based on the competencies he brings to the dance, which contribute to the success of the company. It is that simple. If the veteran job seeker makes it to an interview, he is qualified and has beaten the odds. After landing a job, the benefits of previous military experience will soon surface. Often, the veteran's superior will ask him to tackle problems that will directly relate to experiences similar to those encountered while he was in uniform. In a previous job, I encountered an issue regarding obsolete and low-demand spare, repair parts in our manufacturing plants, and the question of how the company should solve the problem arose. Lo and behold, twenty-five years ago I had been a field-artillery-battalion motor officer and had dealt with the very same issue. As a finance guy, I had not thought about this problem for years when suddenly, it landed on my desk. You never know when a challenge will present itself wrapped in a different scenario but requiring the same skills you needed in boots.

While reading *Boots*, reflect on your days in uniform and remember how you used experiences, knowledge, skills, and abilities to manage many jobs you were never trained to do yet successfully completed. What the military does best is to bring together people with diverse backgrounds and talents, and meld them into one unit through effective leadership. Be proud of that fact, as it is a rare accomplishment in the private sector.

Once in the civilian job, you must continue to take care of those who bust their butts for you in the same way you took care of fellow soldiers, sailors, airmen, or marines. Never forget where you came from. Proudly, you should remember that you are part of the other 1% who raised their right hands and swore to defend this great country. In my opinion, you are the real 1%. You were willing to take a bullet for your previous employer—the military; this quality makes you a rare breed, a minority in the private sector. Consequently, you should be proud and always choose "the harder right," as my father used to tell me, meaning make the choice to take the less traveled, harder road instead of the easy way. One of the best philosophies I have found that explains the harder right is from Jason Falla, Director of Training at Redback One Combat Training Systems:

> Remember that there are two paths in life. One leads to mediocrity and the other to excellence.

> The path to mediocrity is flat and straight. The road is smooth, tasks are easy and effortless and you will meet mediocrity with time to spare.

> The path to excellence is steep and arduous, inordinately lengthy, forcing pilgrims to stumble and fall on every length of the journey.

> Which path will you take? [1]

Always remember, you know more than you think you do. Happy hunting. HOOAH!

The BTL Dirty Dozen

As I began to pull together *Boots to Loafers* (BTL), I started jotting down on paper some of the small things I have encountered over the years. These small things, if not dealt with, can turn into big things that drag you down and divert you from what you are supposed to be focusing on—finding a job. That said, I've compiled a list that I affectionately have named The BTL Dirty Dozen (*The Dirty Dozen* being my all-time favorite movie). If nothing else, refer to this list when you have doubt, feel anxious, or just need a small word of encouragement.

Boots to Loafers® Rules to Live By:

1. **Faith.** Always keep it and never lose it. Be anxious for nothing, but in everything by prayer and supplication with thanksgiving let your requests be made known to God.
2. **Talent.** You bring world-class leadership to the table. Capitalize on that fact. You know more than you think you do!
3. **Steadfastness.** When things get tough, remain calm and stay focused just as you were trained to do. Your peers and senior leaders will be amazed at how unshakable you are under their version of a stressful situation.

4. **Confidence.** Never underestimate yourself. Your work ethic and dedication to what you do will come through in the end.

5. **Process.** Being a staff officer or non-commissioned officer will pay very big dividends for you in the private sector.

6. **Communications.** Learn the language of the private sector. There will be a language barrier—don't fight it. Adapt to it and transform yourself.

7. **Patience.** The private sector seems to have a lot more gray area. Don't be discouraged; it takes some getting used to, and you will succeed.

8. **Change.** From "we" to "I." It is all about you and what you can do for the bottom line. Start your transition early, transform yourself, and then integrate into your new world, your new normal.

9. **Success.** Find Your New True North. Always have a personal growth plan, a contingency plan and an exit strategy in your back pocket.

10. **Networking.** Can't say enough about it. Learn as much as you can about finance, marketing, sales, operations, and supply chain. Become a more valued contributor to your new team and the company.

11. **Ambiguity.** The stage we dance on in uniform! The fog of war, haziness of reality, the potential for misreads, and the mixed meanings of conditions; cause-and-effect confusion—the stage veterans will excel and shine on. Cooler heads always prevail.

12. **Dress.** It may seem silly to some: suits, sport coats, and dress clothes in general—expensive! Not only is it about "what do I need to wear," but also, "what do I need to buy." Look out and don't go crazy or you'll go broke. Watch for sales!

Faith—My Own

Faith

> *When you walk to the edge of all the light you have*
> *And take that first step into the darkness of the unknown,*
> *You must believe one of two things will happen:*
>
> > *There will be something solid for you to stand upon*
> > *or, you will be taught how to fly.*
>
> (© 1976 by Patrick Overton. Used by permission of the author.)

As you may have noticed, faith is number one on my Dirty Dozen list. Without it, through my transition, transformation, and integration into the private sector I would have been lost. As I took this step into "the darkness of the unknown" with *Boots*, I had no fear. My strong desire to extend my hand to those in uniform and my faith in the outcome of this book became my compass. This project defines faith because its success is not in my hands, but within each service member or veteran who reads it. I proceed at this point on faith alone—faith that has eluded me for more than three decades but is now a daily work in progress in my life. As I rebuild the foundation of my faith to weather the storms of life, it is my hope that *Boots* might guide you to a safe harbor outside the gate. The lessons learned from my mistakes and successes, along with my faith that has sheltered me, can certainly teach you to fly.

The lessons learned from my mistakes and successes, along with my faith that has sheltered me, can certainly teach you to fly.

Faith in God as a way of life was fostered by both of my parents. Between the two, however, I believe my father was the one who was more in touch with his faith. I attribute this to his rural South Carolina upbringing. My father was a career army officer with a family in constant motion. We called many countries home and we visited a selection of different churches through the years. Church on Sunday was a Phillips ritual. Of course, all the major Christian holidays were also major church events for our family: Easter, Christmas, etc. Easter clothes were designed and sewn by my mother. As I look back on those days, I cherish the time we spent together as a family seeking spiritual renewal and guidance. In 1964, my father was a battalion commander who had his own chapel and chaplain, and at that time, attending church on Sunday was mandatory for all his officers and their spouses. Those requirements began to die out early in my military career, and I suspect they are completely gone now. The army was certainly different back then.

Although I was raised a Presbyterian, I am now a Southern Baptist and belong to a church in Marietta, Georgia. The congregation is a wonderful mix of young and mature members, many of whom are veterans dating back to World War II. The church has recruited me to work on their annual Veterans Day event, which draws more than five hundred church members, families, and dignitaries. I consider it an honor to lead this event.

In retrospect, God's plan for me was to be a soldier. I had that ambition at a very young age, so when the opportunity came, I jumped at the chance. Anyone who knows me knows that I am a soldier to the bone. Although my journey through life has had its ups and downs, I have had a great ride and look forward to the journey ahead. The key aspect missing from my life, though, was dedication to my beliefs, my faith, and God. My purpose now is to seek understanding and to continue to serve God as he sees fit. My vision includes trying to help other veterans through the lessons I've learned and observations I present here in *Boots*. My advice is to cultivate one's faith. When situations are difficult and you encounter rejection, you should take time, reflect, and pray. When a veteran tries to land that one perfect job, this passage in his hip pocket will lift him:

> *Rejoice in the Lord always. I will say it again: Rejoice! Let your gentleness be evident to all. The Lord is near. Do not be anxious about anything, but in every situation, by prayer and petition, with thanksgiving, present your requests to God. And the peace of God, which transcends all understanding, will guard your hearts and your minds in Christ Jesus.*

> *(Phil. 4:4-7 [New International Version])*

Keep the faith brothers and sisters. It will not fail you.

TRANSITION

The world is round and the place which may seem
like the end may also be the beginning.
—Ivy Baker Priest

transition: Passage from one state, stage, subject, or place to another.

1. SETTING EXPECTATIONS

Before we dive into this, first things first. I'd like to make sure I set your expectations when it comes to the journey you are about to embark on—the job hunt. Here are some eye opening figures compiled by Human Resources expert Dr. John Sullivan[2] about what kind of fight you are about to head into:

- On average, 250 resumes are received for each corporate job opening.
- The first resume is received within 200 seconds after a position is posted.
- 427,000 resumes are posted on Monster.com every week.
- On average, 1,000 individuals will see a single job post, 200 will begin the application process, and 100 will complete the application. Of those 100 resumes, 75 will be screened out by either the automated system or a recruiter, leaving only 25 resumes to be seen by the hiring manager. Based on these resumes, 4 to 6 candidates will be invited for an interview; 1 to 3 of these individuals will be invited back for a final interview; only 1 person will be offered that job; and 80% of those receiving an offer will accept it.
- The average recruiter spends a mere six seconds reviewing a resume.
- Recruiters look at four areas on a resume: job titles, companies you worked at, start/end dates, and education.
- Only 17% of recruiters bother to read cover letters.
- 61% of recruiters will automatically dismiss a resume because it contains typos.
- 43% of hiring managers will disqualify a candidate because of spelling errors on a resume.
- An unprofessional email address will get a resume rejected 76% of the time.
- A resume format that is not scannable can cut your odds of being invited for an interview by 60%.
- Over 50% of applicants for a typical job fail to meet the basic qualifications for that job.
- Unless you have spent time customizing your resume for a specific job, when an electronic keyword search is done chances are against you being selected to proceed.

Remember, a resume only gets you an interview. There is no such thing as the perfect resume. Networking is extremely important; having a strong network that expands into various companies and especially the company you want to work for is significant. In many cases, who you know becomes a key to opening the first door to a job interview. Once you've gotten in the door, it is all up to you to sell yourself. Don't get discouraged. Do your homework and be ready.

. . . occupational licensing requirements in areas such as healthcare to determine how military training, education, and experience can be applied toward earning these types of licenses.

Use the statistics above as a motivator. Many states are stepping up their campaign to help veterans get jobs. Several state legislatures are taking a hard look at occupational licensing requirements in areas such as healthcare to determine how military training, education, and experience can be applied toward earning these types of licenses. Typically in order to qualify for such a license, there are four elements considered: formal education, work experience, scores on the licensing exam, and basic qualifications such as citizenship and residency. As of this writing, thirty-four states have allowed military training, education, and experience count toward these occupational licenses. On another front, the US Department of Labor estimates that by the year 2020, there will be significant job growth in the healthcare industry. The estimates are as high as 1.2 million registered nurses and nearly 400,000 licensed practical nurses. Some states are looking specifically for emergency medical technicians. Additionally, it is estimated there will be a need for more than 300,000 truck drivers. Many states have created programs such as Troops to Trucks specifically to target transitioning military to become commercial truck drivers[3].

The reality is that corporate America is realizing the incredible and extraordinary talents, leadership skills, and problem solving capabilities of our veterans. Many corporations are taking notice and seeking the veteran to become part of the team. The wake up call has sounded and many have heard it.

Military Transition Assistance

Simply throwing together a resume and relying on an impressive military record will not cut it in today's corporate environment. In the following pages, I offer points and insights that are rarely covered in transition assistance classes. My intent is to fill the gaps from all of the transition and outplacement sessions you may have gone through or are getting ready to go through. This is not rocket science, however, it does require your full attention if you want to ultimately get an interview and land a job.

Everyone who leaves the military, from first termers to career service members (officers, warrant officers, and non-commissioned officers), needs to know how to prepare for a whole new world outside the gate. Some of the realities a veteran will encounter in the civilian world may be very disturbing or even traumatic, leaving you angry and ready to give up. Your rank, status, and accomplishments in the military will not impress everyone in the private sector. Awards and decorations all the way up your left breast pocket mean very little on the outside. A hiring manager cares only about the potential employee's impact on the success of her organization. You must take time to reflect upon previous training in the military and apply these skills to your marketability in the private sector. You are making a transition to the private sector, not rehashing your military career or telling war stories. There's a time and a place for all of that, but this ain't it!

Outside the gate, the returning service member will compete with recent college graduates, many of whom have advanced degrees but little or no experience. You will vie for jobs against seasoned managers who have far more experience. I say, so what. I'm here to help stack the deck in your favor. Indeed, veterans offer the private sector some very valuable commodities: loyalty, strong values, discipline, honed leadership skills, adaptability, organization, and diversity, to name a few. Even so, most military transition programs fall way short in letting veterans know just how marketable their abilities and skills truly are.

Here is a fact: most hiring managers, recruiters, and talent managers who have not served in the military know very little about the military culture. Don't allow this to be an obstacle. Use it as an opportunity to educate. The hiring manager or recruiter may not recognize the core set of skills you acquired in the military unless you spell it out for him. You understand, for example, the importance of functioning as part of a team because you have lived and breathed that concept. The ability to adapt instantly to a variety of shifting situations is second nature to a former service member. Most importantly, you know and understand the chain of command—yes, the same ladder exists outside the gate. Often, a service member's reasoning and strong analytical skills have been honed on the battlefield. If that's the case for you, it is why you are ready and willing to take personal responsibility for performance and results. Even if combat was not part of your duty, you received the training to prepare you for such. Your ability to gather as much data and information as possible to make quick, sound decisions is now a natural response. If a potential employer needs someone who can lead from the front, who is accountable and reliable, and who can nurture and foster teamwork, the veteran is the perfect candidate for the job. As I stated earlier, it is up to you to ensure that a potential employer recognizes your skills and potential.

Education

Learning is a treasure that will follow its owner everywhere.

—*Chinese Proverb*

It is often said that there is one thing nobody can take away from you—your education. You should cherish it, cultivate it, and apply it at all times. The military invests much time and money into the professional development of its service members. The ability for you to simply unplug and attend training will be rare, if not nonexistent, outside the gate. It is unheard of to take a year (or more) off from an organization for training and professional education as the military does for such things as the Command and General Staff College, US Army War College, etc. As I see it from my foxhole, the US Armed Forces are world-class at ensuring that their "employees" receive the absolute best training and development possible. The consequences of not knowing your job are dire. We take care of each other.

Most civilian companies, on the other hand, view training and professional development as business expenses rather than as investments in the employees. Often, companies give lip service to development opportunities but fall far short in delivering. My experience has been that companies rely on the employee to learn 70% on the job, 20% online, and only 10% in actual classroom instruction. My personal stance is that this formula does not work to develop the future leaders of a company. It is rare for an employee to have the good fortune of working for a manager who takes a personal interest in her professional development and who earmarks resources (time and money) to train people. Sometimes training and development possibilities turn into a negotiation between a manager and the employee during a performance review.

My suggestion for a transitioning service member is to leverage all the educational opportunities that a new employer provides. Take advantage of internal

US Armed Forces are world-class at ensuring that their "employees" receive the absolute best training and development possible.

or external development courses to increase your knowledge of sales, operations, manufacturing, finance, and other fields of interest; investigate and participate in professional development organizations with which your company has partnered. Capitalize on these organizations and make them part of your professional development plan during an annual performance review. Inquire about any free online training and higher educational opportunities that companies sponsor.

Every veteran should take full advantage of education offered through the GI Bill; this is one of a service member's most beneficial opportunities. My undergraduate degree was funded by the GI Bill and helped me obtain a great career in a Fortune 50 company. Eighty percent of my education costs were paid by the GI Bill. You can find all the details about GI Bill benefits, including on-the-job training and apprenticeships, at www.GIBill.va.gov. If you are still in uniform and preparing to "punch out," or exit, you should take full advantage of the tuition assistance offered. What a deal! Also, if pursuing an undergraduate degree while in service, at least complete all the basic classes so that upon your discharge or retirement, you can immediately enroll in the core courses needed to complete your degree. A word of caution: all credits may not transfer to another institution. Do your homework.

If you began military service without a high school diploma or GED, you must get it now. It is a must-have for any opportunity in the private sector. Your education will open doors that would otherwise remain closed—that is a fact!

An additional word of advice on this topic: Never leave an opportunity for higher education or additional training on the table. Outside the gate, it becomes much more difficult to find the time and resources to take advantage of some of the opportunities you have while in the military. Remember, you will compete with others who have taken advantage of educational opportunities. You are, however, America's treasure, so don't sell yourself short. Become a life-long learner and add to that treasure chest every chance you get.

2. PREPARING FOR YOUR NEXT MISSION: THE JOB SEARCH

Before we begin, I must offer a complete disclaimer: I am not a human resources professional. I know enough to be dangerous; therefore, as I explained in the Introduction, I have enlisted the aid of my friend Paul Falcone, a HR executive and workforce development professional, to provide his personal experience and knowledge of human resources and workforce development practices throughout this chapter. And since Paul does not have prior military experience, I offer my take on searching for a job as well.

... refer back to these sections as you start to build your personal portfolio ..

Let's talk about the major components that will prepare you through your transition and transformation journey. There is a lot of information here, and it will take some time on your part to truly digest it and to put together all of the pieces. I urge you to refer back to these sections as you start to build your personal portfolio of experiences and begin the process of transitioning out of your boots and into loafers.

Doing Your Homework

Identifying the Dominant and Growth-Oriented Industries

Never before has the industry that you select to work in played such a critical role in your long-term career trajectory. While you have been serving our country, globalization and technology have been wreaking havoc on certain long-established and traditional industries, while creating tons of new opportunities in other, newer industries. An example would be the US Postal Service, which is in decline while the electronic mail industry is growing at a record pace. For another example, look at the healthcare industry. Baby boomers are retiring in the thousands every day and they need healthcare. However, it is getting tougher and tougher to find quality healthcare. This could be an area of opportunity for combat medics or even those without experience who want to move into healthcare because of potential future growth. Time spent on reconnaissance is never wasted, whether checking out a travel route before moving Howitzers or preparing to give a speech on Veterans Day. It is no different when you are researching various industries and potential jobs within these industries. The importance of the industry you choose while transitioning into the private sector is paramount.

The good news is that there is a tool available to help you identify the dominant and growth-oriented industries that will have the greatest demand for new hires with your skill set and interests over the next decade. The Bureau of Labor Statistics' *Occupational Outlook Handbook* projects job growth (a) by the role or title you are pursuing and (b) by industry from 2010 to 2020. As an example to get you started, if you are interested in a career in human resources, public relations, or communications/social media, you can easily determine the projected job growth for these specific titles by industry. Let's go through this step by step:

First. Find the Bureau of Labor Statistics' website at www.bls.gov. Be sure to bookmark this for future reference; it is a fabulous resource, and if you simply know its name, you will be well ahead of 90% of your peers.

Second. Click on the "Occupational Outlook Handbook" link under "Publications" (or you could also access it directly here: http://www.bls.gov/ooh/).

Third. Once you arrive on the Handbook landing page, you will see a list of Occupation Groups in the left margin that include Business and Financial, Community and Social Service, Computer and Information Technology, Healthcare, Legal, Military, and the like. This is where the fun begins and things really start getting interesting.

Fourth. Select your occupational group (field) of interest. Using Business and Financial as an example, clicking on the link brings up a list of occupations including Accountants and Auditors; Human Resources Specialists; and Meeting, Convention, and Event Planners. Clicking on the "Human Resources Specialist" title brings up a quick overview of the field that looks like this:

Summary

Quick Facts: Human Resources Specialists	
2010 Median Pay ❓	$52,690 per year $25.33 per hour
Entry-Level Education ❓	Bachelor's degree
Work Experience in a Related Occupation ❓	None
On-the-job Training ❓	None
Number of Jobs, 2010 ❓	442,200
Job Outlook, 2010-20 ❓	21% (Faster than average)
Employment Change, 2010-20 ❓	90,700

Fig. 2 (Source: http://www.bls.gov/ooh/business-and-financial/human-resources-specialists.htm)

Keep in mind that the average position in corporate America will grow somewhere between 12% and 13% over the next ten years, or roughly 1% per year. The fact that the HR Specialist role will be growing at a rate of 21% shows that it is moving at a clip about twice as fast as the average job in America over the next decade—encouraging news!

Fifth. Here is the most important part: Click on the tab at the top of the page that reads "Job Outlook." At the bottom of that page, you will find a section that reads "Job Prospects," and you will find the following call-out box as well:

Employment projections data for human resources specialists, 2010-20

Occupational Title	SOC Code	Employment, 2010	Projected Employment, 2020	Change, 2010-20		Employment by Industry
				Percent	Numeric	
Human Resources, Training, and Labor Relations Specialists, All Other	13-1078	442,200	532,900	21	90,700	[XLS]
SOURCE: U.S. Bureau of Labor Statistics, Employment Projections program						

*Fig. 3 (Source: http://www.bls.gov/ooh/business-and-financial
human-resources-specialists.htm#tab-6)*

Clicking on the spreadsheet (XLS) in the last column will open a projection, by industry, of how the HR Specialist role will fare from 2010 to 2020. You will find in the first column of figures the percentage change (growth or loss) of the HR Specialist role over the next decade in each particular field.

Relative to the 12–13% job growth average over the next ten years, which is the average for all roles in corporate America (growing by roughly 1% per year), here is what job growth for HR folks looks like by industry between 2010 and 2020:

Title	Percent change
Management, scientific, and technical consulting services	73.5
Home health care services	72.1
Services for the elderly and persons with disabilities	65.7
Wireless telecommunications carriers (except satellite)	41.4
Software publishers	35.7
Waste collection	30.3
Telephone call centers	22.3
Wired telecommunications carriers	-4.8
Motion picture, video, and sound recording industries	-9.1
Federal government, excluding postal service	-12.8
Newspaper publishers	-21.7
Postal service	-27.8

Fig. 4 Growth of HR Specialist Role in Selected Industries, 2010–2020
(Table by Paul Falcone, based on data from www.bls.gov.)

Overall, there are 300+ industry categories to consider. Looking to get your foot in the door of the movie business? Be careful because the trend is negative to the tune of about a 1% job loss per year. Has newspaper publishing always been an area of interest where you wanted to launch your HR career? Not so fast—it is creating job losses at 2% per year for HR wannabes like you.

Then again, you will see that if you focus on wireless vs. wired telecom, the percentage growth morphs from -4.8% to +41.4%. Likewise, if you shift away from newspaper publishing to software publishing, the growth index jumps from -21.7% to +35.7%. See how that slight shift in focus could provide you with enormous opportunities while keeping you in a related field?

Finally, notice the top three growth areas in figure 4—they are all traditional STEM (Science, Technology, Engineering, and Math) categories, and two of the three involve healthcare. Not being a math or science major does not mean that you cannot benefit from the overall job growth trends in those particular fields; simply focus your efforts on transitioning into one of those industries or a subset of them. After all, HR, accounting, finance, IT, operations, research, and a host of other disciplines are transferable across industries, so give yourself the greatest chance of career success by pursuing an industry that is growing by leaps and bounds. Of course, the path you ultimately decide to take may depend on your network connections, local economy, and the like. But do not launch your job search without having at least a general idea of growth prospects and trends in both your intended discipline (e.g., human resources) and target industries.

Every employer is looking to gauge your level of informed candidacy as well as what is known as the candidate desire factor.

An important point about gathering all of this information: Every employer is looking to gauge your level of informed candidacy as well as what is known as the candidate desire factor. They are expecting you to know what you want and why you want it, as well as how you will get there. One mention of the fact that you have researched the dominant and growth-oriented industries in the *Occupational Outlook Handbook*, and they will be impressed beyond belief! It is a great resource, a fascinating area of study, and as close to a crystal ball as any of us will come in this lifetime.

I would go as far as saying that the data you gather from this research is about 50% of what you will need to narrow down options for the next career you will want to pursue. The other 50% is made up of a lot of intangibles, such as where you want to live, family and health considerations, work-life balance, and such.

Tapping into the Hidden Job Market

The term "hidden job market" is typically associated with job creation in the fastest growing and most respected organizations in America. But more than that, it is where you will find the most socially-responsible, well-respected, ethical, employee-friendly, fast-growing, and innovative companies on the planet—some of which may be right there in your own backyard, yet you are simply not aware of them.

The whole idea of a hidden job market used to be shrouded in mystery—accessible only to the wealthiest among us and those with access to the greatest connections. Well, the Internet has solved that mystery for us once and for all, and as you will see from the list of employer-of-choice websites below, identifying the strongest companies has now become a true operational focus of many organizations whose resources you will find helpful during your job search.

Identifying the dominant and growth-oriented companies in America is not as hard as you think with these tools in hand. Simply locate companies in your geographic area or industry of choice from these various indexes, and you will not only gain critical insights into the overall job market, but you will also be armed with a very flattering way of introducing yourself to a prospective employer. For instance, you might try something like this:

Ms. Employer,

I took the liberty of researching your organization before reaching out to you by email and was very impressed to find that you were ranked by Forbes as one of the world's "Top 25 Most Innovative Companies." What an outstanding achievement, and I am happy to include a link to the Forbes list below.

[LINK]

I know that strong companies always look for high performers, and I would be honored if you would consider my resume (attached) for any potential [TITLE/ROLE] openings at XYZ Corporation where I might be able to make an immediate contribution. After having completed twenty years of military service, I am looking to transition into the private sector. I will respectfully add that I believe that I could make the same contributions to XYZ that I have successfully made to the US Navy over the past two decades, and being associated with XYZ would be an honor and a role I would cherish.

Thank you so much for your consideration and continued success.

Sincerely,
Paul Falcone

Grow your core list of companies slowly—adding one or two companies from a particular website or magazine issue—and before you know it, you may have twenty-five to a hundred companies that you have researched and where you have introduced yourself. This is an instant way to build a network in the private sector even if you have never lived in a particular part of the country or have no prior private sector employment experience. A lot will depend on your willingness to relocate, of course, but you may just find some successful new start-ups flourishing right in your own backyard!

The suggested sites listed below are just the beginning. You will find many more listings that focus on, for example, the best companies in a particular sector or industry, or those that stand out for their customer service. So have some fun with this, and understand that this is exactly how headhunters pursue new companies and develop client relationships. This is a smart, strategic way to approach a job search, and you will really stand out among your peers because very few job candidates have the wisdom to present themselves in such a favorable light. Here are some key websites to get you started:

For easy access, you can find all of these links at www.bootstoloafers.com.

- **Traditional Resources**
  - "Fortune 500" from *Fortune* magazine: http://money.cnn.com/magazines/fortune/fortune500/
  - "S&P 500 Index" by Standard & Poor's: http://money.cnn.com/data/markets/sandp/
  - "The Forbes 500s" from *Forbes* magazine: http://www.forbes.com/2003/03/26/500sland.html
- **America's Fastest-Growing Companies**
  - "Fortune's Fastest-Growing Companies" from *Fortune* magazine: http://money.cnn.com/magazines/fortune/fastest-growing/2012/full_list/index.html
  - "Fastest-Growing Companies in the Fortune 1000 by Revenue" from *Fortune* magazine: http://money.cnn.com/gallery/news/companies/2013/05/06/500-fastest-growing-revenue.fortune/index.html
  - "The 100 Fastest-Growing Companies" from *Fortune* magazine: http://money.cnn.com/magazines/fortune/fastest-growing/index.html?iid=bc_sp_toprr
  - "Inc. 5000" from Inc. magazine: http://www.inc.com/inc5000/list/
- **Global and Internationally Based Organizations**
  - "Global 500" from *Fortune* magazine: http://money.cnn.com/magazines/fortune/global500/2012/snapshots/6388.html?iid=bc_sp_toprr
  - "The International 500" from *Forbes* magazine: http://www.forbes.com/2003/07/07/internationaland.html
  - "The Global 1000" from *Bloomberg Businessweek* magazine: http://www.businessweek.com/stories/2004-07-25/the-global-1000

- **America's Most Respected Companies**
  - "America's Most Promising Companies" from *Forbes* magazine: http://www.forbes.com/most-promising-companies/
  - "World's Most Admired Companies" from *Fortune* magazine: http://money.cnn.com/magazines/fortune/most-admired/
  - "The World's Most Innovative Companies" from *Fast Company*: http://www.fastcompany.com/section/most-innovative-companies-2013
  - "America's Best Small Companies" from *Forbes* magazine: http://www.forbes.com/best-small-companies/list/
- **Best Companies to Work For**
  - "100 Best Companies to Work For" from *Fortune* magazine: http://money.cnn.com/magazines/fortune/best-companies/?iid=F500_sp_toprr
  - "Best Employers for Workers Over 50 Winners" by AARP: http://www.aarp.org/work/on-the-job/info-06-2013/aarp-best-employers-winners-2013.html
  - "2012 Working Mother 100 Best Companies" from *Working Mother* magazine: http://www.workingmother.com/best-companies/2012-working-mother-100-best-companies
  - "2013 Best Companies for Hourly Workers" from *Working Mother* magazine: http://www.workingmother.com/best-company-list/138503
  - "2013 Best Companies for Multicultural Women" from *Working Mother* magazine: http://www.workingmother.com/best-company-list/140533
  - "Best Places to Work" by GlassDoor.com: http://www.glassdoor.com/Best-Places-to-Work-LST_KQ0,19.htm
- **Specialty Designations**
  - "The World's Most Innovative Companies" from *Forbes* magazine: http://www.forbes.com/innovative-companies/list/
  - "25 Top Companies for Leaders" by CNNMoney: http://money.cnn.com/galleries/2011/news/companies/1111/gallery.top_companies_leaders.fortune/
  - "Inner City 100" from *Fortune* magazine: http://www.money.cnn.com/magazines/fortune/innercity100/
  - "Flexible Fortune 500 Jobs—Best Companies List" by flexjobs.com: http://www.flexjobs.com/company-guide/fortune-500

- ° "The Green 50" from *Inc.* magazine: http://www.inc.com/green/
- ° "The 25 Best Companies To Work For If You Want To Get Promoted Quickly" from *Business Insider*: http://www.businessinsider.com/ best-companies-for-advancing-your-career-2012-9?op=1
- ° "The World's Most Ethical Companies" from *Forbes* magazine: http://www.forbes.com/sites/jacquelynsmith/2013/03/06/ the-worlds-most-ethical-companies-in-2013/

- **Top Veteran-Friendly Employers**
  - ° "The Top Ten Employers for Veterans" from *Forbes* magazine: http://www.forbes.com/sites/jacquelynsmith/2012/04/23/ the-top-employers-for-veterans/
  - ° "Best for Vets 2013: Employers" from *Military Times*: http://projects.militarytimes.com/best-for-veterans/ best-employers-for-veterans/2013/
  - ° "Best Veteran Employers: A Top-35 List" by Military.com: http:// www.military.com/veteran-jobs/career-advice/job-hunting/top-35- veteran-employers.html
  - ° "Featured Employers List" by Hire A Hero: http://www.hireahero. org
  - ° "Federal Contractors and other Vet-Friendly Empolyers" by Vet Central: http://vetcentral.us.jobs/veteransmembers.asp
  - ° U.S. Customs and Border Protection careers: http://www. cbpcareers.com
  - ° "Ranked Top 100 Military-Friendly Employers" by MilitaryFriendly.com: http://employers.militaryfriendly.com

- **Other Websites for Identifying Veteran-Friendly Companies with Current Job Openings**
  - ° Military.com: Monster Veteran Employment Center: http://www. military.com/veteran-jobs
  - ° MilitaryHire.com: http://employers.militaryhire.com/?gclid=CMqc l4KombkCFQxyQgodASMAMA
  - ° MilitaryVetJobs: http://militaryvetjobs.jobs.careercast.com/?gclid=C Nb8xuGimbkCFap7QgodkScATg
  - ° HireVeterans.com: http://www.hireveterans.com
  - ° CareerCast: The Best Jobs for Veterans in 2013: http://www.careercast.com/jobs-rated/best-veterans-jobs-2013

- ° The Mission Continues: http://missioncontinues.org
- ° G.I. Jobs: http://www.gijobs.com/default.aspx
- ° My Next Move for Veterans: www.mynextmove.org/vets

In addition to the websites listed above, here are a couple of government resources that may be of interest to you during your transition:

- **Joining Forces—Taking Action to Service America's Military Families:** http://www.whitehouse.gov/joiningforces
  - ° Employment resources for veterans
  - ° Military spouse license portability
  - ° Helping veterans and service members transition to civilian careers
- **VOW to Hire Heroes Act of 2011 (United States Department of Veterans Affairs):** http://www.benefits.va.gov/vow/
  - ° "The Veterans Opportunity to Work (VOW) to Hire Heroes Act of 2011, provides seamless transition for Service members, expands education and training opportunities for Veterans, and provides tax credits for employers who hire Veterans with service-connected disabilities."
- **US Department of Labor—Veterans' Employment and Training Service (VETS):** www.dol.gov/vets
- **Feds Hire Vets (US Office of Personnel Management):** fedshirevets.gov

O*Net Online is a treasure trove of information about careers, and you will also find a section on Military Occupation Classification/Skills (equivalencies). You can find out more at www.onetonline.org. Note that the Dictionary of Occupational Titles (or DOT, as it is commonly called) is a standard resource that has been used for decades to help identify various roles available in the private sector. Historically, however, it focused more on manufacturing-related positions, while O*Net is dedicated more to jobs in the information age.

If you enter "ex-military job hunting" into your Google search engine, you will find additional re-

> O*Net Online is a treasure trove of information about careers, and you will also find a section on Military Occupation Classification/Skills (equivalencies).

sources, such as www.hireds.com. The good news is that these sites are proliferating and changing all the time. The more challenging news is that you could easily suffer from information overload. Therefore, make this as simple on yourself as possible: Dedicate two to three hours to reviewing these various sites, and then simply focus in on one or two that seem to feel right and fit your personality. Exhaust those initial one or two sites before exploring others. Whittling down your resources is important when there's so much to choose from.

Finally, should you need more resources than the rich supply above for any reason, simply conduct a Google or Ask.com search to learn more about leading companies and organizations looking to hire veterans in your field of specialty or geographic area.

Discovering Company Culture

What exactly is company culture, and how do you find out more about it in advance of an interview? Well, as you might guess, it is not that easy to nail down. Some organizations are known for their very individualized corporate cultures. Jack Welch at General Electric (GE) was legendary for his "rank and yank" system, meaning that all employees had to be categorized (or "force ranked," as the system came to be known) into one of three buckets following a 70–20–10 model:

- 70% of senior leaders should meet or exceed performance expectations at any given time
- 20% should be stellar, exemplary performers (i.e., the top tier)
- 10% of employees should be removed from the organization at any given time (or at least, at the time of annual performance reviews) for not meeting expectations and in order to make room for new talent.

The theory was that all senior executives would want to get into that 20% bucket to ensure ultimate career success, and no one would want to be in that 10% bucket because termination would surely follow.

That is a fairly draconian methodology for rank-ordering senior leaders, and one could argue that it lent itself to an "it is not so much that I should win, but that you should lose" type of mentality. Then again, GE produced more CEOs for other companies than any other organization in history. So argue as you may that it was an exceptionally challenging and demanding culture, it produced results rarely matched by any other organization in the United States.

Disney is an organization that historically was defined by a pervasive corpo-

How do you find out a company's culture prior to joining the organization?

rate culture. While this has changed over the past decade, in the '80s and '90s, Disney had a saying along the lines of, "If you don't show up for work on Saturday, don't even think about coming in on Sunday!" I think that one saying sums up a lot about Disney's organizational culture at the time in terms of expecting a 24/7 time commitment from its leaders. Can you imagine what it would be like working for an organization with that type of expectation?

Are these corporate cultures right or wrong for you? That depends. Sometimes foregoing a personal life for a few years to gain the name-brand recognition of a GE or Disney is worth your while. Here is the rub: How do you find out a company's culture prior to joining the organization? And, considering the cultural norms of the military, a 24/7/365 environment, what kind of commitment are you prepared to make in your "second" life, your new true north?

There is an additional important caveat to keep in mind. More often than not, the overall organizational culture of the company is not as critical to you as the culture of the department in which you will be working. After all, very few organizations have corporate cultures like GE and Disney that create a pervasive work experience transcending all other factors. That type of work environment usually only exists when there is a very strong CEO at the helm who insists on creating a culture based on his values. Few CEOs, however, are that egocentric; most typically allow individual (i.e., division and department) leaders to create their own mini-climates, of sorts, and those typically trump the bigger corporate culture issues you might expect to face. So to refine our question a bit, how do you find out the departmental or divisional culture that you will be working under if you join a particular organization?

First, you will be able to find out more about macro, corporate culture issues on sites like GlassDoor.com, CafePharma.com (for the pharmaceutical industry), and the like. Further, you will find additional information on company cultures at locations such as Yelp.com, Salary.com, Payscale.com, and Indeed.com. As you might guess, websites are proliferating like rabbits in an attempt to decipher companies' corporate cultures. Let me caution you: they all self-report, meaning that there is not much editing going on other than what current employees (and more often, ex-employees) choose to say about those organizations. Therefore, keep the information that you learn from these websites in perspective when interviewing, but don't let it overly influence your decision to accept or reject an offer. Instead, think of this intelligence as due diligence data points to compare with your real-life experience during the interviewing process.

... keep the information that you learn from these websites in perspective when interviewing, but don't let it overly influence your decision ...

Finally, you will naturally find out more about the micro culture that exists in a department where you are interviewing by asking questions that will help you decipher the true company culture in the group where you will be working. Questions like this may help:

- How would you describe the culture of your department or group?
- What makes your department unique and distinctive relative to other areas of the company?
- If you used three adjectives to describe group dynamics on your finance team, what would they be?

That kind of subjective feedback can only come from in-person interview questions and discussions with current or prior employees who serve under a particular leader.

Constructing Your Resume

Now on to the fun stuff. One of the most perplexing challenges facing you has to do with resumes. What do you write? What should they look like? How do you make your resume the equivalent of a DMZ (demilitarized zone) so that lay employers can relate what you did in the service to what their companies do today?

The good news is, it's easier than you think! While you will probably want to invest in a resume writing coach (fee can range in the hundreds of dollars) to help you customize your corporate calling card and put your best foot forward, this section will get you 80% of the way there. The key, though, will always be in customizing your resume to make it feel and look like you; your writing style, content selection, and formatting are as unique as you are, so this is an important exercise that bears due consideration.

A note of caution about resume writing: ask three people about your resume,

Reviewing the technical training programs and job descriptions from previous assignments while in the service can help you discover your strongest interest.

and you'll get four opinions. Resume writing is a combination of art and science, a document that is uniquely you, yet reflecting a profile of skills, experiences, and abilities that fits a general pattern of workers—whether in the military or in the private sector. So while you may not have had a need to translate your skills and experiences into private sector or civilian terms before, this will be an enlightening experience that helps you define yourself succinctly and in a very focused way. Consider your resume a guidepost to lead you through your career—a short overview of who you are now and what you have to offer a prospective employer, of course, but also a personal development matrix to help you see and prepare for your next move in career progression. In short, it is your calling card that will get you in the door of a prospective employer. It will take time to pull together, so be patient.

Skills and Abilities

Analyzing Officer Efficiency Reports (OER), Enlisted Efficiency Reports (EER) and Non-Commissioned Officer Efficiency Reports (NCOER) will be helpful in beginning a skills inventory list. You must also take into consideration all of the additional duties you performed in uniform. Reviewing the technical training programs and job descriptions from previous assignments while in the service can help you discover your strongest interest. Which job allowed the use of favorite skills and abilities? These should be included in a skills inventory. A realistic look at personal skills and abilities will give you insight into selecting a career or occupation.

The best way I have found to capture this information is in the STAR (Situation, Task, Action, and Results) format. The details on the STAR format will be covered later in the book, but here I'll give you a high-level look at it to get you started.

Although STAR is primarily used for interview responses, I have found it extremely helpful in organizing my thoughts when it comes to detailing what I have actually done in a given job. First, let me explain each point of STAR.

Situation. Describe a past situation or task that had to be accomplished.

Task. If the task or situation was accomplished, what was the goal or objective?

Action. Describe the actions taken by you to address the situation. Providing an appropriate amount of detail and remaining focused on personal actions should be your goal. Provide the specific measures you took and your actual contribution.

Result. Explain the outcome of your actions. This is not a time for shyness. You should take credit for your results. What happened? How did the situation end? What did you accomplish? What did you learn? If possible, the answer should demonstrate that your actions produced multiple positive results.

. . . keep your STARs updated to use in future interviews.

Now, dig out all of those OERs, EERs, and NCOERs, analyze them in detail, and build your STARs. It is a tedious process that takes a significant amount of time to complete, but the exercise produces results and makes sense as it helps you organize your thoughts and outline what you have actually done. Next, while you are conducting your research, look for a list of common, corporate-America core competencies. To some of you,"core competencies" is likely a new term. These are the skills that are necessary to be able to do a particular activity or job. At the company level, these are skills that the company does very well and that make it better than other companies. You can start aligning your STARs to these competencies. You have now started building the information you will need to begin your resume. What you have also done is started building a new portfolio of information that will help you prepare for an interview by better organizing your thoughts so you can answer interview questions. The STAR format will help focus your thoughts on past situations and actions. I suggest taking it even one step further: Once you have been hired and started down the path of integration, keep your STARs updated to use in future interviews. Consider doing this at the end of each year. You never know when your next opportunity might come along.

Translating Military Jargon and Terminology into Private-Sector Equivalencies

Fear not: There are plenty of resources available to help you translate your military achievements into civilian parlance. To find a number of military skills translators that can help you do this, visit the US Department of Veterans Affairs website at http://vetsuccess.gov/public/military_skills_translators.html. You will want to focus on "de-militarizing" your resume by replacing such terms

Life transitions can certainly be difficult, but when we look back on them years later, we learn that life is at its fullest during these times.

as "command" with private-sector equivalents like "lead" and "supervise." Don't be overwhelmed by all the choices; spend 10–15 minutes looking through the various military translator tools that are available on this site, and simply pick the one that you're most comfortable with. Bookmark it, and work with that one from that point forward.

An important note before we venture too far down this road: This may be the first time you are engaging in this type of exercise, but it is meant to be fun and self-illuminating. Tying your military achievements together and presenting them to a civilian audience in layman's terms adds an extra twist to this exercise, but it is nothing you cannot master and excel at with a healthy dose of self-critical insight. So enjoy this gift of moving forward in finding your new true north, fully expecting it to be challenging but ultimately very rewarding.

Life transitions can certainly be difficult, but when we look back on them years later, we learn that life is at its fullest during these times. We learn all about creativity and good karma, empathy for others, and survival skills of a whole new and different sort. And going through transitional career challenges will help you help others down the road by paying it forward, so to speak. In fact, one day you will probably think back to your first time sitting down to compose a resume that is fit for civilian consumption and realize how far you have come since those early steps toward transformation and integration into private industry.

A warning: Don't fall in love with your resume! You are probably going to end up with several versions before too long, and that is absolutely normal. Do not keep saving only one version in different ways; save all of your various versions as they make their way through the self-editing process. Customizing your resume to suit particular jobs is the way to go, emphasizing different aspects of your career experience. So simply create a separate folder on your desktop or on your hard drive labeled "Resumes," and begin saving versions of your drafts as follows:

Resume_YourName_1

Resume_YourName_2

Resume_YourName_3, and so forth . . .

You could replace the "1, 2, and 3" above with dates or areas of functional responsibility ("Leadership," "Customer Service," "Logistics," "Operations," and the like). In fact, you might save a resume for each particular company where you submit an application like this:

Resume_YourName_ABC Company

Resume_YourName_XYZ Company

You get the idea. Save your resume multiple ways, play with the formatting and content, and know that you will benefit from that flexibility down the road by utilizing the various iterations as new job opportunities come your way.

What to Include and Exclude

Here is a brief overview of what you should consider including on your resume from top to bottom:

1. Contact Information
2. Executive Overview (optional)
3. Core Leadership Qualifications
4. Professional Experience
5. Additional Experience (if applicable)
6. Education, Certifications, and Foreign Languages
7. Technical Skills
8. Professional Designations and Achievements (if applicable)

And that's about it. Most professional resumes include these key subject areas and little else. I'll show you what these look like on paper in the samples that follow.

Now, here are some of the don'ts when it comes to resume writing in general and what you will want to avoid documenting on your resume:

- Objectives. These are usually spelled out in your cover letter and often add very little value to a typical resume.
- Year of high school graduation. Big whoops—employers are not supposed to know your age, and since most people graduate from high school at eighteen, this inadvertently provides companies with your age.
- "References Available Upon Request" or names and contact information for your references. This comes later in the process and takes up unnecessary space on the resume.

As you can see, the don'ts list is fairly short and straightforward, which is always a good thing. Now the question is, how do you put it all together and what will your new resume look like?

Format and Content

First, follow these guidelines for formatting your resume:

- Font: Times New Roman
- Font style: Regular
- Font size: 12 point or 11 point, depending on spacing needs
- Text color: Black
- Margins: 1 or 1.25 inches at top and bottom as well as left and right (although this can also be adjusted depending on spacing needs)
- Format: MS Word document most common; PDF version also acceptable

That was easy enough. Now on to what the sections themselves might look like in a private sector resume, again using the example of a human resources professional.

1. Contact Information. Your contact information should be formatted at the top of the page like this:

PAUL FALCONE

Los Angeles, California 91355
C (310) 555-1212
Paul@PaulFalconeHR.com
www.linkedin.com/in/paulfalcone1

A few notes about the above: First, notice that the name is in bolded caps to help it stand out. Second, notice that there's no street address listed—only the city and zip code. That is for security reasons these days, with resumes floating all over the Internet; it is perfectly acceptable to leave out your street address, although you can include it if you prefer. Third, you will want to include a cell phone or home phone number, or both, as well as an email address so that it is easy for employers to find you. Note that the second and/or third page of your resume should include your name and cell phone number at the top as a header. Finally, notice that the web address of Paul's LinkedIn profile is included here with his other contact information. We will discuss setting up your LinkedIn profile later when we talk about using social media in your job search.

2. Executive Overview (optional). Here is an example of an Executive Overview, again dedicated to a human resources career path:

> *Accomplished Human Resources Executive having spent nine of the past twelve years with XYZ Company and with twenty years of highly progressive experience delivering value-added services in extremely fast paced, dynamic organizations undergoing tremendous change and growth in both domestic and international and union and nonunion environments. Diverse industry experience in the entertainment, financial services, and healthcare fields in both publicly traded and privately held companies.*

Notice that it includes years of tenure with a particular company, the industries in which this professional has worked, and other aspects of his experience that prospective employers would want to know about, including union, international, as well as public and private company experience.

3. Core Leadership Qualifications. This is a section you should have some fun with. If there is one thing you are schooled, trained, and versed in, it is selfless leadership, so let this section shine! Here is another human resources example to give you a feel for what a private sector resume might look like:

CORE LEADERSHIP QUALIFICATIONS

- Full-Spectrum / C-Level Recruiting
- Employee & Labor Relations
- Training & Organizational Development
- Human Capital Metrics & Analytics

- International Human Resources
- Mergers & Acquisitions / Due Diligence
- Corporate Governance / SOX Compliance
- Executive Compensation

Fig. 5 (Example courtesy of Paul Falcone)

4. Professional Experience. This is the biggie, so let's break this down. First, on a private sector resume, each company where you worked, its location, your job title, and your dates of employment are typically formatted in a specific way. As an executive or senior leader candidate in the private sector, you will also be expected to include information about the company itself—its size in terms of revenue and/or number of employees, international scope of operations, or special recognitions. Therefore, professional experience on an executive's resume might look something like one of these three examples:

Golden Equity Advisors, Beverly Hills, CA   ***2010 - present***
    An \$8 billion private equity, mergers and acquisitions firm ranked by *Forbes* in 2005 as the
    32nd largest private company in America with 40,000 employees worldwide.
    <u>Director of Human Resources</u>
    Job description then begins here . . .

XYZ Cable, Los Angeles, CA   **10/2004 – 9/2011**
XYZ Cable (NYSE: XYZC) is a Fortune 200 cable/Internet/digital telephone distributor with \$19 billion in revenue and 47,000 employees. The West Region consists of Southern California, Colorado, and Hawaii, with \$3 billion in revenue and 8,000 employees.
<u>Vice President, Human Resources</u>
Job description then begins here . . .

Famous Pictures, Hollywood, CA   **1998 – 2005**
A \$4 billion, 2500-employee subsidiary of the entertainment operations of \$25 billion Vanguard Entertainment, one of the world's largest entertainment and media companies.
    <u>Director of International Human Resources (2002– 2005)</u>
    <u>Director of Staffing and Employee Relations (1998– 2002)</u>
Job description then begins here . . .

Fig. 6 (Examples courtesy of Paul Falcone)

Let's take a brief look at how companies, dates, and titles are set up in the examples in figure 6. The first example at Golden Equity Advisers includes revenue, headcount, and a *Forbes* designation to show that the company is dynamic, growing, and hugely successful. That's not bragging—it is simply publicizing the organization's achievements and overall market niche.

You will notice that the company description information is in 9-point font. That is typically too small for a resume, but it is used here to offset the company description from the rest of the resume—an acceptable creative alternative. Notice also in the first example that only the year of initial employment (2010) is listed rather than the more typical month and year (e.g., 9/10 or 9/2010). That's up to you; just keep in mind that the longer your tenure in a particular role, the more it makes sense to include only the years involved. For shorter tenured assignments, the month and year would make it easier for the recruiter or employer to understand just how much time you spent in the role. Remember, 2010–2011 could be one year or two: 1/2010 to 1/2011 equals one year, while 1/2010 to 12/2011 equals two years.

The second example at the cable company includes the revenue and employee count for the entire organization nationwide as well as the west coast region that this individual was responsible for. Also included is the trading symbol for the company's stock since this is a publicly traded company.

Now let's look at the third example (Famous Pictures) since it has a bit of a twist. The individual held two roles at this company—four years in the first role and three years in the second role. As such, you'll find the macro dates in the far right column where it shows 1998–2005. The macro dates are important because you want to get credit for all the years with that organization—otherwise, someone reading your resume may inadvertently assume the positions were with two separate companies, and you could look like a job hopper. To avoid that, the micro dates are placed to the immediate right of each title held so that this individual gets credit for his career progression in addition to his longevity with the company.

When describing the roles you held at various companies, it is important to keep a few rules in mind:

- **Rule 1.** Create a contextual framework around your responsibilities by creating a mini organizational chart of sorts. Show who you report to and how many people you supervise like this:

  <u>Vice President, Human Resources</u>
  Reporting to the senior vice president of human resources in a 150-person HR department, supervised a staff of 40 HR generalists (three director-level reports and 37 extended reports) and managed a budget of $4.7 MM.

  <u>Director of Labor Relations and Staffing</u>
  Reported to the Vice President of Human Resources and supervised a staff of eight.

Fig. 7 (Example courtesy of Paul Falcone)

If you don't directly supervise anyone, simply list the functional person that you report to like this:

Vice President, Human Resources (West Coast)
Reporting to the studio general manager in addition to the SVP HR for XYZ Networks in New York, served as Famous Players' highest-level HR generalist as well as head of West Coast staffing for parent company XYZ Networks.

Fig. 8 (Example courtesy of Paul Falcone)

- **Rule 2.** Narratives or bullets? There are always lots of questions as to whether a narrative job description on a resume makes sense or if prospective employers prefer a bulleted format. There is really no right or wrong answer here. It is strictly up to you. In fact, you may want to use both: use the narrative to describe your overall responsibilities and bullets to highlight your achievements. Using the Famous Pictures example from figure 6, it might look something like this:

Director of International Human Resources (2002– 2005)

Director of Staffing and Employee Relations (1998– 2001)

Reported to the Senior Vice President of Human Resources, ensuring that all compensation and benefit programs and policies were administered in accordance with international protocol and regulations. Initial post managed the employee relations and recruitment function for a client group of 1200 employees on the studio lot and 800 employees in 19 TV stations in the U.S. and Canada. Latter role oversaw 500 internationally based employees in 12 territories in Europe, Asia, and Latin America.

° Ensured that international pay practices, bonus programs, merit budgets, stock options, pension plans, and expatriate relocation policies were administered in accordance with international employment, pension, and tax regulations.
° Spearheaded relocation of the Home Entertainment HQ office from London to Los Angeles and developed retention/severance/relocation financial models for all international transfers.
° Implemented worldwide layoffs in light of statutory obligations for notice periods, enhanced redundancy packages, retention bonuses, and compromise agreements.
° Served as the responsible officer for all H1, L1, O1 and TN nonimmigrant visas as well as green card / permanent residency applications.

Fig. 9 (Example courtesy of Paul Falcone)

Just remember that you want your resume to speak for itself and be fully understandable to a reader who knows absolutely nothing about you. One quick look at the narrative section above and then the bullets below will reveal very quickly the scope of this individual's responsibilities within the context of being an international HR person.

- **Rule 3:** Chronological or functional resume? Short answers work best: chronological. Prospective employers want to see how your career has mapped out and progressed over time, so the chronological format—which shows your current role first and your older positions further down the resume—provides a quick snapshot of your career progression and current capabilities. It is the format expected in the workplace 98% of the time, so do not get confused when you hear about functional (sometimes referred to as "flunctional") resumes as an alternative. Why "flunctional"? They are too difficult to read and decipher, so most employers pay less attention to them, which makes a candidate's chances of being short-listed that much harder.

  Can a functional resume ever come in handy? Yes, but you have to first understand how they came about. When stay-at-home parents decided to return to the workforce after a ten-year break or when older adults with no prior work experience whatsoever decided to launch their first job searches, they couldn't use a chronological format because their employment history was nonexistent. An alternative strategy was created to demonstrate the many skills that the individual acquired over the years as a student, full-time homemaker, parent, and the like, the idea being to sell those skills without attaching them to any particular employer or point in time. It was simply a listing of life skills that hopefully could be translated into a workplace environment. So in short, yes, a functional resume can be very helpful, but it should only be used by individuals who cannot make a case for using a chronological resume because they have little recent, practical job experience. Those of you transitioning from a military to a civilian career path do have prior experience—military experience—and should stick with a chronological resume format in almost all cases.

- **Rule 4.** Following are a few general rules and guidelines to keep in mind when creating the job description portions of your resume.

  ° First, remember that current positions should be described in the current tense (i.e., lead, manage, negotiate) while past positions should be described in the past tense (i.e., led, managed, negotiated).

...resumes only need to go back about ten years.

°Second, resumes only need to go back about ten years. The assumption is that anything older is probably outdated. So if you are a career veteran, show your entire service history in the macro dates section, and then show your various roles and titles in conjunction with their micro dates. Once you have covered ten years of your most recent experience, you can simply write a short paragraph to cover prior experience like this:

Prior: Spent seven years as a [Title] and three years in the [Name] division, responsible for various roles such as . . .

Fig. 10 (Example courtesy of Paul Falcone)

That should be all you need to cover the first ten or twenty years of your service, leaving the last (and most recent) ten to be described in full-blown narrative and bulleted formats.

° Third, avoid "comma" descriptions in your narratives. Too many workers mistakenly assume that a resume is a month-by-month, year-by-year accounting of exactly where they were at any particular point in time. Not so—the resume is a selling tool that helps you demonstrate your achievements and accomplishments working in particular roles and handling certain responsibilities. Think of it this way: If an admin's resume reads: "Responsible for drafting memos, answering phones, filing dossiers, and providing customer service," your initial response should be, "So what?" That's what every admin in the world does. Imagine you are this admin: What makes you stand out as a result of your having done those duties? Is the company where you're working now a better place for the contributions you've made over time? And can you somehow link your achievements to saved time, increased revenue, or reduced expenses?

Now apply that rule to your own situation: Does your "comma resume" simply list what your duties were, or does it come alive with achievements that are codified and quantified? Can a prospective employer see your historical resume and achievement profile and project how that might be applied to her company as a benefit and potential solution to current challenges? Remember, your resume isn't meant to be a rap sheet that answers where you were at any given point in time over the past ten, twenty, or thirty years. Instead, it is meant to be a tool that highlights what you have done and what you are capable of doing in the future.

. . . quantify your accomplishments

° Fourth, quantify your accomplishments in terms of dollars or percentages whenever possible. Employers want to see 20% reductions in turnover, 4% increases in profitability margins, $200,000 savings in systems implementation efficiencies, and the like. Your prior military experience may provide you with opportunities to quantify the results you achieved.

° Fifth, dedicate the most time on your resume to your most recent activities. The farther back you go, the shorter the job descriptions should be, because that older experience probably is not as relevant to what you are doing today. Candidates sometimes look for symmetry by providing approximately the same amount of content for all roles on their resumes. Instead, highlight the current content more than older materials as well as what is special about your experience. For example, in figure 9 above, a good deal of time is spent highlighting international HR as well as mergers and acquisitions experience—not because those activities were all that recent but because those are hot skills in today's job market. So use your best judgment, but bear in mind that *you* get to choose what you want to highlight. There are no right or wrong answers when it comes to what you feel is important and noteworthy.

° Finally, how long should your resume be: one page, six pages, and does it even make a difference? The short answer is yes—too long and you will turn off a prospective employer because you will be viewed as long-winded and full of yourself. But that age-old rule of "your resume should only be one page" was historically meant to apply to recent high school or college graduates. Whether you have had a multi-decade successful career in the military or less than a twenty-year career, as you transition into the private sector, two- and even three-page resumes are perfectly acceptable. If possible, though, keep it down to two since most employers will not read much beyond that unless you really have some compelling content and stories to tell.

5. Additional Experience (if applicable). A section on additional experience may make sense if you teach, publish, serve on community or military boards, or the like. Here's what this section of the resume might look like:

——————————— ADDITIONAL EXPERIENCE ———————————

**UCLA Extension School of Business
& Management**   **1995 – present**
Instructor (evenings) for the following courses:
 - Recruitment, Interviewing, and Selection
 - Employee Relations and Legal Aspects of HRM
 - International Human Resource Management
 - Business Ethics for Human Resource Professionals

Member, UCLA Extension HR Advisory Council (1998 – 2008)

Fig. 11 (Example courtesy of Paul Falcone)

It is perfectly acceptable to add accomplishments like Black Belt in Tae Kwon Do, Eagle Scout, and other types of experiences or achievements in this section if they are important to you. And yes, things you did as a kid can still qualify if they are special (like becoming an Eagle Scout). They speak to character and an achievement mentality, which typically doesn't change all that much over someone's lifetime. Besides, it will give you and the interviewer something fun to talk about.

6. Education, Certifications, and Foreign Languages. Generally speaking, if you are in your mid-twenties and have been out of school for five years or less, then the Education section belongs at the top of your resume. By contrast, if you have been out of school for more than five years, the Education section usually falls to the bottom of your resume. Note as well that if you recently completed an MBA but you received your undergraduate degree twenty years ago, the Education section still belongs at the end of your resume. In short, Education only goes at the top of a resume if you are fairly light on job experience. Once you have more than five years of practical experience under your belt, then it is relegated to the end of the resume.

Be careful not to overdo the number of schools you attended. Sometimes candidates who do not have a bachelor's degree, for example, show that they attended three different junior colleges and then two larger universities in an attempt to demonstrate that they are college material. Do not approach your resume that way. If you do not have a degree, do not feel the need to overcompensate by showing all the schools you have attended. That strategy could backfire and make you look like someone who does not finish what you start. Instead, show the one school where you completed the most work and add a comment along the lines of "56 of 62 units completed toward an A.A. degree" or something similar. Here are some examples from the private sector:

B.A. in German Literature, UCLA, Los Angeles, CA

Gonzaga University, Spokane, WA
Bachelor of Science, Business Administration
Major: Accounting
Degree Expected: June 2014

DePaul University, Chicago, IL
Bachelor of Arts Degree in Political Science
Cum Laude, Dean's Honor List, Honor Status for three of four years

University of San Diego, San Diego, CA
2013 – present
Two years completed toward bachelor's degree in economics; 3.6 GPA; part-time evening program

Fig. 12 (Examples courtesy of Paul Falcone)

Note in figure 12 that, unlike with the year of high school graduation, it is perfectly fine to include the year of your college graduation or years of attendance. That is because anyone could go to college at any time, and there is really no way to determine someone's age from their college attendance dates. That is not the case with high school graduation dates since almost everyone graduates at age eighteen.

One final note about education: If you have a degree, proudly state it! However, if you *do not* have a degree—even if you are just one unit short—do not try to infer that you have one by applying some slick sleight of hand on your resume. If you are currently working toward your degree, make that known by showing "to present" in the description line (as the last example in figure 12 illustrates). And if you have not been back to school in twenty years, simply write something along the lines of "completed x units toward a bachelor's degree in business." But do not make the rookie mistake of making it look like you have a degree when you don't; that could come off as self-serving at best and outright dishonest at worst.

As far as foreign languages, it is generally a good idea to provide some indicator of your fluency in terms of reading, writing, and speaking on a three-part scale: fluent, conversational, or basic. Here's what it might look like:

German (fluent), **French** (working knowledge)

7. Technical skills. Technical skills clearly make the most sense for IT and other computer/systems professionals, but they are just as important for administrative assistants, accountants, attorneys, and physicians. Remember as well that keyword searches are often focused on particular systems expertise, so it is important that you include as much in this section as possible. Of course, some systems will be more familiar to you than others, so you could again apply a "basic, intermediate, advanced" type of descriptor so that you don't feel like you are overcommitting to software that you have not worked with in a number of years. The sample resumes that follow will provide you with several examples that you can model when drafting your own resume.

8. Professional designations and achievements (if applicable). This is an optional section for anything that speaks to your credentials in your field that you would like to highlight or otherwise call out on your resume. This section of the resume might look something like this:

──────── **PROFESSIONAL DESIGNATIONS AND ACHIEVEMENTS** ────────
- Professional Designation in HR Management, UCLA Extension
- Professional in Human Resources (PHR) certificate, HRCI/SHRM
- Regular Contributor, SHRM's *HR Magazine* (1998 – present)
- SHRM / EMA / PIHRA Annual Conference "Top Rated" Presenter

Fig. 13 (Example courtesy of Paul Falcone)

Successful Military Resume Samples

Now that you have explored the resume-writing world through the eyes of private sector workers and employers, it is time to look at some ready-made samples that you might want to emulate as you put your best foot forward and develop your own resume. Remember that you have some creative discretion to customize and personalize your resume. The tips provided in the previous section will serve as helpful and practical guidelines. The resumes that follow do not exactly match each other in form and content, and that's okay. Cookie-cutter resumes are not what the job search game is all about. A resume coach may be an excellent investment to help you express yourself in the most positive light. After all, there is no reason to reinvent the wheel from scratch when you could borrow from other successful executives who may be a few years ahead of you in their transition into the private sector. Special thanks to Bradley-Morris, Inc.*, the largest military-focused recruiting firm in the United States, for sharing the following resumes in an effort to support our troops returning home.

* BMI can be reached at www.bradleymorris.com and (800) 330-4950.

35

Sample 1: US Army Officer.

Mark Guardino

123 Ashburton Grove / Austin, TX 78751 / H: (555) 555-5555 / C: (555) 121-1212
candidate@us.army.mil / candidate@hotmail.com

PROJECT MANAGER
Currently possesses a SECRET Security Clearance
Served as the lead Project Manager for more than $10 million worth of reconstruction efforts in Iraq

EDUCATION & TRAINING
Bachelor of Science in Information Systems Engineering – United States Military Academy, 2009
- NCAA Division I Athletics - Track and Field Letterman (holds school records in discus and javelin)

HIGHLIGHTS OF EXPERIENCE: U.S. Army – Field Artillery Officer

COMPANY EXECUTIVE / MAINTENANCE OFFICER   2013 - Present
2nd Brigade Combat Team, 1st Cavalry Division – Ft. Hood, TX and Baghdad, Iraq
Plan and coordinate operator and organizational level maintenance and services for 41 vehicles. Project Manager for the 2nd Brigade Infrastructure Coordination Element in charge of planning, coordinating and managing sanitation, road and school renovation projects in Baghdad, Iraq. Also serve as the Personal Security Detachment Officer in Charge and led more than 200 combat patrols in Central and South Baghdad.
- Due to the high degree of discipline within the security detachment, hand-selected to train an Infantry Division and Civil Affairs Company on combat patrolling and operations.
- Manage 40 civic reconstruction projects in Baghdad valued at nearly $5 million designed to significantly improve the lives of local Iraqi people.
- Awarded the Bronze Star Medal for meritorious service while assigned as the Infrastructure Coordination Element Project Manager and Combat Patrol Leader during Operation Iraqi Freedom.

PLATOON LEADER   2011 - 2012
2nd Brigade Combat Team, 1st Cavalry Division – Baghdad, Iraq
Led a 20-soldier Security Section for a personal security detail conducting combat missions in Iraq. Managed all aspects of training, readiness, deployment, and mission execution. Accountable for six vehicles and 32 weapons systems worth in excess of $2.5 million. Planned, prepared, and executed sanitation and school projects for the Joint Iraqi Infrastructure Coordination Element and District Governance.
- Developed the Combat Patrol Standard Operating Procedures for the Battalion used to train the other five patrolling elements within the organization.
- Served as the lead Project Manager for $10 million in project efforts that improved education for 22,500 Iraqi children and contributed to the implementation of a solid waste management program in the Karkh District.
- Enabled the reconstruction management and partnering efforts of over 268 projects with a total program value of over $33 million, an accomplishment achieved by no other unit or leader in the Division.
- Led Platoon on 120 combat patrols throughout Central and South Baghdad. Awarded the Combat Action Badge for actively engaging the enemy in Operations Iraqi Freedom (OIF) 6-8

BATTERY FIRE DIRECTION OFFICER   2009 – 2010
3rd Battalion, 82nd Field Artillery, 1st Cavalry Division – Ft. Hood, TX
Managed the training and operations of a 25-soldier Platoon Fire Direction Center to include the accurate and safe computation of firing data for the live firing of 93 lb. high explosive artillery shells and the training of Fire Direction Section.
- Earned the Top Fire Direction Section Award in the Battalion for the quickest and most accurate fire computation during Battalion Gunnery.
- Awarded the Army Achievement Medal for dedication and selfless service that contributed to the ultimate success of the Battalion.

Fig. 14 Sample Resume of US Army Officer (Resume courtesy of Bradley-Morris, Inc.)

Sample 2: US Navy Officer.

Rob Hollocks
44 London Way, Austin Texas 78755
Fabregas@arsenal.com – FrankF10@yahoo.com – 512.333.3333

NAVY NUCLEAR TRAINED ENGINEERING PROFESSIONAL
Process Improvement and Quality Assurance Trained / Qualified Navy Nuclear Engineer

Detail-oriented, military-trained leader with nuclear engineering training and a proven track record in coordinating trades and completing projects on time and within budget. Solid foundation in mechanical, electrical, chemical and nuclear engineering coupled with demonstrated skill in leading large teams to achieve objectives. Experienced in international training and relations.

Education & Training

BS Physics and Astrophysics, University of Colorado at Boulder, Boulder, CO   2008
- 3.02 cumulative GPA. Graduated with Honors, Math & Physics tutor, Peer mentor.

Lean Six Sigma Black Belt Candidate, Acuity Institute, estimated completion: Spring 2011
Franklin Covey "Seven Habits of Highly Effective Leaders", Everett, WA   2012
Navy Prototype School, Charleston, SC   2009
- Hands-on study of design and operations of mechanical and electrical systems, including causality response in a nuclear power plant.

Navy Nuclear Power School, Charleston, SC   2008
- Graduate level training in Math, Thermodynamics, Chemistry, Physics, Electrical Engineering, Material Sciences, Reactor Dynamics, and Nuclear Plant Operations.

Highlights of Experience

Reactor Mechanical and Auxiliaries Division Officer / Quality Assurance Manager   2011 – Present
USS ABRAHAM LINCOLN, CVN 72, Everett, WA
Supervise, lead, train, and manage two divisions of over 60 nuclear trained mechanics and 20 enginemen in operation, maintenance, repair, and quality assurance of reactor support mechanical systems, four diesel generators, and reactor safety systems for two A4W nuclear reactors. As Quality Assurance Manager, create and verify procedures, validate maintenance practices, and provide jobsite supervision and post completion verification.
- Reduced the number of mechanical safety incidents by 50% after taking over Reactor Mechanical Division. Revamped the ship's carbon steel safety/inspection program, developed more effective training, and established a higher sense of ownership throughout the division, resulting in increased overall safety onboard.
- Safely executed over 2,000 maintenance/repair items, from identification through planning, execution and completion, during a seven-month repair cycle, allowing for early project completion.
- Commended by inspection teams for calm response and leadership during complex casualty situations. Selected to stand Propulsion Plant Watch Officer by the ship's Reactor officer during an intense Operational Reactor Safeguards Examination and Post Overhaul Reactor Safety Exam. Selected to stand General Quarters Propulsion Plant Watch Officer during heightened security/tactical situations.
- Qualified Nuclear Engineer by Naval Reactors (Department of Energy). Consistently sought out to run the most complex plant evolutions and train peers on aspects of plant operations.
- Qualified Propulsion Plant Watch Officer. Led teams of 22 nuclear trained mechanics, electricians, electronic technicians, chemists, and conventional mechanics in the safe operation, maintenance, and casualty response of a critical or shutdown nuclear reactor.

Supply Officer / Weapons Officer / Anti-Terrorism Officer   2009 - 2011
MHC CREW CONQUEST, Ingleside, TX
Managed all aspects of supply operations, including parts procurement and budget control. Developed and implemented training for the Weapons department. Coordinator for weapons and ordinance expended.
- Oversaw a $2M annual budget. Saved the U.S. Navy over $200,000 through extensive parts research and procurement.
- Qualified Officer of the Deck. Responsible for the safe navigation, routine operation, and tactical maneuvers of three Coastal Mine Hunters during day to day, mine hunting, and combat operations.
- Developed and executed a force protection training plan to ensure safe protection of U.S. Naval Vessels ship during a six month Arabian Gulf Deployment.
- Over a 5-month span, trained one Greek and two Egyptian crews on handling, operations, maintenance, and fire-fighting/damage control of 3 Costal Mine Hunter class ships while preparing them to be sold under Foreign Military Sales.
- Commended by inspection team and Commanding Officer for being responsible for passing the ship's Supply Management Inspection and Maintenance Management Inspection with zero inventory and zero financial discrepancies.

Personal Information

Rocky Mountain Rescue team member, 2004-2006.
- Participated in over 300 rescue missions per year.

Fig. 15 Sample Resume of US Navy Officer (Resume courtesy of Bradley-Morris, Inc.)

Sample 3: Junior-Career Level Resume.

Joe Shelby
123 South Ardmore Street
Fort Smith, AR 75601
(501) 555-0000 Cell
Joe.Shelby33@gmail.com

EDUCATION

Duke University, Durham, North Carolina
Bachelor of Science in Political Science, minor in legal studies
Graduated: 05/11/2013

MILITARY AWARDS

Sea Service Deployment Ribbon (awarded twice); Global War on Terrorism Medal; Iraqi Campaign Medal (2-campaign star cluster); National Defense medal; Naval Unit Citation Ribbon; Marine Good Conduct Medal; Combat Action Ribbon; Letter of Appreciation; Expert Rifleman Badge (3rd Award); Pistol Sharp Shooter Badge.

EMPLOYMENT HISTORY

Public Defenders Office- Legal Intern   01/2013-04/2013
Cumberland County Court House, Fayetteville, NC
          Observed and took part in decision making operations during actual court trials, and participated in pre-trail
          interviews of clients and helped to maintain and organize court documents
          Conducted all other expected duties in an office environment

Behavioral Health Clinic- Access Coordinator   06/2012-12/2012
Cape Fear Medical Center, Fayetteville NC
          Insured that all patients had correctly filled all proper legal documentation
          Notarized involuntary committed patients
          Worked with little or no supervision and handled sensitive information in a mature and professional manner

United States Marine Corps- 0311, Infantry Rifleman   01/2006-01/2010
1st Battalion 3rd Marines, Bravo Company
MCHB at Kaneohe Bay, HI
          Conducted two combat deployments to Iraq
          Deployed as SAW (M249) gunner, Team Leader, and Acting Squad Leader
          Training NCO for 10 months
          Member of the Company Level Intelligence Team for 6 months

SKILLS & QUALIFICATIONS

          Proficient in Microsoft Office tools (Word, PowerPoint, Outlook, and Excel)
          Effective at academic and legal research
          NC Cumberland County Notary: commission expires 09/10/2017
          Secret Security Clearance expires February 2016
          Limited understanding of French and Arabic
          Trained in CQB, MOUT, Desert Operation, Sensitive Material Gathering

ORGANIZATIONS

Duke University Political Science Association-Founder and President from 01/2012 to 05/2013
Pi Kappa Alpha- Founding Father of Colony, Alumni Chairman, and Interview Captain from 01/2012 to 05/2013
Pi Alpha Delta International Legal Fraternity- Active member from Fall 2011 to Spring 2013

Fig. 16 Sample Resume of Junior-Career Level Individual
(Resume courtesy of Bradley-Morris, Inc.)

Cover Letters

Most recruiters look first at the resume and then look at the cover letter if further information or explanation is needed.

As a general rule, most recruiters look first at the resume and then look at the cover letter if further information or explanation is needed. That is because the resume gives them an immediate snapshot of your experience, the types of organizations you have worked for, the reporting relationships you have managed, and the budgets you have controlled. Add to that the fact that most cover letters are filled with fluffy, generic information about what a candidate wants to do and what value she brings to the table, and a recruiter—either corporate or headhunter—will defer to the resume every time.

There is one exception, though: When someone is looking to make a career transition, say from finance into sales or military into private sector, then the cover letter becomes more important. That is because now the reverse is true—the information contained on the resume is not an exact match to what the recruiter is looking for, so the recruiter needs to understand what the candidate is hoping to achieve in applying for the position.

Cover letters can be in hard copy or email format, but let's assume that you will be using the email variety because it is so much more efficient to go that way. There is an excellent website where you can find specific rules and tips regarding cover letters, thank you letters, and resume writing, including templates, models, and "builders," called Susan Ireland's Resume Site: http://susanireland.com/letter/how-to/. That's an excellent website for well-respected, free resume and cover letter advice. In fact, one of Susan's standard cover letter templates is labeled "Military Transition," and that is a great place to start.

Your goal in drafting your cover letter will be to translate your historical military skills and abilities into a new, private sector world, demonstrating your future potential. That may sound like a tall order, but it is reasonable and doable because so many who have gone before you were successful in transitioning from boots to loafers. And they all began the same exact way—only without the handy guide and guiding hand that this book offers.

Cover Letter Sample

Let's take a look at a typical sample cover letter that may work for you depending on your writing style and level of comfort and your confidence in describing your skills, knowledge, and abilities.

Dear Recruiter:

Please accept my resume for the Senior Financial Analyst position posted on Monster.com. I am currently transitioning out of the military and into the private sector and I believe that I can make the same contribution to your organization that I have successfully made to the US Army, both at home and overseas, for the past two decades.

I've held progressively responsible accounting and finance positions in the army and I hold my bachelor's degree in business with a minor in accounting from the University of Denver. In my most recent role at Camp [NAME] in [LOCATION], I reported to the [TITLE] and oversaw a team of [#] [TITLES] who focused on [RESPONSIBITIES]. These areas appear to be a close match to the roles and responsibilities outlined in your job posting, which is why I'm very excited to submit my resume for consideration.

I've taken the liberty of researching your organization and reviewing your website prior to submitting my resume, and a smaller, manufacturing and distribution organization in the [INDUSTRY] field is exactly what I am looking for in terms of criteria for selecting my next employer. I hope that my resume demonstrates that I'm a long-term player and a very dedicated and loyal worker. Returning home again to the Raleigh-Durham area makes me realize how fortunate and proud I am of the place where I grew up.

It would be an honor to be considered for this role and the opportunity to join your team. I look forward to hearing from you and hope to have a chance to explain how my skills and accomplishments in the US Army can transfer into future benefits for XYZ Corporation. Thanks so much for your consideration!

Sincerely,
Paul Falcone

Fig. 17 Sample Cover Letter (Cover letter courtesy of Paul Falcone.)

Okay, let's break this down a bit. First of all, if you are not comfortable using contractions in your writing ("I'm" versus "I am"), then feel free to avoid them altogether. The level of comfort and folksiness versus formality that you choose to demonstrate is strictly up to you.

Next, notice the transparency and clarity of your message: I am exiting the military after twenty years, this will be my first job in the private sector, I know what I want (and you are it), and I feel so blessed to be back home. If the company you are sending the letter to is vet friendly, you might even mention the number of deployments you have made. That is a great way to structure your overall message.

The fact that you have researched the organization in advance of forwarding your resume is definitely a perk that will allow you to stand out in the employer's eyes, so be sure and get credit for it by stating that you have done that extra step right up front. And your closing focuses on transitioning from your military past to your private sector future, using your accounting and finance skills as the link in your career progression.

Bravo! Your cover letter has gone a long way toward helping you improve your candidacy, especially since a civilian employer might not understand the significance of your role in the military after having reviewed your resume. With the cover letter, you have made it fairly simple for them to understand your message and goals, and you have given them a way to link your past with your future. Since most employers will look for ways to screen in former military members because the country is currently in pro-support-our-troops mode, as well as because it is simply the right thing to do, you have now given this front-line screener a reason to add your resume to the short list of candidates for further consideration.

And that is probably the healthiest way to look at this. Your goal as a job candidate and prospective employee is to help a recruiter understand how to translate what you did in the past to what you can do for them in the future. Online articles and blogs may tell you that recruiters are simply looking to screen *out* resumes for fear of making a mistake, but that is distorting the truth. It is time to shed some light on that ugly perception.

Is it true that recruiters screen out resumes of candidates who may not be a good match for the organization? Yes, of course—that's a no brainer. And is it true that they do that out of fear of making a bad hire? Yes, of course—what else are they there for if not to make excellent hires for their companies by selecting people who could make long-term contributions and avoiding those who can't? But recruiters are not looking to screen people out for the sake of it. They would prefer to bring in as many credible candidates as possible so that the hiring managers in their organizations have multiple people to choose from. But there is some truth to the perception that recruiters tend to screen resumes out of a sense of fear, and it is simply this: If a new hire comes aboard and does great, then the hiring manager takes the credit; if a new hire joins the company and fails miserably in terms of integrating into the new role or the organization as a whole, then fingers tend to point back to the recruiter for referring poorly qualified candidates (especially if this happens more and more often).

> . . . recruiters want to hire veterans if they can figure out how to make a case for their relevance relative to given openings they are recruiting for.

In loose labor markets marked by high unemployment where there are few jobs and oodles of candidates available, employers can be very choosy. In tight labor markets where candidates are scarce and there are job openings everywhere, it is amazing how flexible employers become in terms of their willingness to train new hires and to allow for a learning curve.

The challenge since the Great Recession of 2008–09 reared its ugly head is that we have been in a labor market where jobs are scarce and candidates are plentiful, which does indeed make it tougher for recruiters to justify hiring a finance person out of the military when she can find someone out of a direct, private-sector competitor relatively easily.

That is easy enough to explain and understand. But it misses the point that recruiters want to hire veterans if they can figure out how to make a case for their relevance relative to given openings they are recruiting for. While you have been away serving our country both here and abroad, the "Star Spangled Banner" and "God Bless America" have graced every kind of ball game or sporting event imaginable. Support Our Troops stickers have been attached to millions of cars throughout the country, and the federal government along with numerous special interests have made it a critical mission to ensure that the general public is aware not only of what you have done for us, but also of what we need to do for you in return. So, the goodwill is definitely out there.

The question is, will your cover letter provide enough meat to help the recruiter screen in your resume? Can you make a cogent enough business case that your transferable skills will transition effectively into this job, your first private-sector role? Bear in mind as well that some employers may be hesitant to hire someone straight out of the military because of the cultural adjustments that are typically necessary to complete the transformation. It is tough enough to learn how to navigate a new job in a new company; in an employer's mind, having to also get used to the private sector's way of doing things may simply be too much to ask of a veteran, so the employer reasons that it would be better to hire you in your second job in the private sector rather than your first one out of the gate.

Assuming you can agree that those are reasonable concerns, your next step is to determine a strategy that will help you overcome those natural fears on the part of an employer. First, don't be afraid to make your cover letter a bit more informal and comfortable. The assumption on an employer's part is that you are going to be running around saluting and calling everyone "Sir" and "Ma'am." So don't come across as overly formal. A comfortable writing tone in your cover letter will probably serve you better. For example, don't open your cover letter with "To Whom It May Concern." That is too corporate speak and impersonal. You certainly do not want to open your cover letter with "Dear Gentlemen" or "Dear Sirs." Yikes! Probably 60–80% of the people you will deal with in human resources or the recruitment world will be female, so your all-male introduction would be an immediate red flag.

And be careful not to try to come across too smart. People who write about their ability to "strategically leverage human capital assets" rather than saying that they are effective leaders who build teams based on trust and selflessness simply won't get many responses from an employer. I don't even know what it means to "strategically leverage human capital assets," and candidates who describe themselves as "thought leaders" and "change agents" typically end up turning off recruiters and hiring managers who just want to hire *people*—and nice people at that! So go ahead—put on your friendly face when approaching prospective employers and recruiters. Know that they may be a bit hesitant to invite you in for an interview because, despite the fact that they want to help veterans and do their part, there is a risk that you might not work out in the role you are applying for.

But you are no different from anyone else going through a major life transition. If you were transitioning out of college and into your first full-time role, you would face similar challenges. If you were attempting to change career paths and move from one discipline (e.g., finance) to another (e.g., marketing), you would face recruiters who have similar concerns. What if you had been with your most recent company for twenty years and were laid off because it closed its doors and declared Chapter 7 bankruptcy? Wouldn't recruiters worry that you would be too used to working for one company and culture and might have difficulty transitioning into a new environment? Oh, and don't forget about those folks who have been laid off three or four times since the Great Depression of 2008–09 hit. Don't you think that a recruiter might be thinking that those folks have been laid off too many times despite the bad job market and that they might not be good performers or might not get along well with others?

Corporate America has been on a right-sizing, streamlining, and efficiency binge since 2008, and that trend probably is not going to end any time soon.

The bottom line is, take a deep breath and realize we're all in this together. Corporate America has been on a right-sizing, streamlining, and efficiency binge since 2008, and that trend probably is not going to end any time soon. Making your cover letter and resume represent you as someone comfortable, safe, cool to hang with, and full of motivation and engagement will go a long way in assisting recruiters and employers to help you find a new home.

A second strategy called the Law of Large Numbers can help you through the job search challenges that await you as well. Since a company is not rejecting *you*, per se, but the pedigree or experience history that you represent, you will come to realize that your only defense against the inevitable rejections that will come your way lies in putting volume on your side. The more companies you contact, the more rejections you will generate—but also, the more acceptances. To put another twist on how people have traditionally reviewed the rejection that comes along with a job search campaign, *you actually want to increase the number of rejections you get!* This is because increasing the number of rejections is the only way to increase the number of acceptances.

With that somewhat nonconformist thought in mind, remember that you cannot let five (or one hundred) rejected resumes get in the way of your successful job search campaign. You simply cannot know all the ingredients that went into a particular search assignment or the company's past history in trying to fill that particular opening. You won't normally receive any follow-up from the company about why you were not seen for an interview or ultimately selected for a job, but let's pull back the curtain on how these things sometimes play out behind the scenes:

"We couldn't get to all eight hundred resumes that came in. After we reviewed the first two hundred, we had enough candidates to develop a short list."

"Our new recruitment assistant made a mistake querying the database because she used the wrong keywords. We never got to see top-tier resumes that fit our exact specifications, and we didn't realize that until the search was over and we'd filled the position."

"We were going to hire John Doe, but just then, the company president's son got out of jail, so we gave him the role instead."

"She was the perfect candidate, but since she was referred by an executive search firm, there was a $50,000 fee attached to her $150,000 salary. We decided not to pay a fee and ultimately went with the number two candidate."

The list goes on and on about quirky situations and exceptions to the rule. In the search business, for example, contingency recruiters are measured by the number of outbound phone calls they make every day, since that is the only way to ensure success. Here's how their ratios typically work:

- 50 outbound phone calls = 1 qualified candidate
- 3 prescreened candidates over the phone = 1 viable candidate they can refer to a client company
- 8 interviews with client companies = 1 offer

So again, remember the Law of Large Numbers and let greater exposure increase both your rejections and acceptances. By playing a volume game with your high quality resume, you will let the ratios take care of themselves in terms of the number of acceptances you generate. So how do we generate more and more opportunities to forward resumes to prospective employers? Glad you asked!

The New Millennium Job Search

The days of looking in the classified ad section of your local paper and submitting one resume for one job opening are long behind us. That job search strategy only worked well in the days before globalization and technology forced Americans to compete internationally for local jobs at home—after all, call center representatives who hear from you about trouble with your cell phone, cable television service, bank account, or just about anything else are often in India, Brazil, or other countries. Thanks to the Internet, we can now compete in this global market using tools that help us promote ourselves exponentially. It's all about evolutionary change at revolutionary speed; this mass-marketing job-search capability will help you compete on a scale never before known to mankind.

With your sample resumes and introductory letters all prepared, it's time to develop a job-search strategy by the numbers. Remember that you will want to employ most of these resources at the same time. That is how you will gain the most exposure and coverage in the shortest amount of time, to allow the Law of Large Numbers to work in your favor.

Job Boards

Job boards are the new version of classified ads in newspapers from the olden days. On these websites, you will see long lists of bona fide job descriptions for companies' current available openings. For that reason, they make the most sense in terms of your first step of a job search. Just remember that they should never represent the *only* step of your job-search campaign because their methodology is passive: you submit a resume and hope to hear from someone. That's so twentieth century. The twenty-first century is all about proactive outreach, which I'll talk about in a moment.

The most popular job boards in use as of this writing include:

- www.Monster.com
- www.Indeed.com
- www.USAJobs.gov
- www.JobFox.com
- www.Hound.com

- www.CareerBuilder.com
- www.SimplyHired.com
- us.jobs
- www.Net-Temps.com
- www.CollegeRecruiter.com

There are an overwhelming number of options to choose from, so let's do this the easy way. First, rely primarily on the job boards listed earlier in the section on "Tapping into the Hidden Job Market" to focus on job openings with veteran-friendly companies. (All of the websites mentioned throughout this book are also listed for your reference in Appendix 3.) After all, if certain organizations are going out of their way to attract veterans—whether they simply believe in the cause or need to do so for their affirmative-action outreach efforts—why not start there, especially since there are plenty to choose from?

That doesn't mean, however, that you should ignore the larger boards listed above. Rather than trolling for openings on these mega job-search boards, reverse your strategy just a bit: Upload your resume to the largest job-search sites and get free job alerts matched to your experience and location. Now that's working smart! For example, Indeed.com and SimplyHired.com are website aggregators, meaning that they search other websites for job openings that match your criteria. They then email you daily or weekly (depending on your preferences) with postings that are close to what you are looking for. Hound.com and several other sites will do this for you as well, but Indeed.com and SimplyHired.com are the most well known for their aggregating abilities.

While you are there, post your resume and make it searchable. This way recruiters conducting keyword searches will be able to find you even if you do not know who they are. Again, this is a very smart and proactive strategy on your part. One caveat, though—every time you upload your resume, you will be asked to create a user name and password to tie your resume to your current email address. Create a simple spreadsheet with the date of your resume upload to help keep track of all of these "resume ambassadors" you're generating and remember when and how you set them up. Here is what your simple spreadsheet should include:

1. Job-board name
2. Job-board web address
3. Date account created
4. User name
5. Password
6. Security questions and answers associated with account
7. Resume version/name uploaded (e.g., Resume_YourName_Monster)
8. Website help info (email address and 800 phone number)

Each entry should take you about a minute, but it is a great way to track and measure your proactive outreach efforts. You will also know how to remove your resume from those sites once you have found a new position.

Social Media
As Richard Bowles so eloquently puts it in his book *What Color is Your Parachute, 2014 Edition*, "Google is Your New Resume." In other words, we are all

traceable to a high degree nowadays because of our online profiles on LinkedIn, Facebook, and Twitter (just to name a few). Most employers will take the time to check out your online profile by doing a Google search before you come in for a meeting. And what they find out may be telling. Despite the courts battling over what constitutes an invasion of privacy versus what is fair game when it comes to job applicants' personal social media, the reality is that practically everything you have ever posted on the Internet is viewable. And while it could take decades for the courts to come to some fair and agreed-upon resolution as to what is allowable in this ever-changing world of social media and Internet tracking, assume that you will be researched on Google and LinkedIn (at the very least) by the time you walk in the door at many companies—especially the more senior you are in terms of your title.

> . . . assume that you will be researched on Google and LinkedIn (at the very least) by the time you walk in the door at many companies . . .

This can be a disadvantage if the materials you have posted in the past negatively reflect upon your character or your judgment in terms of some of the decisions you have made, however you can use social media to your advantage as well by building a strong web presence via LinkedIn and Facebook. And you can literally let the entire world know that you are looking to transfer from a military career path into a private sector role. In fact, when you think about the exponential power of the Internet to catapult your exposure to recruiters and prospective employers, the possibilities are amazing.

By the way, if while checking out your own Internet profile you find something questionable that you would not want prospective employers to see, type "How to remove an item from [NAME]" into your Google search box, filling in that [Name] space with Facebook, LinkedIn, Twitter, Pinterest, Plaxo, YouTube, or MySpace. Conduct a little research, and you should be able to find detailed instructions about removing any unwanted comments or photos. Bear in mind though that the Internet is like a spider web of connections, so just because you removed the objectionable item today from the primary site doesn't mean it is not still out there on someone else's site. How's that for making you paranoid? Then again, you can only do so much, so remove the item as quickly as you can so as not to tempt the Fates! Following are some social media tips that will help you with your job search.

LinkedIn has more than 200 million users, many of whom are employers scanning the site for passive job seekers . . .

LinkedIn (www.LinkedIn.com). This is the primary social media website that you will want to focus on because it is considered a professional website and is used primarily for career management purposes. LinkedIn has more than 200 million users, many of whom are employers scanning the site for passive job seekers (i.e., people who may not be looking at job boards or applying to ads, but who nevertheless might be excellent candidates for a particular position). You will definitely want to upload a photo of your face (not your full body from twenty feet away!), and you should add any keywords to your overview that would help a search engine find you.

In addition, under "Current Position," you have the option of writing something along the lines of "Currently in transition" and then describing what you are ideally looking for. LinkedIn is a great resource because it gives you room to tell your story and connect with others—former schoolmates, family members, and old friends. You can also ask friends to reach out to associates in their network who work at particular companies and set up online introductions on your behalf. And there is plenty of relevant information on the "Jobs" tab that allows you to search for all sorts of jobs. Take full advantage of this site and its free resources, and get to know it well before you decide to invest in upgrading your account to premium status. Lastly, while you are setting up your new LinkedIn account, please take the time to join the *Boots to Loafers* discussion group and get involved in the conversation there.

Creating a Vanity URL on LinkedIn. Recall from the previous section on resume "Format and Content" that our sample Contact Information block at the top of the resume included this LinkedIn profile URL: www.linkedin.com/in/paulfalcone1. You will want to include your LinkedIn address once you have an account. When you create a LinkedIn profile, you will be assigned a generic address containing lots of numbers that strains the eye a bit. To avoid having to use this messy address on your resume, create a "vanity URL" that is easier on the eye and that leaves out all those unnecessary digits. To create a vanity URL in LinkedIn, take the following steps:

1. Log in to your LinkedIn account.
2. Hover your mouse over your name in the top right corner of the page and click on "Settings" in the drop down menu that appears.

3. Click on "Edit your public profile," which you can find at the bottom of that page under the "Helpful Links" heading.
4. Click on "Customize your public URL," which you will find on the right side of the page in the "Your public profile URL" section.
5. Once the text box pops up, type the last part of your desired custom URL in the text box, then click "Set Custom URL." Depending on how common your name is, LinkedIn will generate the closest options for you, sometimes placing a 1, 2, or 3 after your full name.

Voila! Your vanity URL will show up on your LinkedIn page from that point forward.

Facebook (www.Facebook.com). Facebook is not considered a professional site, per se, but it is the big daddy of all things social media, with more than a billion users. Besides giving you an opportunity to let others know of your job search desire, you can sign up on pages devoted to job hunting and careers, such as www.facebook.com/jobhunting. You can identify and reach out to people who work for particular companies that you are interested in using Facebook's search capabilities. There is an app available via BranchOut.com that allows you to see where your friends work and to search oodles of job openings.

Additional Social Media Sites. Other sites like Twitter.com (which allows you to convey your "in transition" status in your background), YouTube.com (where you can post a video resume and even create your own channel through a widget at www.widgetbox.com/widgets), and JobShadow.com give you plenty of options for profiling your resume in various ways across the World Wide Web.

Putting It All Together

One who smiles rather than rages is always the stronger.

—Japanese proverb

We have covered a lot of material in this chapter. It is a great deal of work, however it will pay off in the long run. Get your new network up and going. Your family, friends, military associates, childhood schoolmates, former colleagues and coworkers, teachers and mentors, and association comembers are all accessible thanks to the rapid development of social media. Again, don't

Build your LinkedIn webpage carefully, taking advantage of all the bells and whistles to create your candidate profile in the most ideal light.

be overwhelmed by all of this. Simply choose one or two social media platforms and make them part of your job search strategy. For example, if you do nothing more than create a LinkedIn page, you will be well on your way to establishing your Internet presence in the world. Build your LinkedIn webpage carefully, taking advantage of all the bells and whistles to create your candidate profile in the most ideal light. It is better to have a great presence on LinkedIn than a mediocre presence on five different social media sites.

Think about your transition strategically. Create a career spreadsheet that maps out and tracks your job search efforts as follows:

- The first tab of your spreadsheet contains your user names and passwords for all the places where you have posted your resume. It will also include your LinkedIn and/or Facebook account information.

- The second tab keeps a record of the various job postings you have applied for online using one to three job opening websites you like most that focus on military veterans.

- The third tab lists the companies, names, and contact information of the people you have interviewed with—either for current openings or on an exploratory basis. (More on this in chapter 3.)

- The fourth tab on your spreadsheet shows the dominant and growth-oriented companies that you have researched and submitted your resume to.

- The fifth tab contains information from the *Occupational Outlook Handbook* that points you toward the fastest growing industries in your field(s) of interest.

- The sixth tab on the spreadsheet includes your family members and close personal friends who are looking out for you, in addition to associates at local community establishments, fellow church members, and the like.

Of course the list could go on and on, depending on whether you are including job fairs and other events that bring employers and job candidates together.

Whatever your outreach strategy, allow your spreadsheet to guide you each step of the way. It will keep your job search efforts organized and balanced; it will remind you to employ multiple paths of outreach and not get stalled at the passive, "I applied for a job online today" mentality that takes you back to classified ad strategies of the past; and it will help you measure the metrics that lead to more rejections and—more importantly—more acceptances.

. . . interpersonal time spent on the front end of the relationship during the interview is critical to ensuring long-term success in the role . . .

By the time you find a role that matches your interests and skills, you will be able to look back at this beautiful work of art and use it to show your kids and even grandkids how to launch a job search strategy like a pro one day when it is their turn. Learning job search strategy, after all, is part of the gift that this newest challenge in your life is offering you. And every challenge comes with its own reward because it makes us more empathetic and understanding of others. Looked at holistically, this "New Me 2.0" strategy may have challenges—it does for all of us—but it will launch a new you and a new career all at the same time. Embrace the opportunity, be thankful that you are capable of competing, and enjoy the spirit of all you are about to learn about yourself and the private sector as you venture into a new world packed with surprises and new revelations. This is life at its fullest!

3. YOU GOT THE INTERVIEW! NOW WHAT?

Ah, the lovely world of interviewing—even if you have spent twenty years of your career interviewing candidates from the hiring side of the desk, it is not always a lot of fun being interviewed as a candidate. For most of you, interviewing for a new position in an organization will be a whole new experience. You just don't interview for a new job in the military very often unless the new position is working in a major headquarters in a key role—aide-de-camp, or perhaps working for one of the senior service leaders at the Pentagon. However, when a private-sector interview does come your way, you need to be prepared to nail it—it is just that simple.

It is natural to think, "You mean I have to prove to a stranger that I'm worthy to become a member of this team?" Don't fret if you ever feel that way. Still, the interpersonal time spent on the front end of the relationship during the interview is critical to ensuring long-term success in a role, since there is so much at risk for a manager or recruiter during each hiring decision and only so much that a resume can tell him.

The challenge is that every interview is so incredibly different, with some people not knowing how to conduct an interview, others maintaining a "drill sergeant" approach to rigid compliance, and some interviewers doing all the talking and not letting you, the candidate, speak at all. Yet, it is an even playing field for us all because it is where we all start out—on the front end of the selection process with our resumes in hand, smiles on our faces, prefect resume attire to present ourselves, and a readiness for whatever challenges await us. The up side to this entire process is that if you are selected for an interview, the recruiter or HR professional considers you to be qualified for the position. Due to the number of resumes that flow into any organization and the selection process used to establish a pool of viable candidates, if you get the call that you are in the pool, the odds of landing a job just got much better.

There isn't time here to go into every individual interviewing style out there; there are books that deal with this very subject if you want to get more detailed information, including Paul Falcone's *96 Great Interview Questions to Ask Before You Hire* (AMACOM Books), a perennial bestseller that will allow you to take a behind-the-scenes look at the interview questioning process from the hiring manager's point of view. People's interview styles are as unique as their personalities. But how you come across as a candidate in terms of your comfort level, self-confidence, self-knowledge, and level of career introspection, along with the degree of your ambition and your excitement about the position, really makes an incredible difference. Bottom line: your attitude will make a huge difference in the outcome of your job search and subsequent interview. So let's cover some of the key areas that you will likely face in a typical interviewing environment and prepare you to put your best foot (or, loafer) forward to ensure that you stand out as a rarity among your peers.

Prep Work: Do Your Research

Candidate, know thy company! Well, at least know enough about it to engage in healthy discussions and ask intelligent questions. It used to be that to research a company in advance, you had to spend hours at the local library and, in many cases, order books and magazine articles that could take weeks to arrive. Fortunately, today the Internet does all the legwork for you; as a rule of thumb, you will want to spend at least an hour preparing information on each and every company where you are scheduled to interview. To make the data gathering process easier, use this outline to gather your thoughts (The Coca-Cola Company is used here as an example):

Company Research Overview	
Company Name (include Inc., LLC, or other legal entity information)	The Coca-Cola Company and Coca Cola Refreshments
Industry	Consumer Goods, Non-alcoholic beverage
Physical Address & Phone #	One Coca-Cola Plaza, Atlanta, GA 30301 404-676-2222
Website Address & Findings: Company philosophy, mission statement, target consumer markets, primary vs. secondary product lines, tenure of senior executives, community service goals and charities supported	www.coca-cola.com
Parking Instructions (Costs)	No cost. Go to front gate on North Avenue and the guard at the gate will instruct me where to park.
Year Founded	1886
Annual Revenue	Net Operating Revenues of $48 Billion, Operating Income of $11 Billion
# Employees (domestic vs. international)	CCR is approximately 70,000 The Coca-Cola Company is about 150,000 worldwide
Headquarters Location	Same as above
# Locations (both national and international)	In over 200 countries around the world
Top 3 Competitors	Pepsi, RC Cola (owned by Dr. Pepper Snapple Group), a variety of local brands around the world
Industry Trends (SWOT[1] Analysis, Growth Prospects)	http://www.bls.gov/ooh/
Other	

Fig. 18 Company Research Overview Worksheet

. . . quote your sources so that the interviewer is made aware of the time and effort you took to research the organization . . .

Publicly Traded Company Research Websites

As you might suspect, there are multitudes of resources available to track and trend publicly traded company performance. First, it is required by law; second, and more significantly, there is a big incentive to get private investors to purchase public companies' stock, so simply choosing one or two of the resources below should provide you with ample information to help you come across as an informed candidate during an interview. Just be sure to quote your sources so that the interviewer is made aware of the time and effort you took to research the organization before coming in for your interview. After all, if you do the research but the interviewer doesn't realize it, you lose the credit for your efforts.

As you research a company, make note of these important facts:

- Stock's ticker symbol
- Exchange on which stock is traded (NYSE, NASDAQ, etc.)
- Current stock price
- 52-week low/high range of stock price
- Price/earnings (P/E) ratio
- Expected earnings growth

These are the best websites to use in researching publicly traded companies:

- Zacks Investment Research (www.zacks.com/screening)
  ° Make note of Zacks industry rank and buy/sell recommendation
- Hoovers (www.hoovers.com)
- US Securities and Exchange Commission (SEC)—EDGAR Company Filings (http://www.sec.gov/edgar/searchedgar/companysearch.html)
- Bloomberg Businessweek, for recent company news (http://investing. businessweek.com/research/company/overview/overview.asp)

Privately Held, Small Company Research Websites

Private companies can be challenging to research because they are secretive about their business information, but there are ways to penetrate their veil of silence by referencing their corporate websites, online business directories, news sites, online trade and professional journals, and websites specifically intended to evaluate privately held companies. You will have to be creative, though, because unlike with publicly traded organizations, the goal is to keep private information private. These resources may help you learn about private companies:

- Business.com (www.business.com)
- PublicRecords.com (www.publicrecords.com)
- Yellow Pages (www.yellowpages.com)
- Better Business Bureau (www.bbb.org)

Nonprofit Research Websites[4]

The nonprofit world is surprisingly robust. The US nonprofit sector consists of about eleven million workers, or 7% of the entire US workforce, with roughly two million nonprofits in existence today. It is estimated that twenty- to thirty-thousand new nonprofits are launched every year, and the cumulative revenue for this sector is approaching $700 billion, or roughly 9% of the US gross domestic product. So don't discount opportunities in the nonprofit sector by any means. To learn more about a nonprofit where you are considering interviewing, visit one of the following sites:

- Guide Star (www.guidestar.org)
- Charity Navigator (www.charitynavigator.org)
- Better Business Bureau's Wise-Giving Alliance (www.bbb.org/us/charity/)

Company-Culture Websites

Proceed with caution when viewing the sites below. Clearly any time a website creates an open invitation for workers to log on and share their thoughts about their experiences as employees of particular companies, it is bound to get overly negative comments, especially when workers use sites like this to vent. In addition, websites that publish open-source salary data are not validated or confirmed by one unifying entity (like a compensation consulting firm or government agency); they simply invite workers to share their salary information anonymously, and salary ranges are typically very broad (sometimes with a 100% spread), depending on respondents' tenure, education, licensure, and the like.

Still, social media sites like LinkedIn and Facebook are making it much easier to get the scoop on what is going on at particular organizations and what it is like to work there, so the websites below may have some limited usefulness in putting the pieces of the puzzle together, especially if you see overall trends and patterns in the responses. Just bear in mind that most people don't log in to say how much they love their company—they usually log in to vent about their frustration, so give these sites only limited credibility:

- glassdoor (www.glassdoor.com)
- Jobitorial (www.jobitorial.com)
- PayScale (www.payscale.com)
- Salary.com (www.salary.com)
- Hallway (www.hallway.com)

Take the one-sheet Company Research Overview in figure 18 with you on all your interviews once you launch your job search. When invited to ask questions at the conclusion of your meeting, be sure and ask two or three smart questions based on the research you have developed while preparing for the meeting. Remember that there is a difference between "smart" questions and "filler" questions. Filler questions take up time and fall into the "conversation for conversation's sake" category. For example, this is a filler question: "What year was your company founded and how many employees do you have?" Smart questions, based on your research, involve the interviewer at a different level: "I read about some of the challenges your industry is facing from online competitors. How are the brick-and-mortars responding?"

Phone Screens

With the multitude of online applications rolling out on the Internet, most corporate recruiters and hiring managers have developed a first-line-of-defense screening mechanism that is a big time saver for them: telephone interviews. If someone does not pass this initial smell test (e.g., he doesn't speak well, he puts his prior supervisors down, or he appears to have little career direction or ambition), then a short, ten-minute phone screen just saved an hour or two of the hiring manager's time as well as a little money on the back end because she doesn't have to engage in an elongated, in-person interview, pay for the candidate's parking, offer coffee and engage in small talk, etc.

> . . . corporate recruiters and hiring managers have developed a first-line-of-defense screening mechanism that is a big time saver for them: telephone interviews.

The question is, what are employers looking for in order to screen in or screen out a candidate during the initial telephone interview? The answer is actually pretty simple: they want to make sure that you can articulate what is in print on your resume, that you have a fairly comfortable communication style and aren't too over the top in terms of your responses (i.e., not too funny, militaristic, politically oriented, etc.). So the rule to follow is simple: just be yourself. Don't overthink your telephone screen meeting, just as you shouldn't overthink your in-person interview. There is a fairly consistent telephone interview screening matrix that employers often use; let's take a behind-the-scenes look at this tool—make sure you review its content prior to any upcoming telephone screening interviews.

Employer Telephone Interview Screening Matrix	
Candidate Name: **Position Applied For:** **Today's Date:**	
I. Current/Prior Company History & Job Knowledge	
Revenue and size of employee population	
Company niche: primary vs. secondary product lines/competitive ranking	
Size of team supervised /titles of staff/structure	
Supervisor title/department or divisional structure	
Salary progression: starting vs. current base salary	
Bonus target percentage/next payout date	
Deferred compensation structure: stock options, restricted stock units, other profit-sharing/next payout date	
401(k) match vs. defined-benefit pension plan participation	
Software systems currently in use	
Primary reason for leaving	
Current schedule (hours, travel percentage)	

Employer Telephone Interview Screening Matrix	
Next move in career progression if candidate opts not to leave/timeframe to make a change	
II. Success Profile	
Career progression in role from when first hired until now	
Greatest achievement (in terms of increasing revenue, decreasing expenses, or saving time)	
Educational credentials/certifications	
Foreign languages/international experience	
Self-admitted shortcoming/areas for development	
Last performance review score (identify scale measures)	
Understanding of our company based on prior research/level of "informed candidacy"	
III. Self-Assessment of Individual Needs	
3 criteria in selecting next company or position	
Other pending offers on the table	
General salary expectations (base, bonus, total cash compensation)	
Timeframe/availability to resign	
IV. Other Notes	
"Red Flags" of concern	
Overall suitability for position	
Invite for an in-person interview?	

Fig. 19 Employer Telephone Interview Screening Matrix (Example courtesy of Paul Falcone)

No particular recruiter will ask all of these questions, and many may raise issues that are not included on this checklist. Still, corporate recruiters, operations managers, and headhunters generally follow a script like this before progressing to an in-person interview. In addition, considering these types of questions will help you prepare answers for your in-person meeting, so be sure and practice your responses so that you are comfortable answering questions like these if they come your way. The importance of rehearsal cannot be overstated. As part of your transition process, you must be prepared to answer questions about yourself, your goals and objectives, your willingness to relocate, and such. Rehearse these answers until they are "canned." It is critical for you to get to a point where answering these questions becomes second nature.

Courtesy and Exploratory Interviews

There is a big difference between "courtesy" and "exploratory" interviews. A courtesy interview takes place when someone refers you to a company so that you can meet with a member of the management team or the Human Resources department in order to expand your network, pick his brains about career options, and get general career advice from a successful professional in the business world. Courtesy interviews are an important part of anyone's job search because you never know what they can turn into. Referrals from one company to the next, an email about a new job opening that crosses the employer's desk five minutes after you leave the office and that sounds like a great fit for you—you name it. Doing preliminary meet-and-greet interviews is a smart strategy and should be part of every candidate's repertoire.

An exploratory interview, on the other hand, is a lot more serious. A company will often meet with prospective candidates for exploratory interviews when there is either an opening that is not yet announced or when there is a plan to increase headcount by creating a new position within the organization. In cases like these, exploratory interviews give employers an opportunity to assess the talent market and identify what it is that they really need. More often than not, the employer falls in love with a particular candidate and then builds the new job around that person, so to speak.

As a matter of fact, this is where the headhunting business offers the most value. Both contingency recruiters, who are only paid if companies hire their candidates, and retained recruiters, who are paid fees for their consulting services regardless of whether client companies hire their referrals, work on filling job searches when there are particular vacancies within organizations. On the other hand, smart headhunters often identify a really strong candidate, build a marketing plan around that individual, and then call companies to see if they would have an interest in meeting with that individual on a proactive, exploratory basis. A headhunter's pitch during such a phone call might sound something like this:

> *Ms. Employer, my name is Paul Falcone, and I'm an executive recruiter with the XYZ Search Firm. I've identified a divisional controller who works directly for one of your competitors and who knows the key players, industry trends, and key financial measures in your industry. We believe he's geared for progression in his career and that he could make the same contribution to your organization that he's currently making to his present employer.*
>
> *When we identify a candidate who stands out as a rarity among his peers and has just the right education level, industry experience, licensure, and the right type of personality, we ask him for a short list of companies where he would be proud to work. This individual identified your organization right off the bat, and in circumstances like that, we look to schedule an exploratory meeting with that company to see if there might be a special fit. I know that strong companies are always looking for strong players, especially at this level, and I'm wondering if you'd consider sitting down with this individual on an exploratory basis to see how he'd be able to take your organization to the next level.*

If you are straight out of the military, then headhunters may only be a limited resource for you at this point. That is because headhunters typically earn their fee by identifying candidates out of direct competitor companies for the client organization they are recruiting for. However, in today's environment, a number of major corporations are publically announcing their intent to hire veterans, so your odds of securing a headhunter are a bit better. When you start researching headhunters, simply ask them how many veterans they have placed in roles and whether they assist in the transformation, meaning do they coach, teach, or mentor you in interview prep and run mock interviews. Even if you are not in a position now to work with a headhunter, it is good for you to understand how search firms operate, because they may play a more significant role in your career a few years after you transition into the private sector. This scenario will also help you better understand the significance of an exploratory interview.

In short, if you are scheduled for an exploratory interview, prepare just as you would if you were interviewing for a bona fide, posted job opening. You never know what may come of an exploratory interview, but the headhunter's strategy is simply one of getting your name and qualifications to the HR professionals before the formal need arises and the job gets posted. After all, if a headhunter can engender enough of a sense of curiosity that the client company wants to meet with his candidate, there is probably something going on at that company that the public is not aware of. Otherwise, the employer wouldn't take the time to meet with anyone. In fact, in certain situations, headhunters' proactive outreach efforts are so early that the company's Human Resources department may not even be aware that there is a job opening under consideration. No doubt about it, interviewing on an exploratory basis can pay big returns if your timing happens to be right.

. . . prepare just as you would if you were interviewing for a bona fide, posted job opening.

Dress for Success

Dressing properly for an interview is very important but can get rather expensive, so let's walk through this together. Remember a simple rule: dress for the interview, not for the job! You may know that everyone at this company dresses in jeans and a T-shirt most days, but that doesn't mean that you should dress that way for your interview. The interview tells the employer that you know how to dress for success and that you clean up well, so to speak, regardless of the organization's daily dress-code expectations. Of course, much of this will depend on the type of company where you are interviewing, so be sure and ask what the appropriate attire would be (traditional versus relaxed) for your first meeting. The following guidelines for both men and women are a good place to start.

Men's Standard Dress
There are typically two modes for interviewing: formal (business suit and tie) and relaxed (sport jacket and open neck). Assume that the default will be a busi-

Assume that the default will be a business suit and tie.

ness suit and tie. The goal here is not to turn you into a fashion consultant or ask you to run out and buy a $1000+ business suit. You should be able to purchase a handsome, designer-name suit at one of the major retailers for about $300. Add two shirts and two ties, along with a sharp belt and loafers, and you are probably in for another $300. On the other hand, a number of wholesale outlets will sell you three of everything—suit, tie, shirt, socks, and belt—for under $1000. Don't be hesitant to visit your local Goodwill or consignment store if your personal circumstances don't allow you to spend hundreds of dollars on interview clothes; you may be able to cut these prices by up to 80% and still look great!

Depending on your budget and your penchant for name-brand designers, you should be able to dress to the nines for anywhere from $500 to $1000 without a problem. Go with a solid color—navy or dark gray—although a light, pinstripe look should work fine as well. Your long-sleeve, collared shirt should be white or another light color coordinated with the suit, but bright colors should be avoided. Ties, on the other hand, can be bolder, and a red or yellow, solid or patterned tie is very common.

When I retired from the military, I didn't even own a suit. I had a blue blazer; khaki pants; a white, button-down-collar shirt; a tie (maybe two); and a pair of civilian shoes. When I moved into the private sector and started interviewing, I had to buy a couple of suits with all the trimmings. If you get a job in an organization where men wear suits every day, this can get rather expensive very quickly. A "business casual" dress code (slacks, sport coat, and a collared shirt) will reduce the cost of dressing for work, while "casual" (golf shirt and slacks) is even cheaper. The point here is that dressing for your new life should not throw you into bankruptcy. Be smart, look for sales, pay attention to what others are wearing, and space out your purchases.

Forgo aftershave. There is simply too much risk that the interviewer may be hypersensitive to strong smells. In addition, little or no jewelry tends to be the norm, with the maximum topping at out three items: wedding ring, college ring, and watch. You will want to don a neat, professional hairstyle, with your hair away from your face, and be sure to trim your nails prior to the meeting. It goes without saying that shaving before an interview is highly recommended; shadowy beards may make for handsome actors pretending to be doctors on your favorite network drama series, but that is not the look you want to portray when putting forth your best effort to land a job.

Avoid flashy cuts in the jacket or skirt that might appear to show too much skin; frivolous lace should be avoided as well.

And make sure your socks are long enough! There is nothing worse than when a man crosses his legs and you can see the hair on his leg because his socks are too short when his pants leg recoils. Make sure to shine your (typically black) shoes before your interview. It makes no sense to put so much work into the appropriate interview attire only to forget to polish your shoes and, as a result, have them stand out as beaten up and out of style.

Finally, go through a head-to-toe appearance check to make sure you have left no stone unturned: sharp belt that is not overly worn, crisp shirt that has preferably been dry-cleaned, and tailored pants with a fine crease. Think of this entire process as putting on your new uniform, making sure it is all put together properly—gig line straight and dress-right-dress. Nothing new here on proper appearance. You will feel like a million bucks.

Women's Standard Dress

A fashionable two-piece suit or two-piece dress ensemble should be worn by women for most corporate-type interviews. Avoid flashy cuts in the jacket or skirt that might appear to show too much skin; frivolous lace should be avoided as well. Hemlines should end just above the knees, but you have some flexibility to go a bit longer. Coordinate your matching accessories appropriately; accent scarves, belts, and purses should match the tone of the overall image you are trying to convey. Remember as well that understatement and modesty are what you are striving for when it comes to interviewing. Your entire appearance from head to toe should come across in the vein of "less is more" and "please focus on what I'm saying and what I've accomplished rather than on what I'm wearing."

Sensible shoes are important. Spiked high heels risk making you stand taller than all other human beings you will meet that day and do not convey a professional image. Fashion consciousness should not compete with career consciousness in terms of the message you are creating. Generally speaking, wear a lower heel and avoid extreme new styles. Also, be sure to wear a pair of shoes that you are comfortable in; breaking in new shoes on the day of the interview can lead to unintended consequences like pinched toes and calluses, not to mention slips and falls.

For more of a blue-collar type of workplace, you can sidestep the suit and go with a two-piece business dress. Pair a sleeveless shirt with a jacket, or a top with a matching skirt in a simple color scheme of solid blue, black, or grey, or a light print. Nothing too ostentatious, since you are not dressing for the cameras and the red carpet—you are dressing to impress and to land the job.

Jewelry should be on the light side—simple and classy always trumps hanging baubles and loud statements. Overall, jewelry should complement, not compete with, your overall professional look. Avoid flashy bracelets or oversized rings, and opt instead for a simple necklace or chain with matching earrings. A conservative watch adds a professional touch.

Forgo perfume. Too many people appear to be developing allergies these days, and it can be very uncomfortable for an interviewer with a super-sensitive nose to make it all the way through the meeting if there is even a hint of perfume in the air. It is better to be safe than sorry, and skip the perfume altogether. Likewise follow a less is more approach when applying makeup. Pancake foundations and bright lipsticks or eye shadows will arguably lose points for you because they detract from the professional, modest, and conservative impression that is expected of candidates during an interview.

Tattoos, Piercings, and Other Forms of Body Art

Few companies have policies that specifically restrict or forbid tattoos, nose rings, eyebrow posts, and the like. And most employers will tell you that they personally respect a person's right to don those accoutrements as he sees fit. After all, it is your body and your life, and no one should be able to tell you otherwise.

. . . there may be some hesitation to extend a job offer for fear that you don't know how to distinguish effectively between what is appropriate in an interview setting and what is not.

Here is the reality of the situation, though. In the world of interviewing, body art can hurt your chances of landing a new job. Even if an interviewer has no personal bias against your right to adorn yourself as you see fit, and even if that interviewer happens to personally like the particular expression you have chosen and how you have chosen to display it, there may be some hesitation to extend a job offer for fear that you don't know how to distinguish effectively between what is appropriate in an interview setting and what is not.

Sure, a veteran who was recently discharged from the service after an impressive career run may experience the desire to self-express now in ways that the military did not condone or allow. But showing too much of that self-expression during the interview process can potentially damage your candidacy, because interviewing in the private sector—much like in the military—has its own set of norms and expectations. So, tone it down. The mission at hand is to get a job. Don't lose sight of the goal. When in doubt, remove the piercing and cover the tattoo. It is simply one less potential negative regarding your candidacy. Then again, if it is that important to you and something that you consider a fundamental part of who you are, just understand and accept that it may hinder you in certain—though not all—situations from time to time.

What to Take With You

First, be sure to take along eight to ten hard copies of your resume for each and every in-person interview that you attend. That may sound like overkill, but you never know how many people you will be introduced to once you arrive at the work site. Nothing is more embarrassing than sitting there with your hands in your lap while the interviewer is calling people and looking in her inbox to find the resume that she was given prior to your arrival. It is uncomfortable for her, awkward for you, and it starts the meeting off on an odd note.

Instead, think how nice it would be for you to say, "Would you like a hard copy of my resume?" And the interviewer would kindly respond, "You know, I'd love one. I know I've got it here somewhere, but by the time I find it, you could have started working here already!" And there you have it—landmine avoided without any drama. Do not assume that because you applied online or had a telephone interview with a screener prior to this meeting, your hard-copy resume will follow you wherever you go once you arrive. That is a rookie mistake that should be avoided at all costs.

You do not need a super-expensive leather briefcase, but keep your resume copies and company notes, including the Company Research Overview in figure 18, in a nice, 8 ½" x 11" portfolio pad with a professional looking pen.

This way, if the situation arises where you want to share some of your research with the interviewer, everything will be neatly organized and easy to find. On the back of the Company Research Overview worksheet, jot down two or three questions to ask the interviewer when invited to do so. (More on that to come.) Showing up organized, prepared, and neat not only makes a great impression, but also helps you feel confident and engaged during the meeting.

The Two-Minute Drill

Think about this potential scenario, which has happened to me many times: You are heading to your office when the president or CEO or other senior executive joins you in the elevator. He says, "Tell me about yourself" or "What you are working on?" After the blood rushes to your head and you switch into crisis mode trying to come up with a somewhat intelligent answer, you blurt out something. Fifteen or twenty floors later, the conversation is over, and you either blew it or made a great impression.

The old saying "first impressions go a long way" is true, which is why you need an elevator speech, otherwise known as the two-minute drill. This concept takes practice, but once you have it nailed, you are ready. It gets its name from the fact that you probably have a person's attention for a short period of time. Other situations where this concept will pay off: a social event where a senior executive asks you the question over a drink; a question asked during an interview to break the ice; a conference that you are attending; a bar conversation; or even on the street with a stranger. These are all situations where the two-minute drill comes into play.

In preparing your two-minute drill, don't simply summarize your resume. How boring! Your drill should be passionate, personal, interesting, and most of all, brief. It should be a quick introduction with some key, basic points of information that can be conveyed in two or three floors of an elevator ride, not thirty. Once you have created your drill, practice it with someone and ask that person for feedback: "Was my drill interesting? Are my career goals clearly defined? Am I displaying energy and passion about my experience and career? Most importantly, am I demonstrating how I will make a difference to the position and company?" Keep refining your drill, and practice it until you can say it in your sleep. You may find that your two-minute drill is not a one-size-fits-all for every situation or event, so once you feel comfortable with the first one, create a couple more.

Here is a simple example of just such a situation that happened to my wife: She had just been downsized (i.e., let go) from a company and could not stand just sitting around looking for a job, so she went to her local gym and asked if they needed any help. They said they did, however, the position was being the person who opens the gym at 5:00 a.m.! She told them it would not be a problem and to sign her up. Her reasoning was simply, who goes to the gym at 5:00 a.m. before they go to work? The answer: a lot of business men and women. One particular gentleman came in each day like clockwork. My wife struck up brief conversations with him, and, over time, he started asking her a lot of questions about herself. Why was she wasting her time opening the doors of the gym? What had she done in other jobs? What would she like to do? As it turned out, this gentleman was the editor of the city newspaper, and after numerous conversations—two-minute drills—one day he said, "Come down to the newspaper and let's see how we can find you a real job." Fast-forward about two months and my wife was working for a major newspaper, where she stayed for more than three years.

A few lessons to be learned: First, you never know where your next job will come from. Second, you never know some days who it is you are actually speaking to. Third, have your two-minute drill ready to go at all times.

Understand Your Interviewer

There are no right or wrong interviewing styles. Put another way, there are as many interviewing styles as there are interviewers. It is all a matter of what interviewers value and look for in candidates, and how they make their interviews fit their natural communication styles. Paul's interview style is very informal: It is more of a "sit on the couch, peer to peer, get to know you and help you know us" type of approach to interviewing. His goal is to discuss what a candidate is looking for and how the open position may serve as the next step in her overall career progression. Paul typically offers cookies, licorice, and a can of Coke (I am a loyal employee!!) or bottle of water to make a candidate feel at home. His logic? Only if a candidate is totally comfortable with him will she divulge her true, innermost job-hunting secrets. In his mind, if a candidate responds, "Well, normally I wouldn't share this on an interview, but . . ." then he knows that he's gotten to the real person behind all the interview hype. And that is his goal, plain and simple.

Some companies take interviewing very seriously and don't allow for much individuality among their management ranks.

To gain another perspective on interviewing, my style as an interviewer is very similar. Although there are a set of questions that need to be asked during the interview, I do not always follow the script. Similar to Paul, I like to get to know the candidate and get underneath all the formalities. It is important to understand what the candidate has done in relation to the job he is interviewing for and to ensure he is a fit within the company.

Fit, from a corporate or business perspective, is probably a new term for many of you. Essentially, it refers to how an individual fits into the company's culture. Paul and I both understand how stressful an interview can be on the candidate; it is also stressful on the people across the table asking all the questions. From my perspective, it is all about getting the right candidate who can do the job as well as being a good fit for the company, and usually also about stretching the person a bit so he can grow professionally.

Is there a right or a wrong interview style, per se? Of course not! It's simply a matter of what best suits a person. On the other hand, some interviewers forget to follow a simple rule: to let candidates do 80% of the talking, saving their own questions and comments until the end. When interviewers do forget that rule, your "interview" becomes not much of an interview at all; you simply sit there, nod your head, make good eye contact, and smile. If you get a job offer after a Chatty-Cathy interview like that, though, you may need to slow down the process so that you can better understand what the job is all about.

Interviews can be quirky. You have probably heard about those off-the-wall interviews in which someone is asked questions about the size of the world's population, his favorite character on a TV show, or a song that best describes his work ethic. Fortunately, those wild and woolly questions are highly exaggerated in the media and won't come your way in a real-life setting very often, but if they do, don't shy away. Have some fun with the interview and try to place yourself in the best light.

Some companies take interviewing very seriously and don't allow for much individuality among their management ranks. They basically want everyone asking the exact same questions the exact same way. Their logic? If we ask the same questions in the same way to all candidates, then our candidate selection process will be fairer, easier to document, and able to withstand legal scrutiny if we are ever audited by the Equal Employment Opportunity Commission or Office of Federal Contract Compliance Programs. While that logic may be understandable, the real purpose of interviewing is not to avoid a lawsuit; it is to identify and select the most qualified candidates for a particular job opening within an organization. Hopefully companies that take such an extreme approach to the candidate selection process at least allow their hiring managers some level of flexibility to show their personalities during interviews by customizing the questions somewhat.

Okay, now that you know that interviews can take all sorts of forms and formats—long (two hours), short (ten minutes), formal versus informal, asking versus telling—how can you prepare for some of the most common questions that will be coming your way? Let's look at how to approach this topic from the receiving end. Life is all about perspective, after all.

What Interviewers Are Looking For

This section of the book is written for you as a job applicant who is preparing for a private-sector interview in order to find a great job. But once you have been hired, you can use these very same questions and strategies as an interviewer to help identify and select strong candidates who you feel will be able to make a positive contribution to your company. Most interviewers, whether they realize it or not, are looking for basically the same things in the candidates they interview: a technical ability to do the job combined with, more importantly, a good fit between the individual's personality and the company's corporate culture. Here is how some of those macro issues may find their way into a typical interview scenario.

Employer Rule 1: Gauge the Candidate's Level of Self-Awareness. Expect employers to open their interviews with a question like, "Now that you're out of the military, what are you looking to do, and how do you see a role with our company helping you meet your long-term career goals?" You may get that type of first question fairly often, so be prepared to launch from the thirty-thousand-foot level right off the bat. It is a logical opener as well as a respectful icebreaker and a question that is easily fielded utilizing your two-minute drill strategy.

A variation on that theme may be something along the lines of, "Walk me through your progression in your military career, leading me up to the last role you held." A follow-up query might sound like, "What makes you stand out as a rarity among your peers?" and progress to, "What would your most respected critic say of your strengths, areas for development, and future potential as you transition into the private sector?"

Employer Rule 2: Look for Compatibility, not Just Likeability. Hiring managers tend to hire in their own images, but as they look beyond immediate chemistry and focus on the open position, expect questions like, "How sensitive are you to accepting constructive criticism?" or, "How much structure, direction, and feedback do you generally prefer on a day-to-day basis?" and, "Do you generally ask for permission or forgiveness when making decisions?" as well as, "Tell me about a time when you may not have erred on the side of caution when you should have." Unless the employer is focused on matching the candidate's personal style to her department's corporate culture, she may end up with someone who can do the job technically but is totally out of sync with the rest of the team. Poor fits, who end up in resignation or termination ninety days or six months into a new assignment, rarely occur because of a technical mismatch; they are almost always the result of a cultural mismatch where a new hire simply doesn't fit in.

Employer Rule 3: Assess the Candidate's Desire Factor. There is no excuse for candidates not having researched a company, its achievements, competitors, and challenges prior to an interview. Still, some candidates do a far better job than others in terms of articulating their understanding of who they are and why they are so excited about joining a particular organization. Expect employers to ask questions like these to isolate those who are hungriest for the opportunity that they offer: "Why would you want to work here, and what do you know about our organization?" "What makes us stand out in your mind from our competitors?" "If you were to accept this position with us today, how would you explain that to a prospective employer five years from now? In other words, how would this role with our company provide a link to your future career progression?"

From the employer's side of the desk, the goal is to keep a keen eye out for compatibility in communication, pace, constructive criticism, and work-hour commitments based on candidates' responses.

With answers to these very broad, open-ended questions in hand, you will be ready for just about anything that any interviewer could throw your way. Understand that these are tough questions, and they are not easy for anyone at any level to answer, whether a long-term corporate careerist or a newly minted military retiree looking forward to opening his second chapter in life. From the employer's side of the desk, the goal is to keep a keen eye out for compatibility in communication, pace, constructive criticism, and work-hour commitments based on candidates' responses. Once you transition from candidate to employer, remember that every interview gives you an opportunity to share your wealth of knowledge and experience with others; if you simply see the meeting as a chance to give a gift to someone else—whether you hire that person or not—you will find that the communication becomes a lot more natural and enjoyable on the giving (i.e., employer) end. So do not be shy about being comfortable and being yourself when you are on the receiving (i.e., candidate) end. Remember, you are in search of your new true north, and every opportunity to share your gifts with others is a step closer to the goal.

Typical Interview Questions

Traditional Interview Questions. Traditional interview questions include the following:

- What did you like best/least about being in the military and the various roles you have held?
- Who was your favorite/least favorite superior and why?
- What do you see as your long-term career goal, and what do you think you will be doing five years from now?

Holistic Interview Questions. Holistic interview questions look to the whole person in terms of gaining a greater understanding of how that individual sees himself and his various roles throughout his career. Questions like these are typical in a holistic interview:

- What are the broad responsibilities of an artillery officer?
- What other duties or responsibilities did you have?

These simple questions can be very telling.

Achievement-Anchored Interview Questions. Most employers look for achievements when reviewing candidates' resumes and will typically raise the matter during the interview itself. Achievements can be "hard" or "soft," depending on the role and circumstances. For example, sales executives are charged with increasing revenue, plain and simple. They have their feet on the gas pedal at any given time and must know how to gun it on occasion. Finance managers, by contrast, have their feet on the organizational brake, looking to cut expenses and save time. So those roles are typically easy to quantify in terms of dollars and percentages; something either went up or down during those employees' tenure, and depending on the level of responsibility they held, they were either on the cause or effect side of those changes.

But it is not so easy to quantify hard-core revenue increases or expense savings of employees in other fields of corporate America, like human hesources, research and development, or field operations, for example. Of course, these individuals have crucial roles to fulfill, but their contributions are not easily evidenced or codified by quantitative results. Because the line between cause and effect gets blurrier for these middle matrix roles, it takes a bit more work for an interviewer (as well as a candidate) to define the impact of their contributions.

Let's look at the human resources (HR) example: A strong HR team impacts the company culture in many ways, including the way leadership, communication, and teamwork occur on a daily basis. Learning and development teams, for example, build training programs that espouse the company's people philosophy, and HR generalists embedded in their operational groups or at the corporate headquarters office demonstrate an appetite for allowing and encouraging mistakes versus merely tolerating (or ultimately firing for) them. The problem is that a really successful HR team is evidenced by, well, *nothing*. No lawsuits, minimal turnover, few if any workers' compensation claims, no union organizing efforts, etc. So companies sometimes reason, "Why do we really need an HR team in the first place? What do they do anyway? We don't have any problems!" Then they lay off the HR team members, only to find themselves up to their eyeballs in alligators two to three years later with union organizing attempts, excessive turnover, and the like.

The question for you is, how do you quantify the results of your actions? This is one area in which military parlance does not translate very easily into private-sector lingo. If demonstrating hard, quantifiable achievements is challenging for you because you cannot simply morph them into nice little packages of dollars or percentages showing increased revenue or decreased costs, then it is time to look to soft achievements and determine how to sell them to your benefit.

73

Soft achievements may include the equivalent of an employee-of-the-month award, an on-the-spot bonus, or an acknowledgment by leadership or peers that you stand out among others at your level. Think of a college graduate who holds a black belt in Tae Kwon Do, speaks two foreign languages, runs the college radio program as the volunteer news director, or serves as editor of the law review. Those are outstanding achievements because they demonstrate leadership and community involvement, but they have no direct monetary impact that can be easily quantified on a resume.

Looking at this another way, hard achievements can be bulleted in a separate section on a resume, whereas soft accomplishments are typically woven into the narrative of the resume's job description:

- Hard Achievement Examples:

    ° Acknowledged as the Top Battery Commander for consistently exceeding training requirements and ranking in the top 10% of all company-grade officers in the division.
    ° Received an award from the division commander for receiving the highest physical training scores in the division for the last eighteen months.

- Soft Achievement Example:

    ° Reported to the chief of staff and led a team of four direct (supervisor level) and sixteen extended (section leader) reports; served as the interim chief of staff on a regular basis and represented the commanding general at senior-management staff meetings.

Can you see the value of the soft achievement as well as the challenge in making it a freestanding bullet on your resume? It does not quite lend itself to a freestanding, bulleted format, does it? Well, the same goes for your interview discussions; they may not be as evident as hard achievements, but weaving your soft achievements into the conversation is exceptionally important. After all, using the example above, the chief of staff felt so comfortable with you running the ship in her absence and representing her during management staff meetings that she could travel more and feel total peace of mind that you were manning the helm in her absence and keeping the ship's sails all moving in the right direction. There may not be a direct monetary link to that type of accomplishment, but it is just as important—if not more important—than other more visible, hard achievements that come up during the interview discussion.

> **Rehearse how you would respond to questions and be sure also to avoid slang terminology.**

The bottom line is that during an interview, you need to demonstrate, in a humble manner, what made you stand out as a rarity among your peers and how you were acknowledged. Don't make the interviewer dig too deeply for those accomplishments; while it is noble not to brag about yourself, you have to give yourself the advantage of translating your military coups and kudos into a narrative—both written and verbal— that a prospective employer can understand and relate to.

Speech, Language, and Appropriate Use of Vocabulary

It goes without saying that you want to avoid any military acronyms that a civilian might not understand. But more than that, you have to remain aware of explaining your achievements and accomplishments in layman's English so that employers will be able to understand your message clearly. Rehearse how you would respond to questions and be sure also to avoid slang terminology. This is no different from what you had to do before preparing for a mission—rehearsal is never time wasted. Examples of slang responses to avoid are "yeah," "uh huh," and filling in your responses with "so," "um," and "like" when you start stumbling. Even if the company seems laid back and relaxed, you do not have permission to act or sound unprofessional.

Here is an example of Paul's from the private sector. As a recruiter in health-care early in his career, Paul was working at a hospital that had a lab focused on the human genome project. When interviewing a post-doctorate research fellow under consideration for a particular bench scientist role, he explained upfront, "Please answer my questions in layman's terms. The last time I took biology and chemistry was in high school, and I can't say they were my favorite subjects. Still, I'm going to have to explain your achievements and goals to the principal investigator who's hiring for this position, and I'd appreciate it if you'd speak slowly and explain things to me as you go. Would that be okay?" And to that humble request, he always got a resounding "Yes, of course!" That set the tone for the interview from that point forward. After all, everyone likes to teach to a certain degree, and giving people an opportunity to speak about themselves in layman's terms presents both a challenge and an opportunity to reflect on how much they've accomplished in their careers.

Now picture this: You are interviewing for a private sector position, perhaps for the first time in your career, and all your responsibilities and achievements occurred in a world in which very few civilian leaders ever spent a day in their lives. How do you translate your achievements to someone who does not understand the basics of what you do, who does not appreciate the context within which those hard-fought accomplishments were won, and who cannot relate to the experiences you are sharing?

. . . too much military lingo and you could possibly alienate your audience and raise issues about your ultimate fit . . .

The answer is simple: go back to the research scientist analogy—someone who did not study science beyond high school chemistry and biology can still be an effective interviewer *if* the candidate explains things clearly, draws relevant analogies, and is patient in walking the interviewer through the conversation so that he has a higher level of understanding. This will no doubt take some time and patience on your part, as it is a critical skill that may not come so easily. But simply keeping your intended audience in mind—without talking down to them—so that they have a broader, simpler understanding of what you have accomplished is a great mindset to interview with and an excellent advantage for you in terms of demonstrating what makes you the special individual that you are.

This is important too: Don't answer every question with "Yes, Sir," "No, Sir," and "Absolutely correct, Ma'am." Granted, in the south and some other parts of the country, addressing others like this is a sign of respect. But too much military lingo and you could possibly alienate your audience and raise issues about your ultimate fit with the non-military public. Likewise, it's not "O-eight-hundred." It's "eight o'clock." Acting a bit looser and lightening up is an important part of the transition for any returning veteran. Be sure to make those you interview with feel as if they can get to know you and befriend you. A more casual, conversational tone may go a long way in helping others feel a more immediate bond with and connection to you, especially when meeting you for the first time.

Behavioral Style Interviews

A behavioral interview question, also referred to as a behavior-based question, asks you to give more detail about a particular situation so that an interviewer can create a real-world context around your response. For example, if an interviewer asks, "What is it that you like least about being a manager?" you may respond that you really dislike having to fire people. And that is a fine answer. But the interviewer probably is going to want to discuss that a bit more. So she may continue with questions like this:

> *Yeah, I can imagine. That's always a difficult thing to do—I don't like terminating anyone either. Let me ask you this: when was the last time you had to terminate someone for cause, and what were the circumstances that led up to your decision to recommend termination?*

Can you see how that logical follow-up question asked you to provide more detail and make your response more concrete? Now here is an example of how a simple question like that could wind its way into some pretty interesting areas of discussion regarding the way you look at the world:

> *Okay, so when you think about what happened in that circumstance, was there anything you could have done differently? In retrospect, did you leave any stone unturned or feel like there may have been more to the story than that?*

> *So could there have been a circumstance that might have led you to think differently about your decision to terminate or that could have prompted a different recommendation on your part—maybe a final written warning or suspension rather than outright termination?*

> *As you think about it, how could you handle a similar situation differently in the future?*

> *How would you grade yourself on a scale of one to ten in terms of how you handled that? What could have made the experience a ten?*

> *How did your supervisor evaluate your decision in that particular instance? Was your HR department supportive or did they recommend a different outcome?*

As you can see, a behavioral interview can take you off the structured question and answer (Q&A) path and into unknown territory, which is the goal. The closer you stay to the scripted Q&A format of interview questions and responses, the less the employer gets to know the real you. Conversely, the more you veer off the straight and narrow path of pure Q&A interview questioning patterns, the more the real you comes out and the scripted you disappears.

Behavioral interview questions call for on-the-spot self-analysis. There are generally two types of behavior-based interview formats: self-appraisal and situational questions. Self-appraisal queries ask candidates, "What is it about you that makes you feel a certain way or makes you want to do something a particular way?" On the other hand, situational queries look for concrete experience as an indicator of future behavior. The standard behavioral interviewing question typically begins with the phrase, "Tell me about a time when . . ." or, "Give me an example of a time when . . ." or, "Tell me about the last time that you . . . ."

The beauty of this questioning methodology is that it can be applied to almost anything: a candidate's greatest strengths and weaknesses, his leadership and communication style, approach to teamwork, or penchant for asking for forgiveness rather than permission. In short, these types of questions ensure spontaneity because candidates cannot prepare for them in advance. Rehearsed answers to traditional questions go by the wayside in this ad hoc interviewing environment where candidates tell stories about real-life experiences. Don't fret, though—these questioning techniques are not meant to trick you, just to get to know the real you a bit better than might otherwise happen in a thirty- or sixty-minute introductory meeting.

Look at behavior-based interviewing questions, therefore, as a way to tell your story—an invitation from the interviewer to share your real-life experiences and solve workplace problems. And once you transition to the hiring side of the desk, be sure to implement this types of questioning format to ensure that you and the candidate are both on the same page philosophically in terms of how that individual solves problems, leads, and builds strong teams.

Targeted Selection and Competencies

Targeted selection is a natural offshoot of behavior-based interview questioning. Behavioral interview questions ask candidates to go off script and describe in detail how they handled particular situations, how they might have done things differently, how their supervisors critiqued their performances, and what it is about their natural styles that compels them to act in a certain way. And as mentioned above, behavioral questions can be applied to almost any interviewing scenario—what you like most and least about your role, how you approach workflow bottlenecks and employees with challenging attitudes, and so forth.

Targeted selection takes this same interviewing premise and moves it in a more specific direction, focusing on the performance factors or competencies that will be necessary to succeed in a particular job. Let's look at an example.

- **Step 1:** A company that uses targeted selection is looking to hire a front-line supervisor for a call center. HR tasks the management of that call-center team with identifying the core competencies that will make someone successful in that particular role. The management team comes together and defines those critical performance factors that will likely predict future performance and success.
- **Step 2:** The group then develops planned behavioral interview questions that will highlight and add dimension to the core competencies they have identified for the position. Specifically, the group identifies particular job-fit questions that will help distinguish possible matches and mismatches between the various facets of the role and candidates' experiences and preferences. The goal is to ensure consistency by asking the same questions to each interview candidate.
- **Step 3:** With the core competencies and behavior-based job-fit questions in hand, the management team will then record and assess candidates' responses using the STAR system (as discussed in chapter 2).

Candidates can be evaluated and rated consistently by looking at an overall numerical rating for each individual. And while the numerical rating is not intended to be a de facto indicator of which candidate must ultimately be selected (after all, certain areas may be weighted more than others), it makes the candidate evaluation and selection process that much cleaner and easier because everything is outlined so clearly and exceptional considerations can be duly noted.

Now that we have the theory down, let's take a brief look at this from the call-center management's perspective in our example. The leadership team is asked to develop the core competencies that will make a candidate successful in a front-line supervisory role and comes up with the following recommendations and behavioral/situational interview questions that highlight each particular competency.

Core Competency 1: Communication. Here are the performance factors and interview questions the leadership team develops for this competency:

- **Applied Learning:** Clearly shares information and ideas with individuals and groups to help them understand and retain the message.
- **Key Actions:** Organizes and communicates information effectively, maintains audience attention, adjusts communication style to the situation or circumstances at hand, listens well, and ensures understanding.
- **Planned Behavior-Based Questions:**

  1. Tell me about a time when you had to communicate a procedure change or institute a new policy to a group of employees. What was your approach?
  2. Describe a time when you convinced your peers that a new idea you had should be pursued. What was your approach, and what were the results?
  3. Working with others usually involves some form of negotiation. Describe a time when you worked out an agreement with a peer or team member. How did you handle the situation, and what were the results?

Finally, the STAR rating system (previously mentioned in the transition section) is applied and outlined in the supervisor's hiring guide as follows:

Communication	Key Actions
Clearly sharing information and ideas with individuals or groups to help them understand and retain the message.	Organizes the communication
	Maintains audience attention
	Adjusts to the audience
	Ensures understanding

Planned Behavioral Questions

1. Tell me about a time when you had to communicate a procedure change or new policy to a group of employees. What was your approach?

2. Describe a time when you convinced your peer(s) that a new idea you had should be pursued. What was your approach? What were the results?

3. Working with others usually involves some give and take. Describe a time when you worked out an agreement with a peer or team member. How did you handle the situation? What were the results?

Situation/Task	Action	Result	Effective (+) Ineffective (−) Neutral (/)

Follow-Up Questions to Build Complete STARs:

For Situation/Task:	For Action:	For Result:
Describe a situation when . . .	Exactly what did you do?	What was the result?
Why did you . . .?	Describe specifically how you did that.	How did it work out?
What were the circumstances surrounding . . .?	What did you do first? Second?	What happened as a result?
What were you reacting to?	Walk me through the steps you took.	

Fig. 20 Sample STAR Outline for Core Competency of Communication
(Example courtesy of Paul Falcone)

And there you have it: a completed targeted selection behavioral interviewing discussion around the core competency of communication. Now that you understand the basic logic and construct of targeted selection and how it is intended to work, let's look at a finished product for another core competency for the role of front-line call center supervisor: technical skills.

Technical/Professional Knowledge and Skills	Key Actions
Having achieved a satisfactory level of technical and professional skill or knowledge in position-related areas; keeping up with current developments and trends in areas of expertise	Understands technical terminology and developments
	Knows how to apply a technical skill or procedure
	Knows when to apply a technical skill or procedure
	Performs complex tasks in area of expertise

Planned Behavioral Questions

1. What activities have you participated in to improve your technical skills over the last year? How did you incorporate them into your current job? Can you give me an example of how you have used this training?

2. What technical training have you received? Give me an example of how you have applied this training?

3. Tell me about the most complex technical assignment or project you have worked on.

Situation/Task	Action	Result	Effective (+) Ineffective (−) Neutral (/)

Follow-Up Questions to Build Complete STARs:

For Situation/Task:	For Action:	For Result:
Describe a situation when . . .	Exactly what did you do?	What was the result?
Why did you . . .?	Describe specifically how you did that.	How did it work out?
What were the circumstances surrounding . . .?	What did you do first? Second?	What happened as a result?
What were you reacting to?	Walk me through the steps you took.	

Fig. 21 Sample STAR outline for core competency of technical skills
(Example courtesy of Paul Falcone)

83

Other questioning topics that may come your way as a candidate for a call center supervisory role might include: drive, planning and organizing, professionalism, quality orientation, teamwork, and leadership. You will probably be asked about six to eight competencies in all, with two to three behavior-based interviewing questions per competency (i.e., twelve to eighteen questions). Once your interview is complete, the hiring manager will then grade you and your responses using a scoring sheet; any other candidates interviewed for this position will be graded the same way. Just as an FYI, these are the instructions that the hiring supervisor must follow to assign an appropriate grade to each candidate's STAR analysis:

Instructions: Complete each step after the interview.

Identify complete STARs throughout the Interview Guide. (STARS= situation/task, action, result)

1. Indicate whether each STAR is effective (+) or ineffective (-) or neutral (/).

2. Consider the weight of each STAR according to its recency, impact, and relevance to the target job.

3. Determine the rating for each competency. Record it on the line in the lower right corner of each page.

Use the following rating scale:

1 Much less than Acceptable

2 Less than Acceptable

3 Acceptable

4 More than Acceptable

5 Much more than Acceptable

Additional Ratings:

N No opportunity to observe or assess

W Weak Data

Communication

Clearly and succinctly conveying information and ideas to individuals and groups in a variety of situations; communicating in a focused and compelling way that drives others' thoughts and actions. Engaging the audience and helping them to understand and retain the message.

_____ Organizes the communication

_____ Maintains audience attention

_____ Adjusts to the audience

_____ Ensures understanding

_____ Adheres to accepted conventions

_____ Comprehends communication from others

Communication Rating: _____

Fig. 22 Instructions to Interviewer for Completing Targeted Selection STAR Analysis
(Example courtesy of Paul Falcone)

Once each of the six to eight competencies has been graded this way, an overall score can be assigned at the bottom of the form upon completion of the entire interviewing process.

Phew! If this sounds like a lot of work, you're right—it generally is. Targeted selection focuses on sameness and consistency, which certainly helps companies withstand legal scrutiny if challenged by a government agency in terms of its hiring practices. But it is very time intensive on the employer's side. And it is a bit wearying for candidates as well. For example, answering twelve to eighteen "give me an example of a time when . . ." questions can get repetitive after a few responses, and there is a concern that candidates will just make stuff up after a while.

Targeted selection makes the behavior-based question the primary, core interview driver . . .

Targeted selection makes the behavior-based question the primary, core interview driver, which can get tiring after fifteen or twenty minutes, let alone after an hour or more! Nevertheless, many companies employ targeted-selection techniques, along with the STAR evaluation system, so it is important that you recognize this technique when it comes your way. Yes, the questions are very broad and open-ended. Yes, you will be responsible for putting meat on the bones and painting a picture of how you have handled challenges and roadblocks that came your way. But you can also rest assured that if you are being interviewed in a vein like this, so is everyone else, and that is what makes it an even playing field.

And while it can be challenging to field so many questions from so many different angles, you can prepare by disciplining yourself to respond effectively to a barrage of behavior-based questions. Grab a piece of paper or open your word processor and jot down answers to this question:

- How would you respond if asked for an example of a time when you became effective as a leader or individual contributor by demonstrating your abilities in the following areas?

    ° Leadership
    ° Communication
    ° Teamwork and Relationship-Building Skills

- ° Professionalism
- ° Customer Service
- ° Technical Know-How
- ° Adaptability and Change-Management Skills
- ° Conflict Management and Resolution
- ° Diversity Orientation
- ° Ethics, Integrity, and Trust
- ° Motivation
- ° Organization and Planning Skills
- ° Problem-Solving Skills and Results Orientation
- ° Productivity and Volume
- ° Quality
- ° Safety
- ° Self-Development
- ° Staff Development
- ° Time Management
- ° Work/Life Balance

This list of twenty core competencies, while not exhaustive, is pretty close to what you can expect from most employers' questioning arsenals. A simple exercise outlining how you might initially respond and what examples you would provide could go a very long way in helping you field any of the un-rehearsed questions that might come your way during the interview process.

What Questions Should You *Ask?*

Nothing ends an interview on a worse note than when the employer asks the candidate, "Are there any questions I can answer for you?" and the candidate responds, "No, I think you covered everything." Really? *You mean you want to work here for the next five or ten years, and you can't think of one question to ask me as your prospective employer?* reasons the wise interviewer.

No doubt about it, if you are interviewing for a position and do not ask questions, the interviewer

. . . if you are interviewing for a position and do not ask questions, the interviewer will walk away thinking you are either not very motivated . . .

87

will walk away thinking you are either not very motivated to join the organization or at least not sharp enough to fain interest. In short, you will simply experience silence in the form of a rejection letter further down the road.

It is not just a matter of asking questions, though; it is really about asking intelligent, well-thought-out questions that will help you stand out among your peers. The questions posed by candidates should reveal critical insights into their values, goals, and aspirations, as well as their analytical abilities and research knowledge. Let's look at some general rules for what to ask and, more importantly, what *not* to ask at the conclusion of an interview.

Rule 1: Don't Ask Filler Questions. Filler questions simply kill time or otherwise add very little value to the information exchange. Think of these as questions for questions' sake. Anyone with Internet access should not ask the following questions because the answers can be researched in less than five minutes:

- How large is your company in terms of employees and annual revenue?
- How long has your company been in business?
- What stock exchange trades your stock, and what has the recent price been?
- What is your primary product line and who is your primary target consumer?

I know what you are thinking: "I'd *never* ask those questions during an interview. It would make me look foolish to do that." Yes, you are right—but not being prepared to answer basic questions like the ones outlined in the Company Research Overview can lead to embarrassing moments that could kill an otherwise successful interview, so be sure and always do your homework in advance.

Rule 2: Don't Ask Selfish, What's-In-It-For-Me Types of Questions. Avoid questions like these:

- What do you feel this role could ultimately develop into over time, and does your company believe strongly in promoting from within?
- Will the person you hire for this role have his or her own assistant?
- Do you typically fly executives first class, and are there any other travel perks or executive perks that you could tell me about?
- Is a defined-benefit pension plan available? How much does the organization match in terms of employees' 401(k) contributions? Do you offer both traditional and Roth 401(k) options?

The problem with these candidate questions is that they violate one of the simple rules of interviewing: ask not what your company can do for you; ask what you can do for your company. Okay, I'm bending President Kennedy's quote a bit here, but you get the idea. Here is what an employer may be thinking in response to each of those selfish questions above:

- *You're thinking about promotion already? If I were you, I'd worry about landing this job first.*
- *Seriously, you're asking me during your first interview whether you'll have an assistant? I realize you may have been overseas for the past few years—I respect that—but are you kidding? People are lucky to have a job these days. Inquiring about an assistant during the first interview is way too premature. I'm turned off.*
- *You want first-class travel? How about I give you 50–75% travel instead, and then you can focus on how happy and self-motivated you're feeling during that one week a month when you're not on the road. I think I'm sensing a bit of a prima donna entitlement mentality here, and that could really spell trouble for us in the future.*
- *You're asking me whether we have a traditional pension plan and what our match is in the 401(k) plan. Hold your horses, we're not quite there yet. You'd need to be way down the interviewing road before I'd expect you to be focusing on such me-oriented questions.*

The bottom line is, go easy on any questions that focus on what you will be getting out of the relationship rather than putting into it, especially during the early rounds of the interview. You will have an opportunity to ask these questions and more once the company is seriously pursuing you during the final rounds of the offer. That is when they will likely put you in touch with someone from the benefits department to answer your questions about medical plans, monthly premium costs, and the like. Jump to these types of questions too early in the process, and you will likely come across as naïve at best or selfish and entitled at worst.

Rule 3: Do Ask Intelligent, Well-Thought-Out Questions Prepared in Advance. Questions like these will make a positive impression on your interviewer:

- I've had an opportunity to research your organization on the web and in the library before coming in today, and I'd be happy to share what I have found with you. But I was wondering what you believe makes your organization unique. What are two or three things that help you differentiate yourself from your competition?

- What do you believe would really make someone successful in this role? In other words, what two or three things would you want to add to a candidate's background experience or personal style to make that individual an ideal fit for the position?

- In my research, I couldn't identify the names of your top three competitors. Which companies do you focus on when measuring your organization's competitive position in the market?
- I saw in your online profile that you have been with XYZ for four years. What initially attracted you to join the company, if you wouldn't mind my asking, and what do you like most about working here?
- How would you define the organization's overall culture or at least the personality of your department? What do you think would work well in terms of making someone successful from a personality and personal style viewpoint?

What these questions have in common is that they focus on the positive and invite the interviewer to share personal stories and engage in more of a one-on-one conversation. Everyone likes to talk, especially about himself and what makes him or the organization he works for successful and special. Extending that invitation as a candidate is usually a wise move because it strengthens the personal bond and explores common interests.

You can always ask more technically-oriented questions like these as well:

- I understand the primary aspects of the role as you've described them and from what I've read online in the recruitment ad. Can you give me some additional background in terms of the secondary duties involved—maybe things that occur once a quarter or twice a year but that will still be an important part of this position?
- Can you share with me which systems you're currently using and whether you're having any particular systems challenges right now?

Technical questions are fine. Just understand that they usually won't help get an employer to fall in love with you. That type of reaction comes from the emotional types of questions that invite the interviewer to share more with you personally about why they joined the organization, why they still love it, and so forth. Then again, some interviewers may be guarded about sharing any type of personal information, and you will probably sense that throughout the interview. By the time you're invited to ask that type of close-to-the-vest interviewer some questions at the end of your meeting, you may indeed want to limit your questions to only technical matters and leave out anything that could appear to be overly personal in nature.

Likewise, a candidate to become an in-house recruiter with this company might ask position-specific questions like:

- What's the average number of openings that I'd typically be responsible for in this role, and how many projected openings are you estimating over the next six months?
- What percentage of my recruiting efforts would be spent sourcing senior managerial, versus professional or technical, versus administrative support candidates?
- If you wouldn't mind my asking, are you tracking the metrics of your costs per hire, time to start, and source cost analysis? Do you find your metrics trending upward or downward in light of the changes to the economy?

How many questions should you ask an interviewer at the conclusion of your meeting? As a general rule, ask two to three well-thought-out questions, and save the rest for another day (especially if this is a first interview). Use the questions in your arsenal to impress the employer, not just to gain additional data. That is the key strategy underlying the questions you are asking. Be sure to have a half dozen or so questions listed on the back of your Company Research Overview. This way you will never be stumped when asked to pose questions about the role, the company, or the people you will be working with and supporting. Remember that questions make the candidate!

Post-Interview Follow-Up

How do you keep your foot in the proverbial door after you have completed a round or two of interviews or are expecting an offer? Is a thank you note still appropriate, and if so, should it be on stationary and sent by snail mail or is an email acceptable? And can a poorly written thank you note make things worse?

A customized thank you note is not just a well-intentioned, personal afterthought thanking interviewers for their time. Rather, it is a key business tool that you will want to add to your job-finding arsenal. The note's uniqueness allows you to reinforce your strengths, overcome any perceived weaknesses, and share follow-up research with the company to demonstrate your interest. A well-written thank you note typically contains three sections:

> Remember that thank you notes are person-to-person communications, so make your note come alive with your personality, beginning with the opener.

1. An "it was a pleasure meeting you" opener.
2. Either a reinforcement—"I feel I'm particularly well-suited for the job because"—or recovery statement—"Although I'm lacking in one particular area, my skills and experience in other areas will allow me to compensate."
3. A close, "I feel I could make an immediate contribution to your company," coupled with, "And I'm really excited about the possibility of joining your organization."

With this type of winning structure in hand, your thank you note should go a long way toward keeping you front and center in the employer's mind when it comes to evaluating all candidates and coming up with a short list of finalists.

Remember that thank you notes are person-to-person communications, so make your note come alive with your personality, beginning with the opener. Avoid any corporate speak or jargon that sounds overly formalistic like, "Pursuant to our meeting dated August 24, 2013, in which we discussed the mutual benefits that an offer of employment would proffer . . ." Yikes! I wouldn't want to hire that person—would you? When candidates try to embellish how intelligent they are or use big words by talking about "strategically leveraging technology" and such, it tends to be a big turnoff. Keep your opening friendly, inviting, and human. They are not hiring an automaton—they are hiring *you*, a very qualified candidate with exceptional skills and employment history dedicated to serving our country. Let that sense of service and selflessness find a warm way of expressing itself somewhere in the note.

In the main body of the note, you should either reinforce that you are a perfect fit or overcome any objection a hiring manager may have because you don't have an ideal background. Assume there will be doubts about your qualified experience. After all, you are reading this book because you are segueing from a military career and lifestyle to life in the private sector. Even though you may not have exact experience working for a competitor of the company where you are interviewing, you certainly have transferable skills that will apply and fresh sets of ideas that could spark creativity and innovation. Also, if the company did not think you were qualified from the outset, you would never have been invited in for an interview. So focus the second section of your note on overcoming the built-in objection that your experience is not immediately relevant, and make a case for why you can more than compensate for that fact.

For example, if you are being considered for a senior leadership role that oversees union employees, whom you have never led before, this section of your thank you note could focus on the fact that you have lots of experience mediating high-volume, high-pressured staff complaints and have a highly structured approach to handling negotiations. Likewise, if you do not currently possess experience with the computer systems program the company uses, commit to bringing yourself up to speed within your first quarter of employment by purchasing a book and enrolling in a class at a local vocational college.

When it comes to overcoming objections, it is always better to raise the issues yourself and acknowledge them—as well as your proposed solution—as opposed to letting the other party (i.e., the employer) raise them. By acknowledging your perceived drawbacks and how you plan to overcome them, you will be more likely to remain in control of the situation. You will also demonstrate a sense of business maturity and the ability to negotiate well under pressure. In short, if you recognize the objections by holding them up under a light and then logically overcome them by presenting counter-solutions, you will reveal excellent problem-solving skills.

The last portion of your thank you note should include a convincing close that focuses on how much you want the job. Try a close like this: "I've always felt that one of the biggest factors in the selection process is the candidate desire factor. I truly want this position and believe that I could make an immediate contribution to your organization. I would consider myself very fortunate to become a member of your team."

Can there be a downside to thank you notes? Unfortunately, like everything else in life, the sad answer is, yes. Misspelling the interviewer's name or including a typo in the message, could cast enough doubt on your candidacy to convince the interviewer to keep looking for additional candidates. After all, this is a preliminary work product that you are presenting as a prospective new employee. Wouldn't it strike you as odd if the note ended with a special note of *tanks* rather than a special note of *thanks*? Wouldn't it tell you a lot about a candidate's attention to detail if she forwarded you a thank you note referring to you as *Jacque* even though your business card reads *Jacquie*? It would certainly make me wonder, and although it might not be a deal breaker, it could certainly raise eyebrows, which is not the way you want to launch a new job with a new company.

Email format for thank you notes is perfectly fine. It's really more a matter of personal taste whether you want to hand write a letter and mail it via the US Postal Service or whether you simply want to forward an email. Since most everything nowadays is in electronic format, the handwritten note certainly may come across as more thoughtful and sincere. Then again, with the speed of turnaround in terms of decision-making these days, by the time a snail-mail letter arrives, the company may have already made its decision about whom to hire. So use your best judgment, and remember that the content trumps the form of delivery when it comes to thank you notes.

The key to writing an effective thank you note is to allow the letter to be you. It should genuinely express your feelings, written in your own voice. Let your personality shine through. Since you can't just pop back into the office in person to remind them of who you are, your note should remind them of what you discussed and reflect the enthusiasm that you projected during the meeting.

Sell your future benefits based on your past achievements, reflect the pride of a career spent dedicated to the US military, overcome any lingering doubts about your perceived weaknesses, and then close the deal by confirming how much you want the job. Written in this way and placed at the finish line after final interviews are over, your thank you note could be the ideal tool to clinch an offer. An example of a well-written thank you note can be found in appendix 2.

TRANSFORMATION

What you get by achieving your goals is not as important as what you become by achieving your goals.

—Zig Ziglar

transformation: A complete or major change in someone's or something's appearance, form, etc.

4. WHAT IS REBRANDING?

Attitudes

The longer I live, the more I realize the importance
of choosing the right attitude in life.
Attitude is more important than facts.
It is more important than your past;
more important than your education or financial situation;
more important than your circumstances, your successes, or your failures;
more important than what other people think, say or do.
It is more important than your appearance, your giftedness, or your skills.
It will make or break a company. It will cause a church to soar or sink.
It will make the difference between a happy home or a miserable home.
You have a choice each day regarding the attitude you will embrace.

Life is like a violin.
You can focus on the broken strings that dangle, or you can play your life's melody on the
one that remains.
You cannot change the years that have passed,
nor can you change the daily tick of the clock.
You cannot change the pace of your march toward your death.
You cannot change the decisions or the reactions of other people.
And you certainly cannot change the inevitable.
Those are the strings that dangle!
What you can do is play on the one string that remains—your attitude.
I am convinced that life is 10 percent what happens to me
and 90 percent how I react to it.
The same is true for you.

—*Chuck Swindoll*

The previous section of this book outlined a roadmap to get you on your way to securing a job and transitioning back into the private sector. There is no doubt that the transition process will require a great deal of work. There is also little doubt that you will face hurdles, challenges, and sometimes frustrations. Keep in mind that despite the challenges and sometimes broken promises you will experience along the way to your new true north, the United States of America is still a beautiful place to call home! Now, it is time to talk about transformation—the process of rebranding yourself.

Regardless of when you make the decision to leave the military, the transition and transformation process often begin simultaneously. Almost as soon as you decide to exit the military, the process of transforming from a service member to becoming a veteran begins. Your first priority, as discussed in the previous transition section, is to prepare for the job search. Your second priority is to effectively manage the move from military culture to civilian culture. This is what I call transformation. The intensity of the process differs from person to person depending upon individual circumstances. For example, how much planning did you do before you exited the military? What goals were established during the exit strategy?

If you have already taken some of the necessary steps to transition before you left the military, you may encounter solid opportunities waiting outside the gate. This is not an impossible situation. In fact, with time, proper planning, and a transition plan, some of you will walk out of your boots and into your loafers (or flats) very quickly. But even for those of you fortunate enough to experience a quick, easy transition, the transformation process is still important, as you will experience the need to rebrand yourself in many situations: the job hunt, looking for a new home or community, joining a gym, finding a church family, etc.

My transition and transformation process began while I was still in boots, yet I encountered a few interesting turns in the road about five years after retiring and moving into the private sector. Let me tell you about one such event: I remember a conversation with the manager I reported to when I was a finance manager in marketing. Basically, he told me I needed to consider rebranding myself, as feedback from some of my peers indicated they viewed me as hard, inflexible, and difficult to communicate with. Ouch! What he was really saying was that John Phillips was still "the colonel," with a direct communication style and

> Your first priority, as discussed in the previous transition section, is to prepare for the job search. Your second priority is to effectively manage the move from military culture to civilian culture.

> **Rebranding or reinventing yourself is the basis of transformation and starts with the obvious: military language and communication style, home-life events and activities, and of course, the career!**

approach that was not always received well. While my manager validated that I was performing well in the job, he also said my performance would take a huge upswing once I figured out how to reinvent myself. I knew exactly what my manager was saying. The simple truth was that although I was no longer in the military, my communication style did not reflect that I had effectively made the transition. In many ways, I was still in my boots using a no-nonsense, direct, and formal communication style that left my peers a bit uncomfortable. Apparently, my heart was still in soldier mode when I was delivering a message. I needed to learn a completely different style, i.e., rebrand myself. Take note, this did not mean that the soldier in me needed to disappear; rather, it meant that the soldier in me needed to learn how to communicate with a different group of people. My manager did me a huge favor, and to this day, I remain grateful. The real transformation of John Phillips began just eight years ago, and I am happy to report that those much needed changes have helped me to have quite a successful career with that company.

Rebranding or reinventing yourself is the basis of transformation and starts with the obvious: military language and communication style, home-life events and activities, and of course, the career! For all practical purposes, you are rebranding yourself to live, work, and play in a new way—from commissaries to Walmart, from field artillery to finance, and from softball with the guys and gals in uniform to coaching T-ball at the local YMCA. Let the change begin.

Rebranding Defined

Either you deal with what is the reality, or you can be sure that the reality is going to deal with you.

—Alex Haley

Rebranding is one of many new terms you will start to pick up as you make the transition into the private sector. Nothing to be afraid of or concerned about; you've done it many times before, you just never had a name for it.

Here is a quick personal story on rebranding going back to my first days as a soldier: When I graduated from high school, I enlisted in the US Army. The minute the bus door opened and my drill sergeant came on board at Fort Jackson, South Carolina, I knew I was about to undergo a significant change very quickly. What I didn't know was that I was about to learn how to rebrand myself from an immature teenager to a soldier. Although my early years had been spent on army bases around the world as my family moved from one military tour to another, those indirect experiences did not completely prepare me for the rebranding process I was about to undertake. By the time I got off that bus (very quickly, I might add, due to the drill sergeant yelling at me to "get off his bus"), I realized that I would soon learn an entirely new way of life. Several components of change immediately became apparent:

> **Rebranding does not require you to compromise core values; instead, you must reinvent yourself and apply those values in a completely different environment.**

- **Communication style.** Moving into a world where "you speak when spoken to" was my new norm. The best practice for me was keeping my mouth shut, which was hard to do, and simply blending into the crowd with all the other skinhead recruits in fatigues. The communication style was very direct and to the point. There was no doubt in my mind what someone wanted while in uniform—enlisted and as an officer. Being transparent was the norm, and worrying if you hurt someone's feelings was not.

- **Culture.** My new culture was not that new for me since I was an army brat. When I joined, however, I learned the army from the standpoint of being a private. I had been a colonel's son, so the cultural shift for me was seeing life through a different lens at the bottom of the ladder.

- **Attitude.** Attitude is everything—really! My entire attitude completely shifted when I got off that bus. It was serious business, and I was not going to be the guy that stuck out with a bad attitude. Back in those days, you would find yourself under the barracks digging a hole all night simply for having a bad attitude. Attitudes are contagious, so make sure yours is positive.

Those first moments of awareness of what rebranding was all about were lessons that would be played out again some thirty years later as I entered the private sector.

Rebranding does not require you to compromise core values; instead, you must reinvent yourself and apply those values in a completely different environment. You may view the rebranding process as a fresh start with a chance to seize new opportunities, to implement lessons learned, and to capitalize on years of experience while in uniform, making them an advantage in the civilian world. The necessary adjustments differ for each person, so you must do your homework, be adaptable, remain flexible, and use your training to watch, listen, and transform.

So, what does all of this mean? There are two aspects of change that should take place as part of rebranding yourself: the external changes to your appearance and the internal changes in how you communicate and adapt to change. As many of you know from your military training, being aware of and understanding your situation and surroundings is very important. Said in civilian terms, watching and listening to people—how they dress, how they act, how they speak—during simple interactions will tell you volumes and greatly influence your rebranding efforts. I can recall when I made the decision to retire from the army; it was time to take my first step toward transforming myself, so I stopped getting a high and tight every Thursday and let my hair start growing. I hadn't owned a comb for years; it was now time to buy one. The ability to adapt to change is critical. Change is happening all the time in the private sector. Companies are always looking for ways to save money and grow their bottom line (aka profit), which all requires change. Remaining flexible in uncertain times will help you manage expectations as well as your sanity. The fact that you have come from an environment that changes direction often means that these changes should not be an issue for you. This move into the civilian world requires adjustments to specific aspects of life: communication style, status and position, stereotypes and diversity, work life, and home life to name a few. Let's start with the component that will directly impact every facet of your life.

Communication: From Military Language to Civilian Equivalent

One of the most significant challenges you will face is the world of effective communication—verbal and nonverbal. I continue to wrestle with my own communication approach more than fourteen years after leaving the military.

Often, you will face situations involving individuals who are thin-skinned or, in other words, whose feelings are easy to hurt or who are sensitive and require handling with kid gloves. How these types of people interpret your communication approach can result in you being tagged as trouble, too harsh, hard, or even inflexible. As much as that may rub you wrong, you have to avoid the tags and develop new ways to carry on a verbal dialogue, write an email, and use your body language effectively.

Transparency is not always the norm in the private sector . . .

Communication is a two-way process, and therefore, the individual on the receiving end of your words may not accept them the way you intended them to be received. The lesson here is that while you are working to transform your military language over to more suitable private-sector speak, you will also have to learn how individuals you are going to communicate with take their coffee; in other words, do they like to hear from you in a straight-forward and direct way, or do they prefer a more delicate, easy conversation style?

When I moved into the private sector, it took me a few weeks to catch on to what kind of communication style is acceptable. Transparency (perhaps a new word for you—meaning, being more open and honest) is not always the norm in the private sector, and it is a big deal for someone to be perfectly transparent with you on issues. The best way to gauge how you should communicate goes back to what I mentioned previously: watch, listen, learn, and adjust or adapt the new ways of interacting you observe. In most cases, the situation will also dictate how you will need to communicate. If you are being asked to present in front of a large group of employees about the state of the business and the news is not good, you certainly don't want to use a hard, punitive tone with a raised voice. You do not want to talk *at* the group, you want to talk *to* the group. There is a tremendous difference. On the other hand, you do want to be honest, direct, and open, to not sugar coat the message.

Experience has taught me that in most situations related to the business, straight talk on bad news is simply not done. First things first, though—know your audience. This is no different than giving any other briefing; you have to know your audience in order to formulate your delivery. Let me give you a couple of examples of how I have dealt with this type of situation both in the military and in the private sector.

I was a division comptroller, and one brigade was continually overspending their budget each month. The full-year projections of how much they would spend if they continued overspending clearly showed the unit would exceed their annual budget, which was unacceptable. No matter how many times I presented the bad news, each month the same dismal results occurred. Therefore, I first gathered all of the facts, making sure they were indeed facts and not assumptions about what I thought was going on. I then had to convince the division chief of staff that there was a problem, which eventually led to my presenting the information to the two-star commanding general, laying all of the facts on the table—the good, the bad, and yes, the ugly, as well as my recommendations on how to fix the problem. It was a fact-based, direct, completely transparent conversation. After the meeting, the general made one phone call with my recommendation and during the following months, there were zero problems with the brigade. It was made clear to the brigade that if they continued their bad behavior, there was going to be very big trouble. My credibility as the division comptroller jumped exponentially. The only down side was that the brigade commander who got the phone call was very upset (to put it kindly) with me personally.

Now, before I get into how to approach this type of situation in the private sector, I think it is better to set the stage with some key considerations that might influence your method of communication. Consider these things:

- Is the company private or publically traded? If a company is publically traded, controversial results can lead to significant problems with investors and how the company's stock is graded. A privately held company, however, is just that—private.

- What size is the company? There is a major difference between a small company, in which word travels very fast throughout the organization, versus a large corporation with multiple layers of organization, in which word travels slowly and, in some cases, does not reach everyone.

- What is the company's communication style? Many of my friends work for defense contractors filled with former or retired military. In this case, the communication style is not different at all from the way it was while the employees were in uniform.

In the private sector, there are some minor similarities to how communications are handled in the military. I like the old saying that Ronald Reagan had while he was president of the United States: stay fact based and tone neutral. It cannot be understated how important it is to stay fact based. If you have assumptions, state them upfront so that the person or group you are speaking to understands your approach. In a group setting in private-sector business, I have never heard anyone come right out and say something is broken or ever call out a particular person for doing something wrong. It just is not done. Most, if not all, of the communications that fall into this category are done behind closed doors. When it comes to delivery regarding poor performance of a group in the private sector, my approach is to rehearse what I will present to the group, keeping in mind who is in that group. It is important not to direct your briefing to any particular person, to speak in generalities, and most importantly, to have suggestions or recommendations on how to fix the problem. Be prepared to get into the details if asked, but do not pick on one person specifically. Reserve any by-name issues to one-on-one conversations with the leadership of the organization.

Your key take-aways regarding communication in private-sector companies should be to know your audience, always keep emotion out of the conversation, state the facts, stay away from assumptions that are unfounded, and stick to the point. Remember the old rule of holes—when you find yourself in one, stop digging! As you can see, there is a great deal to think about when transforming how you communicate with others outside the gate. If this is an area of weakness for you, find a local college offering a continuing education course on presentation skills or effective communications.

Seeking ways to sharpen your communication skills is important and must also include a focus on listening and nonverbal communication. I have been to meetings during which leaders have a lot to say that truly amounts to nothing more than listening to themselves talk. I walk away wondering what the hell just happened and have no idea what the intent of the meeting was or what was actually communicated—meaning the "corporate tap dance" just occurred. This can be frustrating when you have just exited a world where confusing messages might get someone hurt or killed, but keep in mind that communicating in the corporate world is usually not going to require a medic. Even so, remember that your listening skills and nonverbal language (i.e., gestures) are very important as well.

Listening is equally as valuable a skill as speaking. Let's use an interview situation as an example. The interviewer will note whether you are making eye contact with him, nodding as a sign of understanding, leaning toward him, and not interrupting. These are all positive signs that you are listening. Additionally, if you repeat appropriate information back and answer each question using some of the same references the interviewer made, he'll have a clear indication that you were listening.

Of course, there can be communication barriers at times—for example, accents, noise, fear, prejudice, to name a few. Here is one scenario that someone from the military typically faces, whether a career officer or one who has served four years with eight deployments: You have landed an interview, and the hiring manager is straight out of college and speaks with a very strong accent. Your first thought may be, *Really, a twenty-two-year-old whose communication skills need a little fine-tuning as well is going to decide if I am qualified for the job?* Your body language, attitude, listening skills, and responses will make or break this interview. It is extremely important for you to realize that your service to this country, while appreciated and respected by most, may not be viewed in the same light that you would prefer. The twenty-two-year-old hiring manager is going to look at what contributions you can make to the job he needs to fill. So, listen carefully and remember that your body language can also deter your success.

Body language is often all about attitude. Remember to enter every interview situation with a grateful attitude; smile, shake hands, nod, take notes, and maintain eye contact. All of these gestures are language to the person you are communicating with. A brief course in presentation skills, as mentioned previously, will cover all of these components—speaking, listening, and body language.

At the end of the day, your communication style can open doors just as easily as it can close them. The military environment, sometimes marked by unpredictable and violent situations, dictates the need for quick, concise, and very direct communication with fellow service members. This method of communication can be difficult to find in the private sector. You will find the private sector's more relaxed style of communicating to be confusing. It may also come as a surprise how many people are offended easily. Spend time learning about political correctness prior to leaving the military. The phrase "political correctness" is defined as: "Agreeing with the idea that people should be careful to not use language or behave in a way that could offend a particular group of people."

Communication is the key to every relationship you will have in your life, including relationships with coworkers, friends, and family. I continue to learn how to communicate better through each opportunity to study a situation, understand how a person likes to receive information, and practice before delivering. Time spent driving to an interview or a big meeting can be your best friend as you practice what you will say, how you will say it, and with what tone and emphasis you will deliver it. I don't recommend a lot of body language while driving, though. Save that for when you are in front of a mirror at home!

The best solution for any communication issue you encounter is to talk to someone. If you have concerns about your communication style, reach out to a fellow veteran or a close coworker who may be able to give advice on how to communicate more effectively in a particular situation. Social occasions with friends and family can also provide safe opportunities to learn about how civilians communicate. Trust me—my wife is my sounding board, and when I'm preparing for a presentation, interview, or a one-on-one with a coworker I need to deliver a message to, I engage my wife to listen and provide feedback. She has experience in this area, so I am usually getting sound advice. Find someone who will do that for you.

I think the best way to illustrate this is by relating one particular situation that happened to me. In a situation like this one, your two-minute drill will be an ideal solution: On a nice fall weekend, I was at the local mall with my wife. She needed to buy a new outfit for work because seasons were changing and the colder weather was rolling in. While we were shopping, I literally ran into the chief financial officer (CFO) of my company. Now, picture this: I was wearing a t-shirt with a light fleece jacket, shorts, my Keens, and my *BTL* operator hat. The CFO, on the other hand, was wearing his nicely pressed jeans, deck shoes, a collared shirt, and a nice sweater.

Needless to say, we were both a bit surprised. First things first, I introduced my wife to him. Note that right off the bat, I have communicated to him that I am a very relaxed and easy going person as a result of him seeing what I wear outside the workplace. *What do I say?* starts running through my mind. I typically never saw this man, however, he knew who I was, and I had worked with him before in previous jobs. So, I started with some pleasantries, and he immediately came back to me with the old "what are you doing now?" At this point, there were some major strategies I needed to implement: demonstrate a positive and upbeat attitude, pay attention to detail, be brief (meaning that I did not want to take a block of time to tell my story—I wanted to get to the point), and keep it clean. I made sure I maintained eye contact, and paid attention to what was being said and how it was being said. Lastly, I made sure that this very brief encounter was a two-way conversation rather than just me trying to impress the CFO and not allowing him to get a word in edgewise. It was all over before I knew it, and off I went with my wife, helping her pick out her new outfit. The lesson I learned: you never know whom you will run into or when your next opportunity will fall right in your lap.

Another point to keep in mind: being former military provides you the opportunity to speak a foreign language. It's not French, German, Japanese, or any of the more than six thousand distinct languages on this planet. In fact, military language is unique and generally only understood by those serving in the military. It is filled with jargon, acronyms, service branches, rank structures, and many other constructs that make it difficult for civilians to understand. This is not to say that you have to throw away the language you learned in the military. Rather, you need to find the civilian equivalents for many military words and phrases in order to communicate effectively outside the gate. Some brief examples of this are words such as the following:

- *head* is now *bathroom*
- *dining facility* or *galley* becomes *cafeteria*
- *rucksack* is now a *backpack*
- *low quarters* are simply *shoes*
- *gigline* has no civilian equivalent (I always check my gigline before I go to work)
- you don't take *leave*, you go on *vacation*
- you don't wear a *cover*, you wear a *hat*
- *Bravo Zulu* translates to *job well done*
- *Bundeswehr gloves* or *air force gloves* means your *hands are in your pockets*
- you don't go on *temporary duty* or *TDY*, you go on a *business trip*
- The company won't need a *recall roster*, but will need your *contact information*
- you'll no longer sleep in your *hooch*, but in your *house*

The complete list is extremely long. There are also a variety of military slang terms I won't mention (you all know what I'm talking about) that actually have made their way into the private sector. I am convinced people have heard them in the movies and think it is cool to say them to a military person or veteran.

I have learned an entirely new set of acronyms and language since exiting the military. The *Occupational Outlook Handbook* explored in chapter 2 provides civilian equivalent words and phrases to help you with this task, as do some other resources on the Internet. I will tell you though, it is always a breath of fresh air when I get together with my fellow veterans and we go back to our roots as military guys and gals, talking in our native tongue— military jargon. You will always have it in the back of your mind, and there will be times you will reach back to grab a phrase or term and use it in your new

Struggling with change and varying methods of communication is a normal experience when you move into the private sector.

world, explaining what it means to those on your team. People are more accepting of these newfound phrases or terms when they actually know what they mean and in what context they can use them.

To summarize, look at communication as the vehicle that will take you from your previous role and life to your new one—the new true north. With that in mind, for the most part you will need to discard military language and learn private-sector terminology. You will need to exercise patience and pay particular attention to your surroundings and how others communicate—verbally and nonverbally. You also have to remember that most non-veterans do not understand the military experience, its unique language, or its culture. Struggling with change and varying methods of communication is a normal experience when you move into the private sector.

This particular aspect of your transition and transformation is extremely important to your success outside the gate. Remember, it is vital that you sharpen your all of your communication skills—speaking, listening, and body language. Take time to watch, observe, and learn, just as you were trained to do.

Status and Position

One of the first changes you will be exposed to involves status and position. The military is a culture of order, structure, and a clearly defined hierarchy. For many career military members, especially those who have held positions of higher rank, moving into the private sector is a reality check. Their military positions and ranks have earned them prestige and respect. Their subordinates followed their orders to the letter without question and snapped to attention when they entered a room. (I still find myself jumping to my feet when my manager or a company officer comes to my office. It is in my DNA.) Their positions in the civilian world may not come with the same level of responsibility and authority as their military equivalents, and even if they do, response to that authority is significantly different. Rank in the civilian world is measured by job titles, pay levels, and for some, material possessions and perks. In the business world, military medals for bravery and gallantry in action are replaced by bonuses, stock options, and other rewards and incentives. The rank structure outside the gate is typically as follows:

- **Manager.** A manager can be responsible for controlling or administering people, things, or processes in the company. You are not necessarily leading people simply because you have the title of manager. Note, however, that if you have the term "manager" in your title, your job will score higher for compensation purposes. The military equivalents to this level are non-commissioned officer (E-5 through E-9) and company grade officer (O-1 through O-3).
- **Director.** Directors are also responsible for controlling and administering certain aspects of the company. However when you reach this level, the area of responsibility is much broader than that of a manager. Directors are classified as mid-level executives. It is the same as advancing from company grade officer to field grade officer. From a compensation standpoint, this is the point where you start seeing things such as stock options, stock grants, long-term incentives, etc. Getting to the director level is a big deal, and it is very tough to make that jump.
- **Group Director.** Group directors manage directors and have an even wider span of control or area of responsibility. As with directors, group directors are well compensated. This is also the level at which you are groomed for your next step—becoming a vice president of a company.
- **Vice President.** Reaching the position of vice president (VP) in any company is a major accomplishment; at this level, you are classified as a senior executive. That said, there are VPs of major Fortune 50/100/500 companies and then there are VPs of much smaller companies, whether privately held or public. Once you reach this level, you could be in charge of an entire region of the country or a major division within a company. Suffice it to say, the span of control is substantial; a knowledge base of how business operates and a complete understanding of all aspects of the

business is essential. As with all the other levels within a company, more responsibility means you are compensated in many different ways beyond your regular salary.

- **Chiefs.** These positions include those such as chief operating officer (COO), chief information officer (CIO), chief financial officer (CFO), chief people officer (CPO), etc. These types of positions hold a substantial amount of responsibility and are generally referred to as C-suite or C-level positions. People who make it into these positions are truly at the top of their game and are the subject matter experts for their particular field. They report to the chief executive officer (CEO) and are her primary advisors in running the business. The range of possibilities for compensation is wide open for roles that fall into this category.

Some veterans may welcome this change in status and responsibility while others may view this as a demotion.

Some veterans may welcome this change in status and responsibility while others may view this as a demotion. If you prefer to manage others, to make decisions, and to direct processes and functions, you need to seek employment that immediately allows you to lead. The flip side to that is being what is called an "individual contributor," meaning you don't manage or lead anyone but yourself. There is nothing wrong with that role and frankly, it can be a bit of a welcome break to not manage or lead people for a while so you can catch your breath. There will be plenty of opportunities down the road for you to show you know how to manage and lead people.

No matter where you land in the private sector, you will more than likely have to prove yourself before you move into a position in charge of an entire department or a slice of the country. This is not the case all of the time, but it is the case most of the time. Later in the Integration section, I will get into more detail on leading people and how to effectively manage them in the private sector. Exercising authority in the private sector when your job does not give you that responsibility can result in resentment from coworkers, reprimands from managers, and questions from others about your future success at the company. You do not want to be labeled as the military guy or gal who can't seem to adjust. Trust me, once you get a bad label like that, it will follow you for a very long time and it will affect your upward mobility as well as how you are treated within the organization. Your time to lead will come. In the interim, exercise patience, sit back and observe and learn, as I've mentioned earlier in this section.

In order to effectively transform or rebrand yourself and succeed in the private sector, it is important to understand how status and position are uniquely different from the military. While you learn the differences and begin to understand and respect the status and position of those in the private sector, you may also have to educate others on the status and position you held in the military. Everyone will not understand or show respect for the medals on your chest or the number of deployments you have made. This may simply be because they do not understand. Take it upon yourself to help those you work with each day, as well as those on your team, by explaining things about the military as they come up. Don't hide your background; be proud of what you have accomplished and of the fact that you have served this great country. Take that pride and knowledge coupled with the skills and abilities you have and educate those around you so that they know the truth instead of what is blasted on the local news channel. When doing so, try not to come across as some steely-eyed killer that just came back from the sand box. That will do nothing more than reinforce the stereotype. Instead, lighten up and take the time to walk people through your experiences, what you did while deployed, how you dealt with certain, often hostile, situations, and to explain why you would do it all again if you had to. Create an environment where your coworkers will approach you with questions and not be afraid of you. It's all about attitude, sense of humor, and how your experience is communicated.

Stereotypes and Diversity

Although veterans represent one of the smallest minority groups, they are perhaps one of the most diverse groups. The military represents all segments of society; its members come from all social and economic backgrounds and include every race, ethnic origin, national origin, religion, political belief set, sexual orientation, and marital status.

Companies that employ veterans not only access the unique skills this group brings to an organization, but also benefit by adding individuals to their ranks who have excelled as a single unit, regardless of their preconceived labels. Service members have learned to use each other's talents, skills, and training to function as a team, surviving in dangerous environments without prejudice. The meaning of teamwork is defined by the veteran's experience. This is an exceptional character trait to bring to an organization.

I'd like to approach this in more detail from two perspectives, beginning with the perspective of the employers and HR professionals that each of you will speak with at your first screening opportunity while trying to gain entrance into a company. Never forget one very important fact: a business is in business to make money. The organizational makeup of any publically traded company—i.e., its diversity—is extremely important because it contributes to the bottom line or profit. As a general rule, a company will strive for an inclusive culture and workforce that leverages diverse ideas, talents, and capabilities to create maximum value not only for thebusiness, but for its employees, valued partners, and communities. Diversity leads back to sales and, in turn, to profits of the enterprise.

You should be aware that potential employers tend to stereotype veterans as a result of misinformation and media biases; therefore, many members of private-sector companies must undergo their own transformation to discover the true benefits of bringing this small population on board. Subsequently, rather than placing the usual labels on veterans, they will then recognize them for their service, sacrifices, and talents. Companies that value a veteran's unique qualities have become aware of the powerful contributions they can make and, consequently, have changed their hiring, onboarding, training, and retaining processes for them. My hope is that the information contained here in *Boots* will help educate those corporate leaders, hiring managers, and human resources professionals who have been reluctant to hire veterans due to the stereotyping of their combat experiences. These leaders must also remember that not all veterans have been deployed into war zones. A veteran is much more than what he has seen or experienced; he is a person who has served his country and is now able to use his skills, training, and talents to help a company prosper.

From the perspective of the veteran trying to get her foot in the door, you must be prepared to be prejudged because of your military service, regardless of the size of the company you interview with. I don't say that to be disrespectful. It is merely a warning to raise your level of awareness so you are not caught off guard. As I have mentioned before, you represent the less than 1% of the population that has served this nation in uniform. Our military is a classic example of what a diverse organization should look like. Understand that a workforce in the private sector that is more diverse will help drive workplace, marketplace, and community results, which lead back to profits for the company. As a veteran, you represent an addition to an organization's diverse pool of employees.

Based on recent initiatives coming out of the White House, you also represent up to a $9,000 federal tax credit if you are hired. Taking this a step further, if you are a disabled veteran—even though I know you would rather not have the disability—it may work to your benefit at hiring time. Take advantage of what the law allows when it comes time to secure a job and, ultimately, to keep a job. There are policies within an organization that deal with diversity and inclusion. You will experience such things as hiring pools that require a minority, a woman, and members of other specially designated groups to apply for a position before you—if you are not a member of one of those groups—can even start the interview process. Although these policies vary from company to company, they are always serious business when it comes to hiring people. I have seen committees formed at various levels within a company—from the headquarters to regional offices and even internationally—to discuss statistics on the demographics of the company or to outline and implement initiatives that raise awareness and inclusion of diverse groups.

New initiatives that have started in many companies are called Infinity Groups or Business Resource Groups. These groups are primarily focused around a particular ethnic group or other special group of employees, such as veterans. Groups such as the Asian-Pacific Group, African-American Group, Military Veteran Group, Hispanic Group are a few of the examples I have been exposed to. Their purpose is twofold: raising awareness within the company and educating people about the culture of the groups; and partnering with the business. For example, the Military Veteran Group can partner with the Military Sales organization within a company and advise them on military and veteran matters as it relates to sales. What may work and what may not work in selling to the military? The group may advise on something as simple as ensuring that someone in uniform saluting in an advertisement does so with the right hand and is wearing the proper uniform (you would be amazed at what I have seen and helped fix). The group might also make sure the sales force fully understands the cultural aspects of the military and the wide variety of veteran organizations across the country. The benefits of these groups in any company are endless. If the company you end up working for has one of these groups, join it and get involved. Use it as an opportunity to demystify the myths that are out there about the military and those who have served. This is a daily effort for me personally.

Whether a veteran is inside the gate or out, what matters most is how he uses his capabilities to accomplish great things. It is important for all people, military and civilian, to remain in pursuit of Martin Luther King Jr.'s dream for people to judge each other by the content of one's character[5].

5. ADJUSTMENTS IN WORK AND HOME LIFE

Private-Sector Work Life

Learning to manage the numerous professional nuances encountered in your new workplace is an important part of your successful transformation. Many adjustments you will face in your new career depend upon the cultural aspects of the company and, in some cases, the industry where you choose to work. The importance of corporate culture as well as the cultural aspects of the industry you land in cannot be overstated. As you recall, I touched on these points many times back in the Transition section. Do not discount them; your cultural fit with an organization may mean the difference in your success or failure. Your transformation rucksack should contain the following tips on private-sector work life for future reference.

Attention to Detail
Your attention to detail likely is more intense than that of your civilian counterparts because of your military training and combat experiences. Drilled into every new army recruit's head is the acronym SALUTE (size, activity, location, unit, time, and equipment). When done properly, SALUTE provides great intelligence because a person is paying attention to detail. This is equivalent to having a strong situational awareness or knowing your surroundings, which is a direct tie back to attention to detail. In the world you just came from, it could actually save your life and that of others. In the world you are moving into, it will allow you to stand out and be noticed. These skills are simply not taught outside the gate as a general rule. Your training in this area gives you a distinct advantage in the workplace; however, the absence of it in your coworkers can be a source of irritation and frustration. When this happens, consider it a teachable moment. Take it as an opportunity to share your knowledge and possibly a story or two that reinforces how you have honed these skills.

I recall a situation in which I felt this frustration: An employee of mine continued to make mistakes with the financial statements she had to prepare each month. There were also small format errors that had to be addressed (call me picky, but a standard is a standard and you all know what I mean by that). Instead of getting all bent out of shape about it, I took the time to meet with her and walked her through the financial statement line by line, word by word, number by number. I asked her a number of questions and coached her on how to complete the document, explaining why she needed to make sure it was right. I held her accountable for her actions, but I also helped her fix the problem. I also created a situation in which she took ownership of the problem, thereby ensuring it was permanently fixed and would not happen again. I made sure she knew my door is always open if she doesn't understand something, that all she needs to do is ask. I've never been one to hold against a person the fact that she asks questions. I'd rather someone ask the question and be more productive than continue to make mistakes and have it turn into a performance issue.

Your natural impulse to create order out of chaos may run afoul of the private-sector culture. Use your skill for tolerating and managing ambiguity to your advantage. The fog of war is a common term used for the uncertainty of situation awareness—aka, ambiguity. As a veteran, you have been trained from day one to deal with this beast called ambiguity. The biggest difference in our standing army and any other army on the planet is that our soldiers, down to the lowest level, can make decisions. They are taught to be leaders. Yes, there is a distinct chain of command, however, things happen on the battlefield that force people at every level to step up and take charge. You were trained in the military to tolerate uncertainty and to deal with it through effective planning that includes contingencies. Take those skills and put them to work in the private sector and you will shine. Fair warning though: don't boast about your skills; at the end of the day, it is all about deeds, not words.

Managing Employees

Managing private-sector employees is very different from directing service members. Barking orders and expecting them to be carried out to the letter without question is not the way it works in the private sector. Expect a conversation and taking into account the feelings of your coworkers and associates. Unlike civilian employees, service members do not have the luxury of disagreeing with their commanders, questioning authority, and walking off the job when disgruntled. Since as a service member you have not been accustomed to these freedoms, you must adjust your leadership and communication style to the new workplace. I'll speak to this in more detail in the Integration section.

Social Events

Social events can provide a great opportunity to find your next job or a new community to move to. The military requires payment from service members to attend social events and other sponsored occasions. In the private sector, most company-hosted social events are free to the invited employees or reimbursed through an expense account agreement. These events include holiday parties and team events at a variety of venues ranging from professional sports facilities to go-cart tracks. There is no standard, cookie-cutter type of social event in the private sector. Which events a company team will attend is based on budget, current corporate culture, the state of the business, and the leadership. When expense accounts are used, generally speaking the senior person in the group puts the entire event on his corporate credit card, unless it is a planned event with a contract in place. Acceptable expenses are outlined in an organization's policies and procedures guidelines; if you find yourself in a position to have such a budget, you would be well served to become familiar with these policies.

Soft Skills

Key soft skills that you bring to the workplace are punctuality, excellent attendance, and superior work ethic—traits that are valued by private-sector managers. Think about it: You are coming from a life where you depended on each other in order to survive. You have teammates, and you support each other. You are used to long hours and being in locations that are not ideal and often times even hostile. You have the wherewithal to overcome these inconveniences and get the job done.

I recall many deployments to the National Training Center in California or the Joint Readiness Training Center in Louisiana and multiple REFORGER deployments to Europe. What these deployments all had in common was long hours, meaning very little sleep, nowhere to sleep, and a lot to get done in a very short period of time. What got us all through these different deployments was our support of each other through the entire process. We knew what had to get done. We had a deadline. There were work shifts created and the work got done. When it was time to go down, we would get maybe four hours of sleep and then we were back at it for the next twenty hours. Many times a day turned into days and we got by with cat naps, still getting the job done. I know

I am preaching to the choir, however, my point is that you have been down the rocky road of sleep deprivation and deadlines in adverse conditions. Apply those skills in the private sector with the same passion you did while in uniform and use them to your advantage.

Job Duties

Job duties must be performed at the highest level to meet or exceed the expectations of managers. One of the worst mistakes you can make is to let your hair down once you are out of uniform. A primary reason you were hired likely was not only your leadership capabilities and technical knowledge, but also your soft skills. Therefore, your continued proficiency in these areas is paramount to your success. Most companies rate your performance during annual and mid-year reviews. How you perform the duties of your job, as well as your soft skills, will become part of that review.

Details on performance reviews are forthcoming when we talk about integration, however, it may be worth touching on aspects of these at this juncture. Generally speaking, performance reviews are not used as they are in the military. There is no such thing as your official photo, either. Expect to receive two reviews on your performance during a calendar year—the mid-year review and the end-of-year or annual review. The purpose of these check points is to ensure you are on track regarding the goals you and your manager have agreed will be accomplished during the year. My advice to you is to document everything you do throughout the year in a format that explains the details of the task or situation, such as the STAR format outlined in chapter 2. This will allow you to be organized for the meetings you will have with your manager and will help drive the conversation.

Availability

The private sector does not have lock downs or red, yellow, and green training cycles. The requirements of the job and your duties to fulfill the job will dictate whether you are on call 24 hours a day, 7 days a week, as well as whether you will be required to carry a company-paid cell phone. Typically, salaried management-level employees are paid to be available 24 hours a day, 7 days a week, 365 days a year—the same time required when the employee was in boots. That said, in my fourteen-year career as a manager and director, I have worked very few weekends and have never really been called in for a crisis outside the normal work-week schedule. In my world of corporate finance, for example, we work by a very structured schedule each month, each quarter, and at year end to close the books (i.e., to reconcile all the accounting entries that have been made during that period). We follow a published schedule of the work that needs to be completed by a specific date, including the time each task is due. This is one of the most structured and rigid processes I have come across at the company. There is little to no leeway in the deadlines due to corporate reporting. This especially holds true when it is time to report results outside the company to investors. Do yourself a big favor and ensure you fully understand the requirements related to schedules, time, and deadlines for the job you want so that you'll know exactly what you are getting into.

Conduct

A Code of Business Conduct and Ethics exists in the private sector. Many of the components of any Code of Business Conduct will sound familiar to you. They are very much aligned to the core values of the military. Areas such as integrity, conflicts of interests, dealings with the government as well as competitors, ethics, and compliance are covered in the code. These vary from company to company, but the gist of any code of conduct is to ensure all employees are doing the right thing and not compromising the integrity of the company. This is serious business. Whether off the job, on a business trip, or on vacation, you represent your company. You must not jeopardize a job by exhibiting inappropriate behavior. This is really no different from the standards of conduct you were held to while in uniform. You must exercise good judgment and question the ethical and legal aspects of your actions whenever they are in doubt. Drinking and driving, illegal drug use—in fact, all illegal acts would be classified as inappropriate behavior. The same is true as you perform your daily task in an office setting. Most companies have an employee handbook. Become familiar with it and understand the expectations the company has for all employees.

Personal Life

Your personal life for the most part is just that—personal. Although you are free to share personal information with coworkers, peers, and managers, you should first consider your comfort level with these individuals. I started by sharing the basics with my managers and over time they have learned more about me. I tend to be an open book, meaning I like to get to know other people and what their interests are because, who knows, we may have something in common.

One manager of mine has become a very good friend and has come along on a couple of my spring/fall golf outings with all the guys. Come to find out, we have a lot in common. On the flip side, some people just don't like sharing personal information. It is not like the military, where your manager knows literally everything about you and keeps the information in a small book in his back pocket! You can go for years in the private sector and not know much of anything about the leaders of your group. This has been very strange to me, but it is what it is. The camaraderie you had while in uniform simply does not exist in corporate America. I feel that a good manager takes an interest in the employee, his family, and his outside interests because, quite often, what you do outside the workplace reflects the type of employee you are at work. Common ground with coworkers builds relationships and valuable friendships, which contribute to a more satisfying work environment. A note of caution, however: social media can be the downfall of a career, as was mentioned earlier. If you think your private life is private, think again. Once you post or share information through social media channels, consider it shared with those who could potentially do you harm. Sharing means you've given that information away, and although you may expect a degree of privacy on your Facebook account, others may not respect your desires.

Home Life

Marriages and family relationships are often impacted by the stresses of a military career. We have all been on many deployments—to both hostile environments as well as those that turn out to be little more than major training exercises—and then when we return home, we have to walk on egg shells because we have been gone for such a long time. While we were away, there was one very important, driving force inside us—we longed to be home. The simple things in life that we all take for granted were missing: the cry of a newborn baby, the touch of a spouse or girlfriend, and yes, the comfort of our own homes and all that goes with that.

Truth be told, the day-to-day reality of being home again is not necessarily a welcome period. Often times this new 24/7 world can overwhelm a person rather quickly when on the day before you came home, someone was trying to kill you. Transitioning from a dangerous environment, where it is man vs. man, to the home environment, where your family has been dealing with all the everyday issues of the kids, school, little league, and, more than likely, financial challenges, will test any couple or family. Everything is affected by your transformation from a military to civilian citizen: your entire family, your occupational role, and even fundamental things about you as a person. More than likely, the language you use has gotten worse. Also, you must adjust again to having heat and/or air conditioning, electricity, and being able to just walk to the refrigerator or drive down the street to the local

Once you exchange your boots for loafers, you will have more time at home with your family and friends—a change that can bring a new set of challenges.

fast food joint when you get hungry. It is a time of joyful reunion, painful adjustments, and mending what was broken—perhaps even ending relationships. The Welcome Home banners are put away, and the harsh reality that you are home slowly sinks in.

There is nothing easy about this new norm of being home all the time in the private sector. In your previous life in uniform, being gone on deployments was the norm. You may have been nothing more than a face in a frame to your kids—this fact haunts many of us at times. Spouses have learned to adjust and survive while their other halves are out taking care of the nation's business. Based on my experience, the best way to handle the transformation of your most intimate relationship is to make sure you keep communicating through the entire process. I always have held the belief that you should be able to speak to your spouse about anything—yes, anything. If you can do that without fear of reprisal and can keep the emotional reactions minimized, you can get through anything together and be stronger for it. You have to respect each other, and by all means, maintain a high level of trust with and love for one another. Without those things, you are doomed to fail as a couple, and it will be a very rocky road for you while you are trying to make the transition out of the military, rebrand yourself, and ultimately integrate yourself back into society. You will more than likely miss the more regimented life of the military. After all, at least there you knew what you were up against, what was expected and what to expect. My best advice is to take it easy, focus on the tasks at hand (i.e., finding a job) and your new true north will come more into focus and become attainable.

Absence during deployment, training, and special assignments can place a financial strain on the service member and his family. Preparing your finances long before separation from the military may alleviate some of this stress.

For example, saving a portion of pay to build a transition fund is critical to defray the financial burdens incurred by a protracted job search, relocation expenses, and housing and day-to-day living expenses during your transition.

Once you exchange your boots for loafers, you will have more time at home with your family and friends—a change that can bring a new set of challenges. For example, your spouse is used to you being gone periodically, and now suddenly you are not. There is a strong possibility that your new job (and you will get one) may not have any travel involved in it. I suspect there are two groups of you out there: one group is perfectly fine with never travelling again, with staying home and growing some deep roots; the other group is so accustomed to traveling, it may become boring really quick when you can't hit the road. Your family must be prepared to deal with the fact that you will be home more often. Being home all the time can be a very good thing, especially if you have children in school who participate in sports or other extracurricular activities. There is not a day that goes by that I don't think about all the games my dad missed while I was playing sports. I wanted him there to watch me play football. Forty years later, it still bothers me that he couldn't be there. Take this time now to be together with your family and to enjoy what you missed during your many years in uniform.

This is what most service members have dreamed about and yearned for during their military careers—a life outside the gate that allows them to appreciate and build the relationships that have previously been limited or restricted to email, phone calls, or short visits. Whether inside or outside the gate, establishing open and honest communication between the members of your household is critical to keep families close and committed. This may sound a bit crazy to some of you, but have dinner at the table with the TV turned off, and have a conversation with your family. Be genuinely interested in your children's days, their activities, and what they are experiencing now that you are home all the time. Remember that your being home again affects your kids just as a much as it affects your spouse. For the parent who has been gone all the time, make sure you are in sync with the other parent on how you speak to your children, how you discipline them, and what you need to get involved in. It is just as important for your family to understand what you are going through during this transition and transformation as they did when you were deploying. The transformation is not just about you, it also includes your family since they will be going through this journey with you. At one time or another, all the key components of transformation will play an important role in your personal and home life.

When you were deployed, the strong family network that existed in every unit on military bases provided a support group for your family. These same types of opportunities for support may look a bit different in the civilian world. Once you exit the military, you and your family must build a new support network through family members, new and old friends, and community and social organizations such as churches and veteran's groups (Military Officers Association of America [MOAA], Non Commissioned Officers Association [NCOA], Veterans of Foreign Wars [VFW], American Legion, to name a few). There are other support groups available, but you will have to be willing to reach out to connect with them. Look right in your own community and see if there is a job search networking group that meets at a local restaurant or library (yes, we still have libraries). Interacting with other job hunters at these meetings and discussing the pitfalls of the job search or being home after being gone so long is beneficial. Take advantage of any work and life balance programs offered by your community or by your new company that will enhance both your work and home life experiences. Social events are another great way to meet people and discover new and exciting activities for you and your family to get involved in. Get out there and get involved in your community, your church, and your new job.

Work and Home Life Balance

I believe that I am a pretty good example of a soldier who has experienced a successful military career, transitioned through the gate, transformed into a successful business person, and achieved balance between my work, family, and friends. Work and life balance is extremely important to me, and as a director in a Fortune 50 company leading associates, I try to instill in them an appreciation for establishing a grounded approach to having a work and life balance. Having this balance ensures that you understand what is important in life. Work is a means to an end for me. It is not the center of my universe. The best way I can explain my attitude is that I love to live my life, and my jobs have given me a way to do so. I have been fortunate to see the world as a result of the military and of the private-sector work I have done. I seek adventure, experiencing different cultures in parts of the world many have not seen. Maybe I'm one of the odd ones because I do have a life outside of work. I realize the day will come when I can no longer make the trips I make or do some of the things I do, but, until that time comes, I will continue to work very hard and play even harder.

An important component of any soldier's transformation is reaching a balance between work, family, and life. Chasing this balance is sometimes elusive; many tend to prioritize the wrong things in life. Exercising control over my work and personal life is the fun stuff for me; simply put, I work so that I can play. For me, this is one of the most important aspects of my life outside boots. As soldiers, we lived life in uniform and were subject to be called to any part of the world when diplomacy failed and the next logical step was to insert the military to take care of the nation's business. I love the military and I treasure the time I spent in uniform, but those days ended for me in late 1999.

Now days, I cherish my time off and plan trips with my family and friends. Time spent with my long-time friends, Jim and Jerry, are extremely important to me. We grew up on the gridiron, each trying to land a starting position on the team, and we have managed to remain connected for more than four decades, despite the different paths each of us took both professionally and personally. My relationship and time spent with my brother, Steve, is also valuable to me. My brother respects and honors my service to this country, and I respect and honor his role as a successful businessman. My nephews are a special and a bright spot in my life as well. I love being Uncle John to them and to the children of my friends. It completes a part of me that has been missing, since I do not have children of my own.

Another important passion of mine is completing my bucket list of things I want to achieve during my life, such as traveling to exotic places with my wife, sailing through the Caribbean, rafting or canoeing the rivers of the great West with my brother and best friends, fly fishing in the western and southeastern United States, and golfing with the guys a few times each year.

Every veteran will find his own passions. For some, new careers will become priorities. For others, the freedom to reconnect and spend quality time with family and friends will take precedence. Once out of boots and into loafers, you will be able to do those special things that have been neglected because of deployments or other tours of duty. Creating your own bucket list and accomplishing things that are important will enrich your life and will bring the new normal full circle for you, your family, and friends. Becoming involved with network groups, veteran's groups, churches or charities, civic organizations, and professional associations, can help others like you make the transition by paying it forward. Once you are out of your boots, do yourself and your family a favor and take the time to do those things that you put off for years because of your deployments. The important people in your life deserve to have you around, and you will not regret the time you spend with them.

> **Much of the transformation will hinge on your attitude, support network, and the realization that you will not make this journey alone.**

Finishing Touches

This journey through the transformation phase depends upon one's circumstances, exit plan, and personal goals. Much of the transformation will hinge on your attitude, support network, and the realization that you will not make this journey alone. Having your family involved in the process of altering the lifestyle they have also grown accustomed to is important. As I have said many times, this process is not easy, and it will stress you and your family. Having your immediate and extended family supporting you throughout your journey cannot be overstated. If you have started building your new professional network, make sure you keep them informed and engaged throughout this process. They can provide guidance, coaching, and mentoring that will help you along this journey. Lastly, remember that you are not alone. My words are here to support you and coach you as you need them. My intent is to make sure you are fully armed and equipped to fight your next fight and land that job you deserve.

Never doubt that you possess the training, skills, and experiences to embrace these life-changing processes. Your communication approach may need a little attention and work, your attitude may need to be adjusted at times, but you have what it takes to fine-tune it all and to rebrand yourself for the next phase of life. The strengths you developed during your diverse experiences while in the military—loyalty, values, leadership, discipline, adaptability, along with the ability to bring order to chaos—will serve you well in this next phase of your life. Throughout the rebranding process, hold tight to these traits, as they will shape your attitude for a successful transition and transformation from boots to loafers. It is true that attitude is everything, and it is contagious.

INTEGRATION

Fulfilling the four needs [spiritual, mental, physical, and social] in an integrated way is like combining elements in chemistry. When we reach a "critical mass" of integration, we experience spontaneous combustion—an explosion of inner synergy that ignites the fire within and gives vision, passion, and a spirit of adventure to life.

—Stephen R. Covey
First Things First

integration: The process of making (a person or group) part of a larger group or organization.

6. LIFE OUTSIDE THE GATE

If you have made it this far into the book and are still in the military, you will certainly understand that things are going to be different once you exit the gate. If you have made it to the private sector, you are most likely experiencing all the ups and downs of this new life and desperately need to know how to integrate it all into a positive set of experiences for you and your family. Here are a few tips as you combine all the skills, talents, knowledge, strengths, and more from your days as a soldier into a new set of goals, dreams, and desires: Learn what it means to be flexible. Try not to take things personally—not everyone will understand the role you had in the military. If you have a sense of humor, keep it; if you don't, get one!

Even after more than fourteen years out of the military, I realize that I am still changing, growing, and learning to transition, transform, and integrate. The world outside the gate presents a wealth of opportunities, but they often come with a challenge. I am more prepared and flexible to take on those challenges now than I was those days immediately following my retirement from the military. I am certainly more aware that most of my private-sector peers still do not really know what I did during my twenty years in the military—and that's okay. My professional and personal successes will speak to that, just as yours will! And, my sense of humor has broadened, thankfully. That sense of humor comes in handy often, as leaders of companies will make decisions or, even worse, not make decisions that could have resulted in someone getting hurt on a battlefield. You will be frustrated when this happens, but at least no one is shooting at you when these new experiences occur. This is when your sense of humor will come in handy.

To begin your integration process, it is important for you to have a few basic building blocks on employment practices in the private sector. I'll warn you, this is somewhat dry material, but it will add to your knowledge base when you become a successful candidate for a job.

7. NEGOTIATING YOUR JOB OFFER

CONGRATULATIONS! Take some deep breaths and read on so that you will be prepared for a few additional processes that will require your attention before you receive your business cards.

Before an employer extends an offer to you, salary negotiations typically represent the last barrier to successfully closing the deal. If you can agree on the price your labor represents to the employer, then you can shake hands, set a start date, and be prepared to show up on day one with a smile on your face and a whole new set of adventures, challenges, and learning opportunities to look forward to. But as most career coaches and family members will tell you, be prepared to negotiate the job offer and get the most you can before you say "I do" at the finish line.

That is generally good advice, except for the fact that you won't know much, if anything, about the cards they are holding in their hands or the general wage ranges that a particular company may follow. Will you be paid fairly for what you are going to be asked to do? Will you be underpaid—everyone's greatest fear? Or—gasp—will you be overpaid for the contributions you are about to make? Don't laugh at that last one—it's a real phenomenon. When someone checks the box on an exit interview saying he was overpaid for the work he did, it basically means that he did not get a chance to do what he was hired for, he was underutilized in his role, and he likely experienced high levels of angst and disappointment before choosing to leave the company.

If you were thinking that overpayment meant being paid more than the market should have allowed for someone with your skills and background, just keep in mind that you wouldn't want that either because it could make you a prime target for layoff. The goal is not to find a salary offer that's too hot or too cold. Rather, just like the three little bears in the fairytale, you want an offer that's just right.

So, how do employers extend offers? There is actually a lot more going on in the background than you think, although much depends on the size of the company and the level of sophistication in its compensation planning model. Rule number one is that smaller companies have more flexibility than larger companies when it comes to the salaries they offer. That is because business owners can shell out as much or as little as they want when it comes to offering candidates jobs. After all, who is going to tell them otherwise? It's their wallets.

Then again, large companies may tend to pay less in the beginning but will eventually pay more over time. And when you add the value of their benefits plans along with short- and long-term incentives to the mix, larger companies typically trump smaller companies significantly in terms of overall compensation and remuneration. (Yes, that's a broad generalization, but it generally holds true across all industries and parts of the country.)

What should not be any part of this conversation is how much you will receive in retirement if you are career military.

Many books on finding a job assume that you are negotiating with smaller employers where there is a fair amount of discretion in salary ranges. Therefore, you tend to get advice that lends itself better to negotiating with a smaller employer rather than a larger one, but that clearly misses half the picture. Following are some of the fallacies about salary negotiation you will find in prominent job-finding books.

- **Fallacy #1: Never discuss salary until the very end of the interviewing process.**
Reality: You'll find yourself cold and lonely if you refuse to answer recruiters' or employers' questions about your salary. Most of the time, salary discussions will come up during the telephone, screening interview before you are ever invited into the office. "After all," reasons the employer, "why waste time interviewing someone we can't afford?" Expect the employer to ask you something like this: "John, I don't want to limit you in any way, and please don't mind my asking, but how much were you earning at your last position in the military in terms of base salary and any ancillary compensation items?" That's a valid question because your military salary serves as an anchor in terms of your value to the job market. Yes, it's true that comparing military salaries with private-sector salaries is like comparing apples and oranges, but recruiters and employers have to start somewhere. Make sure you take into account *all* of the ancillary compensation you got while on active duty—it adds up. What should not be any part of this conversation is how much you will receive in retirement if you are career military. It simply is none of their business and should play no part in the decision making regarding compensation in your new role. At this stage, they probably won't ask you how much you are looking for because that is too specific and premature, and you won't know anything about the company, the position, or the benefits yet, but it should not surprise you if they do touch on the subject lightly. After all, they don't want to bring in someone who is currently making $85,000 per year in the military and looking for a $250,000 role in the private sector. That is

probably too much of a mismatch, and the company won't invest the time to educate candidates who have excessive expectations in their first role out of the military.

Here is how you might word your response: "Jane, I'm happy to share with you that my base salary is currently $85,000, but it also included housing and a car allowance as well as full medical coverage while I was serving overseas, so it might be a bit challenging coming up with an apples-to-apples number, since housing and car payments tend to be the highest costs that people have to tackle here at home. As far as my expectations, I have to be totally transparent about that: I'm just not sure yet. A role like the one you're describing to me now, though, sounds like it has a tremendous amount of potential and challenge, and those are my key motivators as I transition from the military to the private sector. Is that a fair enough answer for you at this point?" It certainly is, and you have given the baseline information, along with the housing and auto considerations, without committing to a fixed dollar expectation in the future. Very well handled!

- **Fallacy #2: Employers always start the bidding process lower than they are prepared to go.**
Reality: While it is true that in any negotiation, both parties are on opposite sides trying to find a balance between the cost of labor and the expectations regarding pay, it would be a mistake to assume that every employer is cheap and trying to shortchange you. In fact, it could be just the opposite: You may be going in with an ideal salary number in your head, only to find that your salary offer comes in higher. Why? Because you needed to be brought to the minimum of the salary range, and the number you desired was below it.

You will also see advice stating that if you believe a job range is roughly $60,000–$85,000, start your bidding right below the maximum of the range and negotiate upwards from there. Well, not really—doing so may come across as naive and lessen the value of your candidacy in the employer's eyes. First, it is very difficult to tell how much a position is paying. Even if you are applying for a position in a public company that is posted with a documented salary range, you won't know what your peers in that office are currently making, and their salaries will be the key determinants of how much the company will offer you. This is

Be patient and respectful, and don't fret excessively over salary.

a concept known as internal equity, meaning that a company should not pay a new hire more than existing workers unless there is some rational justification to do so (e.g., the candidate has more years of experience, a valuable certification that others are lacking, a higher level of education, etc.).

So don't try to outthink the employer when it comes to launching your starting number at or just below the top of his salary range. Ranges vary widely—usually 50%, but in higher positions, upwards of 100%— therefore posting that a position at the university pays $65,000–$105,000 does not mean the organization will want to start negotiating with you at $100,000. If the highest person on the team is currently at $92,000 and the group's salaries range from $82,000 to $92,000, there is no way anyone is going to start talking about a six-figure salary with you unless you are exceptionally overqualified for the role and leaps and bounds ahead of the existing staffers in terms of experience and education.

Be patient and respectful, and don't fret excessively over salary. Yes, you have to make enough to live, but the company and the role should take precedence in your analysis over the base salary being offered, because you are looking for a longer-term commitment and career-launching opportunity. Once the employer has a thorough understanding of your current base salary and additional perks, then he will generally start engaging in salary negotiations as you move along in the interview process. You will likely have indications along the way so that by the time you get to the final interview rounds, you will be able to determine roughly in what range the offer will come. And even if you don't get any advance insights into what the employer may be thinking, remember that you are just transitioning out of the military and into the private sector, so the typical employer will realize you are a bit like a fish out of water. Expect the employer to take the lead and mention something like this:

Susan, I'm looking at the salaries of the people on staff along with what we have in the budget. Now, I know the posted salary range shows compensation for that job can go up to $105,000, which it theoretically can, but that's not what we have budgeted. And truth be told, our existing staffers aren't at that *salary either, not by a long shot. So from what I can tell so far, if we were to come in with an offer, it would probably be in the $85,000–$87,500 range. I know that's lateral to what you were earning and doesn't include the offset for housing and car allowances. But I want to pace you through this as much as I can in a spirit of full disclosure and in order to set your expectations correctly. You don't have to do anything with this info right now. I just wanted to share it with you so you can give it some thought. We'll talk more soon.*

- **Fallacy #3: Whoever mentions salary first typically loses the negotiation.**
Reality: I do not recommend that you initiate discussions about salary offers first. That is not your place. Instead, the recruiter will ask you what you are currently making and then decide from there whether you are within the range of the position he is trying to fill. The assumption above comes from the "What's Behind Door Number 3?" mentality, in which everything boils down to the final round of conversations. That is not generally how this is done. But you may find yourself in a situation where an employer says, "Janet, I need to ask you a very important question: at what point dollar-wise would you accept this offer and at what point would you reject it?" If you are asked such a question, then feel free to talk about the offer and your perception. Your response might sound like this:

> *That's a tougher question for me, Jim, as I'm transitioning into the private sector for the first time and don't know exactly how these types of negotiations are handled. I know the $85,000 base salary that I was receiving in the military is my anchor, so to speak, and I get that. I also realize that the premium overseas pay that included housing and car allowances doesn't really count back here in the States, which is understandable. But I'm not sure how to peg myself salary-wise to this role because I don't know what your budget looks like or what the internal equity landscape looks like, so I'd ask if you could take the first stab at this and let me know where you think I'd best fit into your salary structure relative to the other members of the team. Is that something you'd be willing to share with me? Again, I'm really interested in this position and this company, as you know, but blurting out a number or even a range is a bit of shot in the dark for me at this point, so I'd really appreciate your help.*

That is a very well thought out and informed response. You will be speaking the employer's language because you will be hitting on his key

> **You cannot expect your next employer to make up for lost time by offering you a 50% salary increase.**

considerations—salary range, since it is posted for everyone to see, as well as internal equity and budget. The budget for a particular job's salary is typically tied to what the last person in the role was earning. Therefore, if the employer pays you more, there will be a variance he may need to get special permission for. Internal equity and budget are two big considerations that every employer faces when extending offers, so you will probably fare very well for being so honest and well informed.

- **Fallacy #4: I can negotiate an offer that will help me make up for lost time—to catch up with my peers and make what I *really* should be getting paid right now.**

  Reality: Wrong! It is not a prospective employer's responsibility to help you make up for lost time (real or perceived) in your career development. A candidate sometimes feels that remaining with the same company (or branch of the military) for so long has cost him market share, so to speak, because he has been limited by his company's paltry merit increases over the past five years or so. Well, welcome to the club!

  You cannot expect your next employer to make up for lost time by offering you a 50% salary increase. That is a naive way of approaching your job search. Instead, follow a general rule of reason that—assuming you are, indeed, underpaid for the work you do—your next employer may be able to award you a 10–15% (20% tops) increase in your base salary rate. That is more than optimistic in this post-recession job market—although the increase you can expect will fluctuate with the type of work you do and the part of the country you are in. In short, if you really feel you need a 40% or 50% increase to remain competitive, accept this position now and expect to change employers again in two to three years, when you hopefully will snag another 15–20% increase. By doing it this way, you will eventually catch up to your perceived market value three to five years from now.

- **Fallacy #5: I can probably come pretty close to estimating what they will offer me by using the various online search tools available.**

  Reality: Online tools can be helpful in approximating the value of the salary range for the job you are applying for, but their limitations are significant. First, they are self-published, meaning that in most cases, workers upload their salary information without any form of checks or balances from an organization that understands compensation design and analysis, so you are seeing one-off exceptions without any contextual framework.

Second, they provide numbers in a vacuum. A director of human resources at a Fortune 500 company can earn exceptionally more than a senior vice president of human resources in a two-hundred-person organization. Small versus large, private versus public, for-profit versus nonprofit, manufacturing versus service sector—all these factors play considerable roles in determining the fair market value for a particular job.

That being said, if you are going to look into salary data on the Web, here are some sites that might help you when considering salary ranges in general:

○ www.salary.com
○ www.salaryexpert.com
○ www.bls.gov/ooh
○ http://jobstar.org/tools/salary/index.cfm
○ http://stats.bls.gov/oes/oes_emp.htm
○ www.myplan.com

Expect to find exceptionally wide ranges of salary data for jobs with exactly the same or very similar titles. And be sure to avoid making a statement to an employer along the lines of, "I've researched salary ranges on Salary.com, and I believe this job should be paying $x." That would be considered exceptionally naive, shortsighted, and potentially insulting to an employer or recruiter who negotiates job offers for a living.

Exempt vs. Nonexempt

One of the concepts that may take some getting used to in the private sector is "exempt" versus "nonexempt," and that is because it is a fairly confusing concept. Exemption status has to do with how companies classify their workers relative to paying overtime. What exactly does it mean to be exempt or nonexempt for purposes of overtime? Remember it this way: an exempt employee is exempt from the overtime protections and provisions of the Fair Labor Standards Act (FLSA).

The Fair Labor Standards Act was voted into existence in 1938 at the time of the Great Depression and enabled the federal government to become deeply involved in regulating minimum wages for workers who might otherwise be exploited by business owners. The act established overtime wage requirements and defined specific occupations (typically ownership and senior management) that were exempt from the law's protections. It required employers in covered enterprises to pay "time-and-a-half"—150% of the regular rate received by nonexempt employees—for all hours those individuals worked in excess of forty hours per week.

What you need to keep in mind is that if you are in an executive or leadership role within your new organization, you will be classified as exempt and not eligible for overtime pay. Managers, outside sales people, and recognized professionals like doctors and lawyers, for example, are typically exempt and receive no premium pay for working long hours and weekends. That is because they are paid for their results, not the time they put in to reach those results. If you have an administrative assistant or if the company has a receptionist, on the other hand, that person will probably be designated as nonexempt and paid for his time. That means that he receives regular breaks and lunch periods as well as premium pay for overtime, which is typically defined as hours worked in excess of forty per week, though in certain states like California, overtime is any time longer than eight hours in a workday. Nonexempt employees get docked financially if they come in late or leave early, but they earn overtime pay if they work beyond their regular hours.

If you are accepting a leadership position within an organization, understand that when it comes to nonexempt employees, you must recognize the importance of time away from work for breaks and meal periods. Too many unsuspecting employers have found themselves wrapped up in class action lawsuits because they did not realize that they were responsible for ensuring that the nonexempt workers take their breaks and lunches regularly.

Market Base Pay and Incentive Pay

Market base pay, simply put, is your starting salary. It is the amount in your offer letter, the number you sometimes fret over, trying to determine if there will be too much month at the end of your money! Your current base salary in the military will serve as an anchor in determining what your future base salary will look like in terms of your next salary offer because, like it or not, your salary represents the level of responsibility you hold and the impact that you make on an organization. True, translating military dollars to private-sector dollars is very much an apples-to-oranges exercise, but it is still the first place that an employer will want to start. Therefore, do not hold back or refuse to share your current compensation information: it could cut short an otherwise potentially successful interview. Besides, your military pay is public information; a hiring manager can look it up and come up with a ball-park estimate of your compensation.

> ... translating military dollars to private-sector dollars is very much an apples-to-oranges exercise ...

Incentive pay comes in two forms: (a) short-term and (b) long-term incentives. Short-term incentives are typically in the form of bonuses that add to your cash compensation. When you add your base salary plus bonus, you come up with what HR people call "total cash comp." You will always want to distinguish your base salary from your bonus because, while base salaries are fairly secure, bonuses can fluctuate wildly, are discretionary, and are rarely guaranteed. So, if you earn a base salary of $100,000 with a 20% bonus target, you would describe it as follows: "My base salary is $100K, and I have a 20% bonus target, bringing my total cash comp to $120,000." You could then expect a recruiter or employer to ask you about the 20% bonus target: did you receive it consistently, did you ever go over- or under-target (based on your company's performance), and other questions.

Long-term incentives (LTI), by comparison, are typically associated with equity in publicly traded companies and come in the form of stock options and restricted stock units (RSUs) as well as a host of other plans that tie an executive to a company for the long haul. Private employers have their own LTI programs that are non-equity based and can be paid out in cash and in company stock. Whatever the case, these types of plans attempt to tie individual leader performance to the organization's strategic plan and overall performance in some form or another. The specifics of restricted stock, phantom stock, profit pools, performance units, strategic deferred compensation, options, stock appreciation rights, and the like go way beyond the scope of this book. They can get very complicated, so don't be scared to ask someone to explain them to you in detail.

Suffice it to say, though, that if you are being offered any kind of equity participation or long-term, deferred-incentive compensation plan, you are arguably among the top 5% of executives at that organization. And just as you have a bonus target amount for your annual bonus, you will also have an LTI target for any type of equity or LTI award. For example, you might describe your current compensation as follows: "I'm at a $205,000 base salary and have a 35% bonus target and 40% LTI target." That means that between your bonus cash award (35%) and long-term incentive payouts (40%), you will be making 75% more than your base salary. That is a very impressive package! But the LTI package will probably pay out to you incrementally over a specified period of time that is called the vesting period.

8. BENEFITS

Disclaimer: IRS rates may vary over time. Consult the IRS for current rates.

As you will see, benefits play an increasingly important role in the total compensation of workers at all levels. Healthcare costs have grown exponentially due to advances in medical technology and, some would argue, a medical insurance industry that has run amok. Be that as it may, it is important that you understand the various elements of the medical benefits you will be offered, both in terms of the cost and services provided. The goal of this chapter is to raise your awareness of the various benefit offerings available and to help you make selections that are right for you and your family so that you are getting the optimum coverage for a reasonable price. Benefits in the private sector are not necessarily one size fits all as they are in the military.

Medical Plan Options

You will be eligible to participate in a company's health and medical plans if you are a regular, full-time employee. In some organizations, you have to be scheduled to work forty hours per week to receive full benefits—no exceptions. In other organizations, you will be recognized as a full-time employee as long as you work thirty hours a week or more. And yet other organizations have a step process in which, if you work forty hours per week, you will receive 100% benefits coverage; if you work thirty-eight hours per week, you will receive 90% benefits coverage; and so forth, all the way down to 50% coverage for a thirty-hour-per-week schedule. Below that level, you won't be able to participate in the plan. In addition, independent contractors and temporary workers are typically excluded from participating in employer-sponsored health plans, although much of this may be up for debate in the near future.

You can also enroll your eligible dependents for benefits. These include your spouse; children, step-children, or adopted children up to age twenty-six, or disabled children up to any age; and domestic part-ner and eligible domestic partner's children in most cases (although a notarized affidavit will likely be required).

Note that after your initial enrollment upon starting a new job, you gener-ally have to wait for your company's open enrollment window, which typi-cally occurs only once a year, to add new dependents to your medical plan. The exception is for a qualifying family status change, which entitles you to enroll another dependent within thirty days of that event. For example, a qualifying event that will permit you to add someone outside of the annual open enrollment window might be marriage, divorce, birth or adoption of a child, or your spouse's gain or loss of other coverage. So, if your spouse loses his job and insurance coverage, you can add him to your company's plan at that point—but only if you remain within the thirty-day notice period. If you miss that window, you will have to wait for the next round of open enrollment.

Now on to the coverage plans available to you. Take a deep breath—this is going to feel overwhelming, and not just because you are exploring private-sector benefits for the first time. Everyone is overwhelmed by benefits options nowadays because of the changes being introduced by the Affordable Care Act (aka, Obamacare). Physicians' offices, insurers, and company benefit represen-tatives are watching for changes that will impact their patients, clients, and em-ployees—changes that are on a massive scale and will clearly have a significant impact on healthcare delivery as we now know it.

You may be given options of selecting a PPO or Preferred Provider Orga-nization, HMO or Health Maintenance Organization, CDHP or Consumer Driven Health Plan, or some other type of entity that may be specific to your state. Providers like United Healthcare, Anthem Blue Cross and Blue Shield, Aetna, and Cigna all offer programs that fit these various models.

A PPO, for example, is a medical plan that lets you choose between in-network and out-of-network providers; however, you receive services at discounted rates when utilizing an in-network provider. Your copay, coinsurance, and deductible are based on the services provided. Coinsurance is a percentage of the actual cost of coverage that you pay once the deductible has been reached.

When you consider the options available to you under a PPO plan, you will typically see a menu that looks something like the table below.

Benefit	In-Network	Out-of-Network
Deductible (Individual / Family)	$500 / $1,000	$700 / $1,400
Coinsurance	Plan pays 80% after deductible is met	Plan pays 65% after deductible is met
Out-of-Pocket Maximum	$3,500 / $7,000	$7,500 / $7,000
Office Visit Copay	$25 copay	Plan pays 65% after deductible
Specialist and Urgent Care Copay	$40 copay	Plan pays 65% after deductible
Preventive	100%, no deductive or copay	Plan pays 65% after deductible
Emergency Room	$200 copay	Pay at in-network level
Hospital Inpatient	$250 copay; plan pays 80% after deductible	$350 copay; plan pays 65% after deductible

Fig. 23 Coverage Details of Example PPO Plan (Table courtesy of Paul Falcone)

Notice the financial advantages of remaining within the network of existing providers, although you have the flexibility to go out of network to any healthcare practitioner of choice, albeit at a higher cost. A PPO is the "Cadillac" plan of choice and typically comes bundled with a dental, prescription drug, and sometimes, vision plan.

As far as the premiums you might expect to pay for a plan like this, options might include the following:

PPO Premiums	Bi-Weekly Cost (26 pay periods per year)	Annual Cost
Employee Only	$44	$1,144
Employee + Spouse	$114	$2,964
Employee + Child(ren)	$99	$2,574
Family	$180	$4,680

Fig. 24 Costs of Example PPO Plan (Table courtesy of Paul Falcone)

As you can see, this type of plan can get a bit pricey for a family of four, which is why having other options is a good thing.

A Consumer Driven Health Plan, or CDHP, is another interesting model to look at as you shop for insurance coverage. CDHPs typically feature the lowest biweekly payroll deduction, so the premiums are relatively low. It rewards you for being a smart consumer of healthcare, while continuing to provide quality benefits that protect you from the financial risk of significant medical needs. A CDHP is typically coupled with a Health Savings Account that the company contributes to and that can be funded with your own additional pre-tax contributions—meaning that the money you invest can be shielded from taxation, similar to a traditional 401(k) or IRA, which will be explained later.

There are no copays with a CDHP; however, you must meet the full deductible before coinsurance kicks in, except for certain preventive care services and preventive prescription drugs that are covered at 100% and to which no deductible applies. Here is what the coverage might look like in a CDHP plan:

Benefit	In-Network	Out-of-Network
Deductible (Individual / Family)	$1,250 / $2,500	$1,250 / $2,500
Coinsurance	Plan pays 85% after deductible	Plan pays 65% after deductible
Out-of-Pocket Maximum	$5,950 / $11,900	$5,950 / $11,900
Office Visit Copay	Plan pays 85% after deductible	Plan pays 65% after deductible
Specialist and Urgent Care Copay	Plan pays 85% after deductible	Plan pays 65% after deductible
Preventive	100%, no deductive or copay	Plan pays 65% after deductible
Emergency Room	Plan pays 85% after deductible	Pay at in-network level
Hospital Inpatient	Plan pays 85% after deductible	Plan pays 65% after deductible

Fig. 25 Coverage Details of Example CDHP Plan (Table courtesy of Paul Falcone)

As you can see, your deductibles and out-of-pocket maximums will be higher in a CDHP than what you would expect to see with a PPO plan, but the advantage of this type of plan is that the premiums are much lower. Here is what you might expect to pay for a CDHP plan:

CDHP Premiums	Bi-Weekly Cost (26 pay periods per year)	Annual Cost
Employee Only	$24	$624
Employee + Spouse	$63	$1,638
Employee + Child(ren)	$57	$1,482
Family	$101	$2,626

Fig. 26 Costs of Example CDHP Plan (Table courtesy of Paul Falcone)

As I mentioned, CDHPs are associated with Health Savings Accounts (HSAs) that function like IRAs for healthcare, only better: Like an IRA, an HSA allows for tax-free contributions and investment earnings. But unlike with a regular IRA, your withdrawals are tax-free as well, as long as you spend the money on medical care.

Therefore, if you would prefer to keep your premiums lower and to dedicate pre-tax dollars to pay for planned medical expenses, this could be a wonderful option. But if you prefer the "Cadillac" model and are willing to pay almost double in some cases for coverage, then the PPO may make most sense.

Each company's offerings will have different features, limits, maximums, and other stipulations. The Health Maintenance Organization (HMO) represents yet another model: in this type of plan, most physician services require a copayment before the plan pays its share of covered costs. HMO premiums can be expensive, but if you really need its services, your overall financial exposure will be minimized because its model focuses on keeping costs down. The catch? There is no out-of-network option, except in emergency situations. So if you develop a rare form of a disease and know of a hospital that specializes in its treatment, the HMO may insist that you be treated in one of its facilities instead. That is a risk that you will assume to take advantage of lowered total premium costs associated with an HMO.

. . . be sure to read the benefits enrollment guide that your company provides you.

When it comes time to select the appropriate healthcare provider that most closely meets your needs and the needs of your family, be sure to read the benefits enrollment guide that your company provides you. The level of information that typically is provided to employees on the options they have for healthcare is impressive. The models above can be used as a baseline comparison tool to see how your company's benefits offerings measure up. But, do meet one-on-one with someone from the Benefits department or call the carriers themselves; it is important that you understand what you are getting for your money and, even more so, what you won't be getting should you become ill.

. . . find out whom the commissioner of veterans affairs is in the state where you will live and work.

Lastly, keep in mind these three key points when it comes to healthcare: First, if you are coming off active duty, you have probably deployed a few times and may even have been injured. Make sure you retain a copy of your medical records and be sure you are signed up with the Veterans Administration (VA). I understand all the backlog issues they are having, but the most important thing is to make sure you get into their system. You may be healthy as a horse right now but, when you get a little older (and you will), things start to hurt for no apparent reason, which may be service connected. You must make sure you document anything and everything while you are still on active duty in preparation to make claims for disability compensation. Second, find out whom the commissioner of veterans affairs is in the state where you will live and work. This person has an organization of veteran service officers that exists to help you deal with the VA. These folks will be an invaluable asset to you when it comes to compiling the mounds of paperwork you will need for claims or appeals on claims. Use them and thank them for their service. Third, for those who have the option of benefiting from Tricare, please take time to understand what you are entitled to. Tricare will be a secondary insurance to those career military members who elect to also have private, civilian insurance offered by the private-sector company they work for. Make sure when you see a doctor or do anything related to healthcare that you disclose that you have Tricare as a secondary insurance.

Defined-Benefit, or Traditional, Pension Plans

Traditional pension plans are becoming rare in corporate America these days, but if you are fortunate enough to be offered a position with a company that has a defined-benefit pension plan in place, run—don't walk—to the altar and accept the job offer! This benefit trumps all others because it is incredibly valuable in terms of its long-term potential. A defined-benefit pension plan provides a monthly annuity or lump sum payment (you elect which you want) that you receive at retirement; the amount is determined using a set formula that includes your compensation and your years of service with the organization. Typically, you become eligible to participate in the plan once you reach some service milestone (for example, a five-year vesting period), and you are guaranteed* a monthly payout once you reach age sixty-five. In some cases you can start receiving your retirement annuity (if you elect that option) sooner, depending on the plan guidelines.

One difference between traditional pension plans and 401(k) plans is that with traditional pension plans, the company pays the entire cost of the benefit, and there is no cost whatsoever to the employee. If you are eligible for a pension with the military, a private-sector pension is certainly the icing on the cake in most cases. It never hurts to have multiple sources of passive income ("passive" in the sense that the cash flow continually self-generates without your having to contribute), so the option of a traditional pension plan should place any organization right at the top of your list. Another way to look at it—a traditional pension is the gift that keeps on giving!

There are some complicated rules that govern the amount of the payout once the employee reaches age sixty-five, including eligibility-service, vesting-service, and benefit-service calculations. Each company defines its own basic benefit formula that explains how the monthly allowance—much like an annuity—will be calculated, but the retirement benefit is virtually free money because the company remains responsible for investing on your behalf and making those payments once you reach sixty-five (or earlier, if you opt to retire and elect the benefits at a younger age).

* The guarantee may be affected by the company's bankruptcy at some future date. The Pension Benefit Guarantee Corporation, or PBGC, is the government entity that oversees private sector pensions. In theory, its goal is to ensure compliance and proper funding so that retirees receive 100% of the benefits due them. In reality, the PBGC may only be able to guarantee a percentage of the total payout in light of a company bankruptcy. Still, it is free money, so pensions are the most valuable employee benefit around—if you can find a company that offers one!

Typically, only base salary-cash compensation counts toward the pension calculation, as most companies exclude annual bonuses or long-term incentives like stock options and restricted stock units. In some cases, short-term bonuses are included in your total compensation calculation. Additionally, the amount of your compensation that can be taken into account when determining employer and employee contributions is limited. For example, the compensation limitation is $250,000 for 2012 and $255,000 for 2013[6]. A sample calculation formula might look like this: *Average earnings in highest three years of employment multiplied by 2% times total years of service.*

You will be asked to select a payment method best suited to your personal needs. If you are married at the time of your retirement, you will usually be offered a 50% joint and survivor annuity option, meaning your spouse receives 50% of your monthly benefit payment after you die. In exchange for covering two lives, however, the payout while you are alive is much smaller. There are additional options— for example, one that allows you to name someone in addition to your spouse for a contingent annuity option—but the main thing to keep in mind is that the company is footing the bill for this tremendously valuable benefit. This is the same when those retiring from the military elect the percentage of survivor benefits.

Defined-Contribution, or 401(k), Plans

401(k) plans, like traditional pension plans, help you save for retirement. There is one major difference, though—with 401(k) plans, you are saving your own money, which is deducted from each paycheck, and you are fully responsible for the outcome of your investments. Not quite as attractive as the traditional pension plans described above, are they? Be that as it may, 401(k) plans make total sense in today's day and age. When traditional pensions first came onto the scene in the late-19th and early-20th centuries, people simply did not live that long, so the pension payouts were not as much of an issue. Add to that the fact that back in those days, there were roughly sixteen active workers for every one pensioner, and you can see why traditional pension plans played a very important role in elderly Americans' financial well-being from a sustainability standpoint.

Well, times have changed. Between the Baby Boomers and medical technology advances, the old formula has been turned upside down. Average life spans are now closer to eighty years, and beginning in 2011, the first Baby

Boomers, born in 1946[*], began to retire. During the following eighteen years through 2029, roughly seventy-eight million Baby Boomers will retire—approximately ten thousand per day—changing the ratio of workers to pensions from 16:1, when pensions were in their heyday, to 4:1 nowadays. You can see why the math simply does not work: you cannot tax four workers enough to pay for one person's retirement; the liability simply cannot be spread that thin. To the credit of the US government, these trends were identified in the early 1970s when 401(k) plans were first being created.

The 401(k) model works well in terms of its efficiency and incentives. Companies receive tax breaks if they match a certain percentage of employee investments, and workers receive tax breaks if they set aside a particular amount of money for their own retirement. This is complicated by the fact that financial markets go through extreme twists and turns, as the Great Recession of 2008–09 saw investors' total net worth fall by $13 trillion, or 20%, from its level in 2007. Still, the shift from government-sponsored and company-sponsored pensions to worker-sponsored programs makes total sense in light of the demographic changes prompted by the retirement of the Baby Boom generation and the aging of the American population.

I suggest that you begin investing in a 401(k) as soon as you are allowed to in your new company. Pay particular attention to the company-matching aspect of the plan. Once you get your regular deduction and investment choices up and running, you will forget about the 401(k) and it will be on automatic pilot. For those of you over fifty years old, there is a catch-up opportunity whereby you can contribute an extra amount to your 401(k). Refer to the IRS code or your company-plan details for the specifics regarding this benefit. I also advise utilizing a methodology called dollar cost averaging when it comes time for you to invest. Dollar cost averaging is a simple way to minimize risk through a set amount of investments done at predetermined intervals, regardless of the market performance. When the market is down, your purchasing power is greater and you will buy more shares. When the market is up, you will buy fewer shares at the higher price. The "averaging" part comes into play when you take the long-

---

[*] The Baby Boom generation was born in 1946, right after the end of World War II, and saw its official end in 1964 with the launch of the birth control pill.

term approach (investing for years) to this method—regardless of market price or performance, your savings will grow very quickly.

Traditional vs. Roth 401(k) Plans and IRAs

Both 401(k) plans and Individual Retirement Accounts (IRAs) come in two basic flavors: traditional and Roth. Without getting too overly financial in this explanation, simply understand that the difference between the two has to do with tax treatments of the deductions now and of the payouts once you are in retirement.

Traditional 401(k) plans are known as private-sector salary-reduction plans. Along with their two cousins—403(b) plans in the nonprofit sector and 457 plans in the public sector—the salary-reduction element stems from the fact that the money invested by a worker is hidden from taxation. In other words, if you earn $100,000 per year but contribute $15,000 to your traditional 401(k) plan, the government will tax you as if you only earned $85,000 that year. Don't be confused by the terms 401(k), 403(b), or 457; the numbers refer to the section of the IRS code that created and governs them, so technically speaking, they are actually Section 401(k), Section 403(b), and Section 457 plans.

The salary-reduction element exists because employee contributions to traditional 401(k) plans are made on a pre-tax basis. Traditional contributions reduce your taxable income in the year you make the contribution. This is one of the key government incentives built into 401(k) program design: the more you invest in yourself, the fewer taxes you end up paying the government. There is a second key incentive that the government uses to incentivize US workers to save for their own retirement via 401(k) investments: the money you invest today grows tax-deferred until you withdraw it at retirement. Once you retire, you will then pay ordinary income tax on all traditional contributions and any gains.

Roth 401(k) plans work differently because they allow workers to opt to receive their tax incentives at the time of retirement rather than now. Roth plans are not designed to reduce your current taxes. In the example above, if you earn $100,000 per year and invest $15,000 into your Roth 401(k), you will still be taxed this year on your full $100,000 salary. However, the gains on your investments won't be subject to taxation when you retire. That's really tempting, isn't it?

Which one will be right for you? While it is clear that workers nearing retirement and at their peak earning capacity will probably benefit more from the traditional 401(k) plan's advantages, and workers in their early- to mid-twenties will clearly find advantages with the Roth option, those workers in the middle—from ages twenty-five to sixty—will need to look closely at the advantages and disadvantages of both options depending on their specific circumstances. There are tax considerations that you will need to consider. But many of us do not think about diversifying our tax risks throughout our careers and at retirement, which is why having *both* traditional and Roth investments could make total sense in most cases.

The Company Match: Your Key Incentive for Investing

Let's assume you are considering joining a company that provides a 100% match on the first 5% of your pay, and you will be earning $50,000 per year at this company. In that case, the math would look like this:

$50,000 gross annual salary

x 5% investment contribution made to your plan
   (via payroll deduction)

$2,500 amount you invest in your company's plan

x 100% company match (up to 5% of your gross pay)

$2,500 amount that your company contributes to
   your investment

Therefore, your $2,500 investment yields a 100% return, resulting in $5,000 in your retirement account. And here is some more good news: That 100% return does not include any appreciation that your investments may earn over time. In addition, that additional $2,500 amount that your company used to encourage you to invest in your own retirement does not count toward the annual 401(k) maximum. Show me any place else where you could earn a 100% return on your investment!

. . . don't leave free money on the table!

In reality, very few companies match 100% of your investment (although a rare few may match more than 100%). It is more commonly the case that companies match about $0.50 on the dollar, cutting the company's contribution in the example above from $2,500 to $1,250. But that is still an incredible return on your money, wouldn't you say? So, don't leave free money on the table!

But wait—there's more. Investing in your company's 401(k) plan up to the match is basically free all the way around. You heard that correctly—the money that you invest in your company's 401(k) plan up to the matching amount basically costs you little to nothing. Here is how to figure it out using the $0.50 company match in the example above:

$2,500   *Amount you contribute*

$1,250   *Amount the company contributes (50% match)*

$800   *Amount you save at tax time in a traditional 401(k) that hides your salary from taxes (roughly one-third of your $2,500 investment amount)*

$150   *Amount your investment will earn, on average, over several decades assuming a 6% rate of return (but not including compounding)*

And there you have it: Your $2,500 investment benefitted you with an additional $2,200 when you put it all together. The difference, $300, is what you paid to have a retirement account worth approximately $3,750 this year alone ($2,500 + $1,250). Multiply that by thirty years and see if your net investment of $300 was worth it! Of course, you will want to contribute more than what the company match allows (in this case, 5%); investing up to the company's matching portion should be the minimum that you invest. However, that free matching money should incentivize you never to miss an opportunity to capture the free lunch your employer is offering. You will save at tax time, your retirement nest egg will grow, and you will wonder why anyone wouldn't take advantage of this virtually free-money offer that is awaiting him in his company.

Calculating Your 401(k) Contribution

Let's do some more math together: Assume your base salary is $200,000 and you opt to defer the full $23,000 (the maximum amount if one is fifty or older, of course you can choose to invest a much smaller amount) by having payroll deductions made throughout the year from your paycheck. Note that payroll deductions work the same way whether you are investing via a traditional or Roth 401(k). Okay, we have our two big numbers in hand: annual salary and target 401(k) contribution. You only need one more piece of information to calculate your payroll deduction amount—the number of pay periods throughout the year. For the sake of this example, we will assume your company pays on a biweekly basis, therefore there are twenty-six pay periods throughout the year. The figures you have so far are these:

Annual base salary: *$200,000*

Target 401(k) investment: *$23,000*

Number of pay periods: *26*

Next, let's see how much of that $23,000 investment amount will be deducted from each of your twenty-six[*] paychecks:

$23,000 target investment (2013 max)

÷ 26 pay periods

$884.62 contribution per paycheck (goal)

Now this is where it gets a little tricky: You will need to select a withholding percentage (in whole numbers) that comes closest to that $884.62 amount, and this will take a pencil and paper (or spreadsheet) as well as an eraser. So, if you remain with the $23,000 investment goal assumption, here is how you'll figure out how to get closest to that $884.62 biweekly deduction amount:

11% Withholding Calculation	12% Withholding Calculation
$200,000	$200,000
x 11%	x 12%
$22,000	$24,000

Fig. 27 Example Calculation of Withholding Percentage for 401(k) Contribution
(Table courtesy of Paul Falcone)

Obviously, $24,000 is too high (the 12% option), so you will need to go with the 11% option, coming in at $22,000. Now let's divide that number by twenty-six pay periods to see what the actual per-paycheck contribution is going to look like:

[*] Quick note of caution: If your company pays an annual bonus separately, you will actually end up with twenty-seven paychecks during the year, which could throw your calculations off. A 401(k) deduction will automatically be made from your bonus check unless you instruct your company not to make that particular deferral; you will usually have to give at least two payroll periods notice if you don't want the 401(k) investment taken out of your bonus check.

$22,000

÷ 26 pay periods

$846.15 contribution per paycheck (actual)

And there you have it: while your ideal goal would be to invest $884.62 per paycheck throughout the year, your calculation actually brings you to $846.15—about $38 less than your desired goal. It is a good idea to leave some wiggle room because you might get a merit increase during the upcoming year that raises your contributions slightly. The key to determining the appropriate contribution deduction for your 401(k), therefore, lies in getting as close to the ideal withholding percentage as possible. People often fiddle with their 401(k) withholding percentages right up until the end of the calendar year to get every dime they can into the plan without exceeding the maximum limit.

Alert: There Is a Danger to Over-Contributing! If you end up putting more than the $17,500—or $23,000, for those fifty or older—allowed maximum into your 401(k) plan in 2013, you could run into problems. Your employer will typically cap your contributions at that point, but sometimes companies miss that window. And that is when things get complicated because the IRS does not like it when people try to stash more money into their plans than the law allows. Options might include tax penalties in the form of double taxation, return of overpayments (which gets complicated when you file your tax return), or an allowance of the overpayment on a post-tax basis. That may not sound so bad in terms of dealing with your company, but it is absolutely no fun to deal with an IRS auditor, so proceed with caution. Here's what 401kHelpCenter.com, a "knowledge service that monitors and aggregates information related to the 401k industry," advises:

> **Question**: *What happens if I contribute more than the annual allowable limit to my 401k?*
>
> **Answer:** *If you exceed the 401(k) elective deferral limit, you must report the excess as income on your tax return forms for the calendar year the deferral was made as well as on your tax return for the calendar year when the excess amounts are withdrawn. The only way they can correct the mistake and avoid double taxation is to request that the excess be refunded, plus earnings, by the tax-filing deadline for the year in which the contributions were made, for example, by April 15, 2013, for excess contributions made during calendar 2012. In that case, the excess*

contribution need only be reported as taxable income for the year the contribution was made. (http://www.401khelpcenter.com/faq/faq_27.html#.UiySzxYydWg_)

Unless you want to deal with the tax-speak above as well as with a web of complicated IRS red tape, don't go a penny over the annual limit!

Individual Retirement Plans for the Self-Employed

If you opt to go the self-employed route, you'll find additional tax-efficient retirement investment vehicles available that make sound financial sense. This information could easily fill several volumes of books, but here is a quick overview along with additional resources for your consideration if you are looking into retirement plans as a self-employed worker.

SEP-IRAs

A Simplified Employee Pension Individual Retirement Arrangement (SEP-IRA) is a variation of an IRA. Business owners implement SEP-IRAs to provide retirement benefits for themselves and their employees. There are few significant administration costs for a self-employed individual with no employees. If you are self-employed and have employees, all employees must receive the same benefits under a SEP plan. Since SEP accounts are treated as IRAs, funds can be invested the same way as any other IRA.

Employees may contribute up to $5,500 in calendar year 2014, or $6,500 if they are fifty or above. This contribution amount is in addition to the employer's contribution amount. Employer contribution amounts are based on the business owner's annual compensation. The employer can contribute up to 25% of his or her total compensation to a maximum of $52,000 per year. The employer contribution to the SEP-IRA plan is made on a pre-tax basis, which means that no tax is paid on the business owner's contributions until the money is eventually withdrawn once workers reach retirement age. What a great way to reduce taxable income! And while the employer is not required to make contributions every year, in years where contributions are made, they must be equal for all employees. So it is a fairly simple and easy plan to set up and administer, which is why we are discussing it first.

Contributions to a SEP-IRA are tax deductible and serve the same salary reduction purpose as traditional IRAs . . .

As far as tax treatment goes, SEP-IRAs are taxed at ordinary income tax rates when qualified withdrawals are made, just as traditional IRAs are. Contributions to a SEP-IRA are tax deductible and serve the same salary reduction purpose as traditional IRAs in that they lower the business owner's income tax liability in the current year. Note, though, that since a SEP is a form of an IRA, IRA contribution limits apply. In other words, investing in a SEP-IRA will limit how much you can invest in a Roth IRA that calendar year. Your combined IRA contributions—whether traditional, Roth, SEP, or SIMPLE—must remain at or below the maximum allowable annual contribution for IRAs in general.

Overall, the SEP-IRA is arguably the simplest of the three IRA options because the employee controls the plan and the business owner makes predetermined contributions. Employers can institute a SEP-IRA plan even if they have another retirement plan. Just remember that the penalty for exceeding the contribution limit applies to IRAs as well: if you contribute more than the IRS limit, you may incur a 6% penalty on any excess contributions until you remove the excess contribution.

SIMPLE IRAs and Keogh Plans

I'm guessing you thought the SEP sounded pretty simple and straightforward, but you need to know what a SIMPLE IRA is and what a Keogh Plan is as well. A Savings Incentive Match Plan for Employees (SIMPLE) IRA is a tax-deferred, employer-sponsored retirement plan that is simpler to set up and administer than a 401(k) or 403(b) plan, which is why small businesses are drawn to it. Like a 401(k) plan, a SIMPLE IRA is funded via a pre-tax salary reduction, but unlike a 401(k) plan, a SIMPLE IRA is not subject to complicated ERISA regulations. In addition, contribution limits for SIMPLE plans are lower than for most other types of employer-sponsored retirement plans (e.g., $12,000 in 2013 and 2014; $14,500 in 2013 and 2014 if you are age fifty or older).

SIMPLE IRAs require a company match: either a dollar-for-dollar match of an employee's contributions up to 3% of the employee's compensation or a flat 2% of compensation for each employee regardless of the amount the employee contributes. Note, however, that if an employer has another retirement plan in place, then the SIMPLE plan cannot be used.

A Keogh plan, sometimes referred to as a H.R.10 plan, is a similar type of qualified retirement plan used by people who are self-employed or by businesses that are not incorporated. Contributions are tax deferred, making Keogh plans a popular choice for small business owners. Keogh plans have similar tax advantages to other forms of IRAs in that contributions and revenue generated from investments can be tax deferred.

There are two types of Keogh plans: (a) defined contribution and (b) defined benefit. In a defined-contribution plan, a fixed contribution is made per pay period, whereas in a defined-benefit plan, a more complex IRS formula is used to calculate the rate of contributions. The main benefit of Keogh plans versus other IRAs is that they may have higher contribution limits. In 2013, for example, employees can generally contribute up to $16,500 per year, and the employer can contribute up to $32,500 on behalf of the employee, for a total annual contribution of $51,000 (or 25% of annual compensation, whichever is lower). For 2014, the total amount increases to $52,000. However, despite the higher contribution limits, Keoghs are not as popular as other plans because they are more complex to administer and typically require professional help to establish. There is no such thing as a Roth Keogh plan, so all contributions must be made on a pre-tax basis.

So which would you rather establish for your business—a SEP, SIMPLE, or Keogh IRA? You will have to rely on your tax person to get a deeper understanding of the implications of each of these three types of plans for you based on your income level, investment horizon, employee population, penchant for simple versus more complex setup and administration requirements, and participation in other plans. Here is a summary of their guidelines to help you remember how to tell them apart:

- **SEP**: You can contribute as much as 25% of your net earnings from self-employment (not including contributions for yourself), up to $52,000 in 2014.
- **SIMPLE**: You can put all of your net earnings from self-employment into your SIMPLE IRA, up to $12,000 in 2013 and 2014 (plus an additional $2500 if you're fifty or older) in salary-reduction contributions, along with either a 2% fixed contribution or 3% matching contribution.
- **Keogh**: Offers higher employee contribution limits, but is more difficult to set up and administer.

See IRS Publication 560 for additional information on SEP, SIMPLE, and Keogh (listed under Qualified) Plans at http://www.irs.gov/pub/irs-pdf/p560.pdf.

Personal Time Off (PTO)

Most companies recognize the value of permitting workers to take paid time off to disengage from work and take care of their family and personal matters. As such, companies go to varying degrees in establishing time-off policies and in making it somewhat easy for workers to schedule that time without guilt.

Holidays
For full-time and benefit-eligible employees, companies generally recognize the following national holidays:

- New Year's Day (January)
- Birthday of Martin Luther King Jr. (January)
- Washington's Birthday, also called Presidents' Day (February)
- Memorial Day (May)
- Independence Day (July)
- Labor Day (September)
- Thanksgiving Holiday (November)
- Christmas Holiday (December)

Part-time employees usually are not included in a company's vacation, holiday, or PTO program. Each company establishes how many hours an employee must work to be considered full time (40 hours, 34 hours, etc.) and to participate in PTO programs.

In addition to the formal holidays outlined above, some organizations observe "personal" or "floating" holidays that permit employees to take paid time off for whatever reason they deem appropriate. For example, a company that does not recognize Martin Luther King Jr. Day or Presidents' Day in January or February may allow for three floating holidays so that employees can take off on those days or other holidays not formally recognized by the company (e.g., Good Friday). A word of caution: private-sector companies are not required to observe federal holidays. Don't make the mistake I did and not show up for work on a federal holiday without checking your company's holiday schedule; you will probably get a phone call. Additionally, there is no such thing as training holidays like those many of you have grown accustomed to, on which three-day weekends often turn into four-day weekends.

Vacation

Companies differ in the vacation time they allow for employees. Generally speaking, the longer you are with a company, the more vacation time you will accrue. Most companies allow ten vacation days (two weeks) in the first year, which may be extended to three weeks after five years, for example, or four weeks after ten years of service. Officially recognized holidays of the company are not counted as vacation days, nor are weekend days.

The nonprofit sector is typically much more flexible with its PTO allotments than its for-profit counterparts are. For example, a nonprofit may allow four weeks of vacation after the first year of employment. The logic? Since nonprofits historically have had limited opportunity to award bonuses, granting additional time off makes sense. After all, time is a proxy for money in the workplace, so if you can't award a higher base salary or bonus, the additional PTO could help recruit more qualified candidates and raise the level of employee satisfaction and engagement.

One final note about vacation pay: vacation accruals are treated as a vested benefit in virtually all states. This means that, unlike sick time, vacation pay, once accrued, must be paid out at its cash equivalent if you ever leave the company. Storing vacation can, therefore, be a convenient way to save for a rainy day; just don't get to the point where you are maxed out, because you will stop accruing additional vacation time beyond that point. When you reach your max, be sure to schedule some time off so that the PTO clock can start running again and you can begin to accrue new time off.

Sick Leave

Companies typically offer sick leave benefits that allow employees time off on a planned or unplanned basis to care for their health needs—after all, we all get sick from time to time. While some organizations place no cap on the number of sick days that an employee may take off, most use a cap of ten days per year. Companies don't typically grant the ten-day allotment all at once on January 1 of every year. Instead, an accrual rate of 5.5 hours per pay period, or something similar, may kick in as soon as you begin and continue until you reach a maximum accumulation rate (for example, sixty days in your sick leave bank).

Here are the caveats, though: The accrual of sick leave does not entitle you to be excessively absent, as defined by the company's attendance policy. In addition, paid sick-leave time may not be substituted for vacation days or holidays taken, even though you may fall ill during your vacation. Again, rules differ by company and should be stipulated in the attendance or PTO policy. Also, in contrast to vacation days, sick days are typically not treated as a vested benefit, therefore, they are not paid out at the time of termination.

Disability Insurance

Some companies pay for employees to participate in both short-term disability (STD) and long-term disability (LTD) programs, in case they fall ill for extended periods of time. Alternatively, employers can request that employees pay for these benefits.

Short-Term Disability (STD)

STD plans typically replace a percentage of your base pay if you need an extended period of time off for illness or injury, up to a maximum dollar value. A typical plan, for example, might replace up to 60% or 70% of your base pay or $2,500 per week, whichever is less. If you opt to elect coverage, deductions to pay for it are made from your paycheck on a post-tax basis, meaning that paying for the coverage does not reduce your salary in the eyes of the IRS, as is the case with traditional 401(k) plan contributions, for example. However, it is typically the case that if you pay a premium to elect the coverage, the monetary award you receive from the benefit while you're disabled will be tax-free. Some companies handle STD coverage differently: they pay for you to have the STD coverage, but taxes are withheld from your claim payments.

STD benefits typically kick in after you have been disabled for seven calendar days due to an accident or

> **STD benefits typically kick in after you have been disabled for seven calendar days due to an accident or illness.**

illness. You then begin receiving disability payments weekly, directly from the insurance provider, once the claim has been approved. The cost to purchase this benefit is based on your salary. Benefits continue for twenty-six weeks, after which long-term disability (LTD) insurance kicks in.

Do you need STD? I highly recommend it. The chances of an illness or injury sidelining you for several weeks or months is much higher than your chances of dying, yet many American workers load up on life insurance without giving much thought to temporary pay continuation in case of an accident. STD cost for a fifty-year-old California executive supporting a family of four runs approximately $27 per pay period; multiplied by twenty-six pay periods, that's roughly $700 per year.

Long-Term Disability (LTD)

Long-term disability coverage is typically a company-provided benefit at no cost to the employee, but that depends on the size of the company. Larger companies tend to pay for it, while smaller companies may push the premium costs back to the employee or not offer the benefit at all. LTD typically provides for 60% salary continuation after a six-month elimination period (i.e., the period of short-term disability). LTD usually has a maximum payout value per month, currently around $13,000 in many cases. If you become seriously disabled, LTD payments will go a long way—combined with other disability income benefits such as state disability insurance, social security, and workers' compensation payments—in replacing a portion of your monthly income.

Bear in mind that you can purchase a supplemental disability policy on your own if your company doesn't offer LTD coverage or if you simply want more financial protection. A policy that would bring in an extra $2,000 a month might cost a fifty-year-old professional male about $1,200–$1,500 a year. To find an insurance agent who can track down the best deal for you, contact the National Association of Health Underwriters at www.nahu.org.

Life Insurance

Basic Life Insurance

As a private-sector employee, you will probably receive some level of basic life insurance coverage at a flat amount (e.g., $50,000), or in an amount equal to your salary, at no cost to you. A richer benefit plan might offer basic life insurance coverage of three times your annual earnings, to a maximum benefit of $350,000. Keep in mind that the value of basic life insurance greater than $50,000 is taxable and will be added back, or "imputed," to your income on your paycheck statement.

Supplemental Life and AD&D Insurance

In addition to basic life insurance, you can typically purchase supplemental life insurance along with Accidental Death and Dismemberment (AD&D) coverage for yourself and your family. There is typically a maximum amount of life insurance that you can obtain (e.g., $2,000,000) from both the company-provided basic life insurance and any supplemental life insurance coverage that you elect.

Supplemental life insurance and AD&D coverage typically come wrapped together and can range from one times to eight times your annual base salary. One times your salary is typically guaranteed, while elections greater than three times your base salary or amounts over $500,000 (whichever is less), for example, will require evidence of insurability—typically a blood test and urine specimen, along with a few noninvasive tests such as a pulse or heart rate check.

For spousal or domestic partner coverage, you will likely be able to purchase policies in increments of $10,000 up to a maximum of approximately $250,000. For child coverage (ages 14 days to 26 years), the coverage can be purchased in increments of $5000 up to a maximum of approximately $20,000.

The Value of Fringe Benefits

All this information on benefits may be a bit overwhelming, but remember that the value of your "fringe" (i.e., anything other than cash compensation) benefits can make a tremendous difference in the value of the offer you receive. Working in an organization where base salary is the only cash component is a lot different than for a company that offers significant bonus potential (e.g., 25% and higher of your base salary) in addition to equity offerings (stock options and restricted stock units). And a company that offers a traditional, defined-benefit pension plan is the king of the hill—one of the rare employers that could sustain your retirement years by making monthly annuity payments to you, which it saved for and managed through the years while you were going about life doing your own thing.

Likewise, "Cadillac" healthcare plans can hold tremendous value for you in terms of peace of mind and in case of sudden, life-threatening illness, which can befall any of us at some time. The Affordable Care Act will likely be a critical game changer in the healthcare landscape over the coming decade, as the government strives to insure tens of millions of people who have historically been excluded from the insurance system in the United States and who remain vulnerable to a medical diagnosis that could ruin them financially, as well as place a tremendous financial burden on the rest of us.

With all these moving parts—pressures from government to incentivize new consumer spending habits, push down medical costs, and pass along additional expenses to employers—you can expect a bumpy ride over the next decade. That being said, when you look at the value of these healthcare and retirement programs as a percentage of base-salary costs, it is safe to estimate that fringe benefits add anywhere from 20% to 40% of value to your total compensation package. That means that if you earn a base salary of $100,000 and no bonus, your total compensation package will be worth anywhere from $120,000 to $140,000 if you had to replace the various coverages offered in your benefits package on your own. So, before accepting an offer outright, it is always a good idea, therefore, to ask for a benefits one-sheet that provides an overview of what is offered and in what amounts. Compare that information to the material in this chapter to get a better feel for the true value of your offer.

9. SETTING THE CONDITIONS FOR SUCCESS

Now you are in the door starting your new career, which has been your goal as well as my hope for you in writing this book. Whether your role is one of an individual contributor or of a manager leading and directing others, it is time to begin expanding your new professional network. This network should include fellow employees from all aspects of the business—marketing, finance, sales, operations, supply chain, etc. Your motive is to align yourself with others who can provide important insights about how each department works toward achieving the business goals and vision of the company. Start by finding a mentor, or at least identify someone who has leadership skills and can act as a resource and sounding board. An ideal mentor would be someone within the company who has also served in the military. If there is a Business Resource Group or Infinity Group of Veterans in your new organization, join it and get involved. You may also find a mentor within this group.

Here is how I approached the task of finding a mentor in the private sector: While working in the various positions I've held over the years, I met a number of subject matter experts. As time permitted, I invited them to lunch—everyone has to eat after all—and I was open with them. I told them I was retired military and that I was trying to learn the ropes regarding how things got done around the company as well as more about their particular specialty areas. Trust me, when you ask someone to talk about what he does, to help you understand his world of marketing or finance, he will jump at the opportunity. People love to talk about themselves and what they know, so capitalize on that and learn from them. And make sure you don't just go to one person in each of these specialty areas; meet as many people as you can and get to know them. You never know where your next opportunity will come from; it could come from one of these experts you have met.

When I was a soldier, I knew my primary job cold and was trained to deal with adversity and stress under fire and to just get the job done. I suspect you are the same. Yet, there were many jobs that came my way in the military in which I had to dig deep and figure things out on my own. It is no different in the private sector. Reach out and find a network of professionals who can help steer your new course. This effort takes a lot of time and really never ends. Always keep in the back of your mind when you meet someone new, that person might just be the one who helps you get in the door for an interview. Then once you are in your new job, you will be able to determine whom you need to connect with in order to get your job done. When I started at Coca-Cola, it took me a few months to learn how the process of getting approvals worked. Along the way, I started meeting a number of people from all types of backgrounds with different skill sets, and I started building my Coca-Cola network. This did not happen overnight; it may be a while before people will take their time to get to know you. What helped me was my ability to collaborate with others as well as the ability to interact with all people, from the highest levels of the company to the lowest. Those skills came from my time in uniform. Leverage what you know, and do not sell yourself short—you know more than you think you do.

The things that you have done during your military service, whether it was short or long, are just shy of being a miracle, in my opinion. Networking during your service years was certainly different, but no less important, as many of you met face to face with tribal elders, local government officials, and others to make on-the-spot decisions so that your troops were not killed or injured. These same skills, at a much lesser level, can be transferred over to sales, operations, finance, marketing, and even mergers-and-acquisitions negotiations. There are many CEOs in the private sector who would love to have people in their organizations with these types of skills.

All of that said, your transition, transformation, and integration into civilian life will come with challenges. If you have been downrange, you will have moments of extreme frustration at some of the most mundane things you will come across or events that may happen in the workplace—such as meetings that seem to never end in which nothing is decided upon except a need to meet again, for example. Sometimes you will deal with a manager who requires 100% of the information from you in order to make a decision—and still that decision never comes. The mere idea that a combat unit can effectively operate on 80% (or less) information and execute a battle plan will seem miraculous by comparison.

Indecisiveness in the private sector is very frustrating, but manageable. When situations as these occur, reach out to your mentor or someone you have connected with in the company to talk it through. I suspect that you won't sweat the small stuff because you come from a world where things are a bit rough and a lot more real. You may have come from a forward operating base in God-knows-where Afghanistan, where you lived in a bunker with all the not-so-lovely things that go along with that experience, where just getting a shower without being sniped at was the highlight of your day—hey, I've been there, done that. The good news that you will discover quickly is that life outside the combat zone and inside the day-to-day corporate gig is going to be much easier.

Training

Never underestimate the value of your military training. As you start to move through the transition and transformation phases, you will be pleasantly surprised at what you already know and even more surprised at how much of an investment the military made in your training and development. I am not aware of anyone who is fully employed by a company leaving her day-to-day employment to attend graduate school or any other type of training for an extended period of time while still being paid her salary. Such a case might rarely be reserved for very senior leaders within the organization. The investment made by the military services in training its people is the reason we have the greatest military in the world. Training your people pays at the end of the day.

> If you have been a staff officer or a non-commissioned staff officer, you will come to the table with an abundance of training on your resume that will certainly pay off for you in the private sector.

Here is a little finance tip for you: training and development is considered an expense to a company. In the beginning of my private-sector career, I had difficulty accepting this change. But the reality within a company is, when dollars start getting tight, line items like training and development, travel and entertainment, and group meetings are potential targets for freezes or cuts. The unfortunate side effect of this financial maneuvering is that both the company and its employees will suffer when professional development ends. In the long run, when employees have not received professional training and the future leaders of the company have not been developed, the company will flounder. The training versus expense issue is a vicious circle.

Private-sector companies simply don't look at training and development as an investment in their most valued asset as the military does. The current trend in company training is for employees to take more online classes rather than receiving in-person education. You may get an email with a link to a website on which you will take mandatory training for the company. I have seen this type of training for classes on diversity, the company's Code of Business Conduct, and compliance with company policies. Online courses are generally less time consuming than classroom, facilitator-led courses. However, there are obvious benefits to classroom instruction, including the opportunity for face-to-face time with other classmates. A classroom setting is a perfect arena for networking. Look for in-person training opportunities that can help you in your current and future roles.

If you have been a staff officer or a non-commissioned staff officer, you will come to the table with an abundance of training on your resume that will certainly pay off for you in the private sector. On average, a military person spends about 70–80% of his career in a staff-type position. There is not much difference in the role and responsibilities of a staff officer or a non-commissioned staff officer versus a corporate position requiring the movement of documents through the organization to senior executives for a decision. The same due diligence is required in each position to get the action approved. The knowledge, training, and skills you acquired while in boots will be critical for you in a variety of corporate functions, such as collaborating across multiple teams, communicating effectively, and understanding corporate politics in the workplace. The Pentagon used to have a three-ring binder outlining all the do's and don'ts for being a staff officer or non-commissioned staff officer. It is probably all automated now. While there may not be a binder awaiting you in your private-sector role, there probably will be a resource available to you to outline the do's and don'ts for your new job. However in the private sector, you will quickly learn the phrase "on the job training."

Employee Handbooks, Policy and Procedure Manuals, and Codes of Business Conduct

An employee handbook is an overview of the company's policies, practices, and guidelines. This document is specifically designed for employees because it covers many of the basic areas of the employment relationship—hiring, corrective action and termination, compensation, benefits, training and career progression, and who to call if you are injured on the job and want to file a formal complaint. The handbook doesn't spell out the procedures in too much detail because cases can be very different depending on someone's tenure, the impact of the issue on company operations, and the organization's past practices when dealing with similar situations. Instead, handbooks will point employees in the right direction in order to have their needs and requests evaluated on a case-by-case basis, often by the organization's HR department.

Policy and procedure (P&P) manuals, on the other hand, are typically designed for the management team and are not necessarily shared openly with employees. These manuals walk managers through various processes step by step and include detailed instructions in resolving issues. For example, a P&P on corrective action may outline that a manager is expected to respond to an employee's request to lodge a complaint within twenty-four hours, escalate the matter to senior departmental management or HR within seventy-two hours, etc. The added structure and direction contained in a typical P&P manual guides company leadership through the conflict-resolution process using a step-by-step approach that is fairly simple to follow and very black and white to interpret.

An organization's Code of Business Conduct, sometimes known as a Code of Conduct or Code of Business Ethics, is much different, however. The Sarbanes-Oxley Act of 2002 was passed after the tech stock implosion in the summer of 2000. In light of the corporate manipulation of company annual reports and falsified shareholder letters that emanated from organizations like Enron, WorldCom, and Adelphia leading to the stock market meltdown that year, Congress passed the law, which stated, among other things, that the CEO and CFO of a publicly traded company would face mandatory jail time and stiff personal fines if he knew, or should have known, that the information being circulated about his company's financial performance was falsified.

One of the fallout items of the Sarbanes-Oxley Act, or SOX or SARBOX, as it came to be known, is that all publicly traded companies are required to publish a code of business ethics and also train all employees on its meaning and significance. Publicly traded companies all over America rushed to develop corporate ethics statements and train their management teams on its most significant topics: how to escalate a potential conflict of interest, how to institute financial controls and check-and-balance systems to ensure that any wrongdoings will be identified and exposed early on, and the like. SOX touched the human resources world as well because any corporate ethics statement by definition must address the ethical implications of how a company treats its workers. Don't be surprised if, in your new job, you have to take a Code of Business Conduct course on an annual basis. You may also be asked to complete a disclosure statement that solicits any potential conflicts of interest you may have (e.g., a family member working for the same company).

Companies include specific language in their codes of business conduct that address discrimination, harassment, disclosure of potential conflicts of interest, and such. Moreover, business conduct statements reflect not only the *letter* of the law but the *spirit* of the law as well. That spirit connotation makes a business conduct statement much more far-reaching and broader than a typical employee handbook or policy and procedure manual. Managers can no longer play the monkey with his hands over his eyes, ears, and mouth, claiming not to know of unethical conduct simply because it was not made apparent to them.

Privately held companies often publish similar codes of business conduct because doing so is such a smart idea. While not mandated by the government (as is the case with publicly traded companies), the benefits of having a code of conduct have encouraged many private employers to adopt the practice.

10. LEADING IN LOAFERS

If getting the job is step one and keeping the job is step two, then thriving in the job is step three. Transitioning from a leadership role in the military to a leadership role in corporate America will have its own unique challenges, but there is no reason to learn from mistakes when I can give you your very own crystal ball to help you navigate around the landmines. Let's get started with some good old-fashioned defensive strategies, and then we'll move on to a more offensive approach.

Defensive Strategy: Employment Law Basics in the Private Sector

As you transition into the private sector, you will benefit from having a broad-brush understanding of how our employment system in the US works and what aspects apply directly to you, beginning with a brief history of how things got to this point.

Employment at Will vs. Discharge for Just Cause

When our nation was founded in the 18th century, we drew from English law in terms of setting up our workplace standards and expectations. One of the fundamental rights of citizens was that of working—a job was considered a right, of sorts. In fact, the 14th Amendment to the Constitution included language stating that the right to work was so fundamental, it should not be arbitrarily taken away without workplace due process, meaning that an employee could not be discharged from a company without just cause. This right of workers to their jobs remained the law of the land until the Great Depression of the 1930s, when the discharge-for-just-cause-only standard was turned on its head by a new legal concept that came to be known as "employment at will," whereby workers could be terminated at the whims of their employers. Over time, this employment-at-will philosophy became the law of the land and morphed into an employer's right, leaving American workers at the whim of bosses who were often depicted as tyrants. Not incidentally, the 1950s through the 1970s saw the greatest rise in labor unions in our history, the primary driver being that unions promised their members they would no longer be held to an at-will employment standard. US workers flocked to unions because of the perception of fairness that unions espoused: "Join us and your company can't

. . . or even being held individually liable for engaging in what is known as "managerial bad acts."

just throw you out. They'll have to show they had just cause, so you'll know about the problem in writing before you lose your job!" Flash forward to the early 1980s: A California court ruled that there could be exceptions to the employment-at-will doctrine. If a company appeared to engage in certain types of unlawful behaviors, then that company could not claim a worker was employed at will and had no expectation to continued employment. In short, the right to work had been returned to the US worker, right where it originally began in the 18th century.

That California court ruled that a company cannot terminate a worker if the discharge infringes on a protected right or goes against public policy. Specifically, there are four key exceptions to the employment-at-will doctrine:

- **Employment contracts.** If a contract exists, the company must adhere to its terms and conditions, including notice requirements, lest it breach the contract. Where an employment contract exists for a fixed period of time (for example, three years) and is silent concerning grounds for terminating the contract, courts in many states have held that employers have an implied obligation to discharge only for just cause. Similarly, unionized employees are governed by the terms and conditions of a collective bargaining agreement and are not at will.
- **Implied contract exceptions.** An employer may be bound by promises published in the employee handbook or oral promises made at the hiring interview requiring just cause to terminate. In addition, employers are prohibited from discharging long-term employees just before they are due to receive anticipated financial benefits. This is known as an implied covenant of good faith and fair dealing.

- **Statutory considerations.** Dismissals are illegal when based on age, sex, national origin, religion, union membership, or any other legislation established in Title VII of the 1964 Civil Rights Act, the Age Discrimination in Employment Act, the Americans with Disabilities Act, and state law equivalents. Essentially, this means that potential problems regarding race, age, sex, and physical disability may arise any time someone in a protected class is fired.
- **Public policy exceptions.** A company cannot terminate an employee for filing a workers' compensation claim, whistleblowing, engaging in group activities that protest unsafe work conditions, or refusing to commit an unlawful act on the employer's behalf.

Enlisting the Services and Support of HR

Here is a question to consider: what are you supposed to do as a leader in corporate America (if you attain a leadership position) when faced with these kinds of challenges? The solution is to enlist the support of your company's human resources team any time you suspect that someone may need to be disciplined or ultimately terminated. HR is responsible for conducting investigations into potential wrongdoing and helping you decide what the appropriate company response should be based on both the company's policies and past practices. Utilizing an internal third party like HR is always the best way to go because, whenever you do so, you will be deemed to be acting within the course and scope of your employment.

However, if an individual supervisor takes it upon herself to terminate someone without getting approval from either HR or higher levels of operational management, she may find herself in serious trouble, including being immediately discharged for cause or even being held individually liable for engaging in what is known as "managerial bad acts."

Performance vs. Conduct: A Critical Distinction

It is a far different world outside the gate, where the Uniform Code of Military Justice simply does not apply—take for example an Article 15 for misbehaving or poor performance in the military, a very common violation. In the private sector, organizations typically refer to their standards of performance and conduct as a general catch all for all policies, procedures, and workplace expectations and guidelines. But there is a tremendous difference between a performance infraction and a conduct violation, and it is critical that you understand the ramifications of each.

Performance infractions typically refer to problematic performance in the areas of quality, quantity, speed, customer service, and attendance or tardiness (although many companies split attendance and tardiness out from the broader performance category). When problems occur in these areas, companies are expected to provide workplace due process as out-

Performance infractions typically refer to problematic performance in the areas of quality, quantity, speed, customer service, and attendance or tardiness

lined in their employee handbooks and policy and procedure manuals. Specifically, a step system of increased consequences is implemented, whereby each time an additional infraction occurs, it is documented, with each progressive step containing language to indicate the severity of the situation and the consequence that will apply if the problem is not remedied immediately.

Most companies follow a "three strikes and you're out" progressive discipline process that looks something like this:

Step 1:   *Documented verbal warning*

Step 2:   *Written warning*

Step 3:   *Final written warning*

After that final written warning, another incident will typically justify termination of employment. There can be exceptions, of course. A new hire who is only thirty days into a new position with the company may be terminated without prior written documentation or may receive one documented warning, just to protect the company, before being dismissed. On the other hand, a thirty-year employee may be accorded greater workplace due process because of his years of tenure. As an example, this individual may be put on a Performance Improvement Plan (PIP) or given a letter of clarification, which documents the problems without escalating the formal corrective-action chain that leads to termination. In any case, when it comes to performance and attendance infractions, the expectation is that the company follows its policies and accords workplace due process in the form of stepped up corrective-action notices so

Conduct = Ethics = Integrity

that the worker understands what the problem is, what he needs to do to fix the problem, and what the consequences will be if he fails to demonstrate improvement within a reasonable timeframe.

This is not so with conduct infractions. Conduct infractions may lead to immediate dismissal, even for a first offense for which there is no prior corrective action on record. And even if a company opts not to terminate on a first offense, the organization may go straight to a final written warning, in other words, just shy of termination. For example, if an employee engages in theft, then termination would be the result—even for a first-time offense. In such cases, the issue drives the outcome, meaning that the company does not have the discretion *not* to terminate. After all, if Employee A is not terminated for stealing, how would the company justify terminating Employee B for stealing at some point in the future without looking like a discriminatory employer? Ditto for embezzlement, fraud, egregious cases of sexual harassment, and other conduct infractions.

What about someone who falsifies a timecard by showing she worked overtime when the security camera shows that she left the office at 5 p.m. sharp? Since time worked is a proxy for money, she may be terminated, even on the first offense, for timecard fraud because it is deemed no different than stealing money from the company. Most workers don't realize that timecard fraud is a summary offense—an infraction that leads to immediate dismissal. They mistakenly believe that if they get caught, they will simply receive some form of corrective action or formal reprimand rather than be fired outright. They are shocked when they find out they have not only lost their jobs, but their company references as well. And, it cuts both ways: a supervisor who edits a timecard to remove overtime worked in order to meet budget will likewise expose himself to immediate dismissal—for stealing money from the employee.

Conduct = Ethics = Integrity. Companies have very little discretion to retain a worker—no matter how good or efficient—if that individual commits a conduct infraction. Even if the employee in question has been with the organization for thirty years and won the employee-of-the-year award thirty times in a row, one conduct violation and he is out—plain and simple. There are no justifications or excuses. As a leader, you will want to discuss these conduct issues with your team members and make sure they know never to put themselves in a situation in which the company has no discretion and no option but to terminate them.

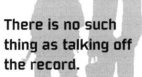

There is no such thing as talking off the record.

Conducting Performance Reviews and Managing Office Politics

People are people, whether you dress them up in military uniforms or don them in blue dress suits and pearls. Therefore, many of the same rules apply to leadership and performance success in the private sector as they do in the military. Following is a short list of considerations that you should be prepared for when transitioning from a leadership role in boots to one in loafers.

There is no such thing as talking off the record. Any time an employee wants to speak with you "off the record" or "in strict confidence," give the following caveat: "I'd be happy to help you, but I can't keep the matter confidential if it has to do with one of three things: (1) discrimination or harassment, (2) potential violence in the workplace, or (3) a potential conflict of interest with the company's operations. In those cases, I'll have an affirmative obligation to disclose what you tell me to other members of management. If it doesn't have to do with one of those three things, though, then I'd be happy to speak with you in confidence"

Why the caveat? Because once any employee puts you on notice as a supervisor regarding a potential problem regarding harassment, discrimination, bullying, or the like, it is the same in the eyes of the law as if they put the CEO of your company on notice. Being a nice guy and protecting someone's confidence about being harassed or discriminated against will come back to bite you big time should a lawsuit ensue. The plaintiff attorney will argue that *the company* was placed on notice and failed to act, meaning that the supervisor not only speaks *for* the company but *is* the company in matters like these.

Don't fall prey to grade inflation when issuing annual performance review scores. In years past, the military has suffered from this same issue when it comes to both officer and non-commissioned officer efficiency reports. If a solider was not rated very high, or maxed out, he would probably not get promoted. In the private sector, a manager often feels guilty for awarding a substandard, overall performance review score at performance appraisal time because she knows (1) it could lead to further disciplinary action, (2) the employee won't be given a merit increase, and (3) that individual could lose out on his bonus.

While it may sound harsh to dole out substandard overall scores on the annual review, you must be honest in assessing an individual's performance and conduct or else it can come back to bite you in a number of ways. This is what a typical overall-grade scoring section looks like in most companies' performance review systems:

5 *Outstanding / Exceptional Performance*

4 *Exceeds Expectations*

3 *Meets Expectations*

2 *Partially Meets Expectations*

1 *Does Not Meet Expectations*

The dividing line is between scores 3 and 2. Award a score of 3 or higher, and you will have validated an entire year's performance—even if that individual is currently on an active final written warning. By contrast, a score of 2 or 1 invalidates the entire year's performance, which is important if you believe that this individual is not a good fit or should otherwise be terminated in the near term.

Let's look at those scores a bit more in detail. A "3–Meets Expectations" score says that the individual is performing at par. If a typical performance review has a dozen individual categories preceding the "overall score" at the very end of the document, then one or two of the individual categories may fall below expectations even though you believe that the individual met overall expectations for the entire review year.

The 2 and 1 scores are a bit more challenging, however. A score of "2–Partially Meets Expectations" shows that, while the individual is meeting expectations in a number of areas, his overall performance failed to meet company expectations. Companies often allow a modest increase (e.g., a 1% merit increase out of a possible 3%) and/or partial bonus for a 2 score. A score of "1–Does Not Meet Expectations" demonstrates that the individual is failing in multiple areas. Companies typically won't allow for a prorated merit increase or bonus in the case of a failed score like that.

Sameness and consistency are *not* the same thing! As a frontline leader in your organization, you should always strive for consistency, but that does not mean you will treat everyone and everything the exact same way.

You don't have to put up with bad attitudes. Attitude is everything! It makes a very big difference in just about every situation. As you move into a leadership role in the private sector, you may be surprised to see the extent to which certain employees suffer from an entitlement mentality, victim syndrome, or other forms of apathy, outright anger, or poor attitude. Are you required to put up with that? Of course

You don't have to put up with bad attitudes. Attitude is everything! It makes a very big difference in just about every situation.

not—but you have to know how to address it appropriately in the workplace. This is a very important part of your personal transformation. It is something you will more than likely have to constantly remind yourself about—namely, that you are no longer in the military, and there is no longer such a thing as calling people on the carpet or chewing someone's behind. You get the picture.

Understand that just because someone is a top performer doesn't mean they won't exhibit conduct that is unbecoming of a model employee. Then again, workers sometimes erroneously believe that if they are solid performers, they are untouchable and can behave any way they want. When facing someone who appears to exhibit a bad attitude, take this three-step approach to fixing the problem from your first sit-down meeting:

- First, don't use the term "attitude." Them's fightin' words. Most courts will argue that differences in attitude are simply the result of differences in opinion or personal style, so rather than angering your workers or risking alienating a judge in a courtroom, simply replace the word "attitude" with "conduct" or "behavior." Whether you are discussing this issue verbally or writing it down in some form of corrective action, making that simple replacement will add automatic credibility to your message.

- Second, use the word "perception" to address the individual's problematic conduct and hold him responsible for his own perception management. Here is an example:

  "William, I wanted to meet with you quietly and in private to share some concerns that I have regarding your conduct—at least in terms of how it appears from my vantage point. I've always believed that perception is reality until proven otherwise and that people are responsible for their own perception management. In other words, regardless of your intentions or how you believe

you're coming across, your behavior may make others uncomfortable or leave them feeling as if they have to walk on eggshells around you.

"From what I can see, I believe you may have a perception problem on your hands. When I first began here, I heard whispers that you could be challenging to deal with, that you might have a chip on your shoulder, and that you tend to push others away. I don't listen to that type of banter, and I'm not judging you in any way, but I do have a right to share my observations as your supervisor.

"I don't mean to hurt your feelings or embarrass you in any way, and I'd ask you to listen to this as openly as possible and not feel defensive, but I'm having a hard time getting along with you. I find that you come across as moody and that you can appear to sulk, and it's difficult to tell how you're feeling from one point in time to another, which makes me feel like I have to be on guard and overly cautious not to upset you.

"That's not really fair to me or to other members of the team. You are an excellent performer and this has nothing to do with the quality or volume of your work. But you are responsible for creating a friendly and inclusive work environment just like the rest of us are, and I can't justify making an exception to our overall sense of teamwork or camaraderie because you appear to become overly defensive all of a sudden. With all due respect, you can come across as a schoolyard bully pushing the other kids up against the fence and daring them to challenge you, and it's really hurting group morale. Can you see why I might feel that way or have that perception?"

- Third, employ the half-circle icon in figure 29 at this point in the conversation to ensure that the employee fully understands that he is responsible for both his performance and his conduct. Draw a circle on a piece of paper, and split the circle in half. Write the word "Performance" in the top half of the circle and "Conduct" in the bottom half so that it looks like this:

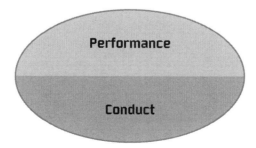

Fig. 29 Performance/Conflict Icon

The conversation might then progress as follows:

"William, I know you're performing well in terms of the quality and volume of your work product, but that only fits into half the circle. The conduct portion is equally, if not more, important. It's the lower half of the circle that speaks to your communication style and willingness to act as a team player and supportive influence, and simply falling back on your performance doesn't justify your behavior. Truth be told, with a record like this, you'd fail your annual performance review because you'd only be delivering at 50%.

"I'm here to help and extend an olive branch, but it's up to you to accept my offer. But we can't have these types of conversations any more, and I really need you to think about whether this job or company is a good fit for you at this point in your career. If it is, then that's great news—I'm happy to re-welcome you to the company and put this all behind us. But if it isn't, then I'd ask you to be fair to yourself and to the rest of us on the team and consider your options for finding other opportunities that will make you happier elsewhere. If you decide to remain in your role with us—and I hope you do—you'll have to commit to me that we won't need to have a conversation like this again. Addressing this once should be enough, and I'd prefer to avoid going down the path of corrective action and ultimately termination for cause, because it's so painful and dramatic. Can you make that commitment to me now, or is it something you'd prefer to think about or sleep on?"

Conversations like these are certainly challenging, but said with the other person's best interests in mind, and in a spirit of goodwill and support, they will accomplish what you are setting out to do—raising the individual's awareness of how he comes across and how he suffers from a perception management problem. These types of conversations should come rather easily to you since they are so direct and to the point. Stay professional, fact based, and tone neutral.

One caveat about a conversation like this, however: Whenever you plan to have a tough conversation with a member of your team that includes options like resigning, it is best to partner with another member of management or your human resources representative. Please make sure you consult with them before you proceed with a conversation like this.

Learn to appropriately address rumor mongers, gossips, and office snitches. When it comes to office politics, the most challenging worm in

> **The path of least resistance is avoidance, but addressing your concerns openly, fairly, and directly will give you an advantage throughout your career.**

the apple will typically be the gossip who fans the flames from the sidelines without getting involved himself. This is the individual who is smart enough to stay under the radar screen but who whispers ideas into the ears of others, assuming ill intentions or pointing out unfairness or inequities that may be more opinion than fact. How you address these office snitches who are wily enough to deny culpability may set you apart from other leaders, who often refuse to engage in these necessary confrontations and allow ill will to fester in the department.

The path of least resistance is avoidance, but addressing your concerns openly, fairly, and directly will give you an advantage throughout your career. When cloak-and-dagger drama seems to plague your team, your best course of action will be to address the matter openly in front of the whole group. Attacking someone's personality, eccentricities, private life, or any other areas of vulnerability is not okay, and it is up to you as a leader to stop that type of behavior dead in its tracks.

Remember, most people in the private sector are not trained heavily in leadership and positive confrontation as you have been via your military training. But survey after survey shows that what CEOs want and need most in their key executives focuses around leadership, effective communication, and teamwork. The types of challenges covered in this section may be frustrating when they occur, but they provide you with a unique opportunity to show who you are and how these matters should be dealt with respectfully, firmly, and in a timely fashion. In short, take advantage of opportunities like these to demonstrate your beliefs and values by modeling behaviors that will help others grow and develop in their careers

Effective Leadership: Your Best Offense

You may fool all the people some of the time; you can even fool some of the people all of the time; but you can't fool all of the people all of the time.

—Abraham Lincoln

People—the Greatest Asset

Taking care of your people does not end when you move into the private sector. Commanding or leading troops is one of the highest honors one can have in the military. It goes without saying, but I'll say it any-way—there are no commanders in the private sector. People do not necessarily jump when you tell them to jump. And by the way, you don't tell coworkers to do anything; you have conversations, set expectations, make sure they understand, set deadlines, and prepare

yourself to be as flexible as a rubber band. Integrating all of your skills from the military along with everything you have learned in this book thus far will give you an advantage when dealing with the many faces of adversity that will surely come your way in the private sector.

As you read in the Transformation section, developing relationships and fine-tuning your communication skills are important components to your success on the job, in your community, and throughout your journey outside the gate. Learning how others will communicate is equally important, as many will have their own unique styles. Don't be surprised if a manager asks you to do something and then follows the request with, "How do you feel about it?" The first time I was asked how I felt about something or if I was comfortable about something, I almost fell out of my chair in disbelief. I honestly didn't think I had heard the person correctly. In the military, I was never asked how I felt or if I was comfortable about a job I was being asked to perform. You will need to fine-tune your people skills early on and to always be willing to learn and grow as you develop new relationships. The good news is, you are trainable and it can be done!

The greatest asset you will encounter, whether you are in boots or loafers, is people. Moving from the military to the private sector will require that you treat people just a bit differently. Your challenge will be to soften your tone, not be as direct in your delivery, and remember that you are not commanding anyone. You may also encounter a completely different set of protocols when approaching people up and down the leadership chain of command in the private sector. Learn what that protocol is through your manager or superior early on. This is all a part of learning to communicate.

Some companies may have a relaxed policy allowing all employees, both managers and non-managers, to make contact with senior-level associates without a strict chain of command. Generally, you will see this in very small companies. Other companies may be more formal and follow a chain-of-command business etiquette, in which communications reach senior leaders through an established level of authority. This is a case-by-case situation that is dependent on the type of industry and/or employer you actually sign on with.

If your role in the private sector is to lead or direct others, do yourself a big favor and make sure your employees maintain a balance in their lives. You should take this on as a personal objective with your team. When you are in charge, you will set the pace. This can be a balancing act for many leaders. Some leaders will have little interest in having a conversation about anything other than work. Personally, I like to work with people who have personal and social lives outside of work, who like to laugh (even at themselves), and who have some non-job-related priorities that they approach with the same passion they apply to their work. The worst-case scenario is working with a person who is the consummate, grim workaholic or the pompous, pretentious professional. I called them "careerist" in the military. They will do anything, including railroad you and walk all over you, to get the next promotion or job opening. Steer clear of these people! As I said before, seek out a coach, teacher, or mentor with whom to share your thoughts and frustrations and to seek guidance. Some of my strongest professional and personal relationships have been formed with those individuals from whom I sought council while at work. I also take time each day to pray for wisdom in everything I do. My philosophy of leadership is similar to that of General Colin Powell, who has said: "Perpetual optimism is a force multiplier . . . Spare me the grim litany of the 'realist,' give me the unrealistic aspirations of the optimist any day."[7] Take the harder right when it comes to caring for yourself and your team, and be the optimist with the unrealistic aspirations!

Redefining Leadership

Leadership training was a constant while you were in uniform. Outside the gate however, you may not experience the same level of commitment to leadership training and focus from your employer. If you have landed a leadership position, congratulations! More than likely you will be eager to learn and grow in this role and perhaps seek additional opportunities to climb the leadership ladder. Be aware, however, that often people are promoted in the private sector for being more technically competent and attaining results (which stems from effective leadership). Utilize what you know and were trained to do; the rest will play out over time. Enroll in any leadership training opportunities that are available to you, but remember that you come to the table with some leadership skills already. If the company that employs you does not offer advanced leadership training, seek it on your own through external sources. Effectively apply the leadership skills you learned in uniform and you will be rewarded by the results of your efforts.

Do not fall captive to e-mail on your Smartphone, or computer; it is not the be-all and end-all of leadership and communication.

Be seen. Be heard. Be felt! Do not be a prisoner to your office. As a leader, your team will appreciate seeing you and hearing from you. A quick walk through the office saying, "Good morning," is a great start. As a young commander, I was always out and about—motor pool; downrange with the troops; on the gun line, talking to my soldiers at all times of the day and night. I was always visible. Leaders who are engaged and interested in their people realize more positive results, both in good times and when the going gets tough. Do not fall captive to e-mail on your Smartphone, or computer; it is not the be-all and end-all of leadership and communication. Go where you can assess the risks and make adjustments by seeing, hearing, and understanding what is occurring in your organization. The German word "fingerspitzengefuellen" means feel of the battlefield, a sense that permits commanders to understand the needs of their troops and to make necessary adjustments. Apply the same principals in the private sector. If you do this, you will be in the minority in whatever company you work for, but your team will yield positive results because they know you care.

So, can leadership be taught? Are true leaders simply born that way, or can you learn how to become an effective leader and get better at it over time? The answer, of course, is there is truth to both statements. Some people are just born to lead, while others admit they are surprised to see how much they have accomplished in their lives and humbly chalk up their successes to hard work, dedication, and good old-fashioned sweat.

Let's discuss three leadership axioms and how you could apply each to your career as a leader in an American industry.

What you want for yourself, *give* to another. For my fellow Christians, this is the injunction from Jesus to "Do unto others, as you would have them do unto you." Think about the simplicity of this idea and its profound con-

For my fellow Christians, this is the injunction from Jesus to "Do unto others, as you would have them do unto you."

sequences. Assume that you are one of the people on your team and ask how you would feel if you were treated a particular way. Remember, you are the first domino—you create your experiences and teach others to create theirs.

You create the culture within your team. If your goals are to have fun, make work enjoyable, give people room to grow and experiment, and appreciate and be thankful for all the blessings in your life, then your people will naturally model that type of behavior over time. Similarly, if you are not trusting, if you inspect more than you expect, if you micromanage and attempt to control everything in your group, then you will create a culture of compliance rather than a culture of creativity and innovation. Keep in mind that creativity and innovation are the golden rings in today's workplace. Pierce your employees' hearts, and you will get 110% out of them because they will want to work harder for you. Create a culture of compliance and strict rule adherence, on the other hand, and you will get no more than 100% out of them because they will do just enough to meet expectations but won't necessarily perform with distinction—there will be no need to since they won't feel that added connection that comes from a supporting, caring, and yes, loving supervisor.

It is said that people join companies and leave supervisors. How many times have you heard someone say, "Wow, I got a new job at XYZ Company and I'm so excited! I always wanted to work there!" only to be followed two years later by, "I can't wait to get out of this crazy company. My boss is a lunatic"? Unfortunately, that occurs all too often in corporate America. Your wisdom and selfless guidance of your team can lead to group stability, engagement, and peace of mind for all those who are lucky enough to serve under you.

Remember that you don't have to be a master to teach mastery. Simply model the behaviors that you believe are important and see yourself as a teacher.

Teach what you choose to learn. Remember that you don't have to be a master to teach mastery. Simply model the behaviors that you believe are important and see yourself as a teacher. You could be a teacher of specific skills, knowledge, and abilities to help someone excel in his career. You could be a teacher of wisdom, showing others how to pick

179

their battles appropriately, address problem issues constructively, and find ways motivate themselves. Or you could be a teacher whose focus lies in both helping the company to succeed, as well as helping your team members grow and progress in their careers. One way to do so might be to rotate your more junior staffers into and out of leadership roles and projects, especially when leading staff meetings. Ideally, your leadership style captures all of these things to varying degrees.

Think back to when you were in boots and how you coached, taught, and mentored those who were under you. How did you give them more responsibility? How did you offer them exposure to senior leaders? These same techniques can be deployed in the private sector. Consider allowing members of your team to lead your weekly or biweekly group meetings—under your guidance, of course. The goal is not to just throw them out there and let them figure it out. Instead, it is to prepare them to be successful in this rotational role so that they get the chance to lead the team and assume responsibility for certain opportunities and challenges that may be plaguing your department or company.

There are three basic steps to a successful staff meeting. First, begin the meeting with a round robin, in which each team member gets to discuss what is going on in her world. It is not only important for individuals to talk about themselves; it is also critical that all members of the staff hear what their peers are doing. Too many times, employees dig holes for themselves and develop an entitlement mentality in which they believe they are doing all the work. Once they hear what everyone else is working on, however, they tend to develop a greater appreciation for their peers' contributions. Their sense of entitlement will typically diminish as a result.

This, by the way, also keeps you in the loop and diminishes that feeling of flying blind. After all, it is one thing to have a problem on your hands; it is another to learn about that problem from your boss rather than from your staff. Regular meetings give everyone the most up-to-date information possible, but the key is to allow your associates to share their information first. Such meetings are not top-down messages from you to them, but rather bottom-up approaches to gathering data and demonstrating respect for people's contributions in the workplace by allowing them the opportunity to talk and share their ideas.

The second part of the staff meeting introduces constructive criticism into the decision-making process. Specifically ask, "What do we need to be doing differently to reinvent the workflow in our area?" The best ideas will always come from the people in the trenches. This is not news to you. You know

> **. . . many employees
> share with Human
> Resources during exit
> interview meetings is
> that they didn't feel
> their ideas mattered.**

from your military experience that if you want to gauge the true health of an organization, you must go to the troops and ask them. They will tell you what is really happening. The frustration that many employees share with Human Resources during exit interview meetings is that they didn't feel their ideas mattered. They went through the motions day-in and day-out but had no real impact or influence over their working environments. This simple invitation satisfies the basic need to be heard and to make a positive difference.

Your goal is to help them focus on what can be done with existing resources. As such, you should give ownership of a suggestion to the individual who raised it. Really encourage your people to look at your current way of doing business and to redefine the critical points where inefficiencies, delays, or outright breakdowns occur. Define a bite-sized plan of action that can be easily implemented and measured, and ask for a volunteer to spearhead the new activity. That is empowerment—the freedom to suggest a better way of doing things and the authority to put your personal imprint on the revisions.

The third element of the staff meeting focuses on what you, as a group, could have done differently in the past week to make the company a better place. This is basically a mini After Action Report (AAR) or, in other words, capturing lessons learned. We are all hired to increase revenues, decrease expenses, or save time. Any lost opportunities to impact the company's bottom line in one of those three ways should be discussed, studied, and revisited in the future. "What could we have done differently?" is a natural counterpoint to your opening question, because it mirrors what is going on in your group at any given time.

Over time, these meetings will hopefully expand from the micro view of work assignments and project updates to the more macro level of organizational impact. For example, your staff meetings may eventually morph into a rhythm that feels like this:

1. What have we done over the past week/month/quarter/year to increase revenues, decrease costs, or save time?
2. What can I, as your supervisor, do to provide you with more support, structure, and direction and to help you achieve your career goals?
3. What are our short- and longer-term goals, and what will be the measur-

able outcomes so that we'll know that you've reached those goals?

In short, you may just find that teaching leadership is as easy as allowing others to lead and then watching their results. Teaching what you choose to learn is often as simple as setting up your employees for success, guiding them until they get traction, and then stepping out of the way.

> ... you may just find that teaching leadership is as easy as allowing others to lead and then watching their results.

Each to his own without judgment. Selfless leadership, or "servant" leadership, as it has also been called, tends to fair much better in today's environment than it did in the past. We all know the tales of Generals Patton and MacArthur from the World War II days, when great leaders led millions of men into battle. But that top-down, almost monarchical approach is not typically well suited for today's private-sector workplace. We are more educated, more informed, and more in tune with ourselves nowadays and expect leaders to lead from the heart rather than with a heavy hand or command[8].

Even business schools advertise their emphasis on teaching students how to challenge their hearts, their values, and their leadership points of view—the most important factors impacting people and profits. The buzzwords in today's business world are human capital assets, talent development, performance management, and employee engagement. In short, we now realize that in our knowledge-based economy, our most critical assets leave the office and go home every night. Our job is to make sure they return to work the next morning, fit and motivated, since human-capital talent remains the key differentiator in successful versus mediocre organizations.

A key to leadership wisdom lies in avoiding judgment. The old "I told you so" mentality does little more than cause frustration and resentment. Workers want to be treated like adults, not children. They want respect, they want to be trusted, they want autonomy, and they want to be appreciated for the contribution they make. In other words, withhold judgment and focus instead on observation.

> Observation, in essence, is simply about the "what's so," while judgment tends to be more about the "so what."

You have every right to observe what you are seeing as a leader in corporate America. Observation, in essence, is simply about the "what's so," while judgment tends to be more about the "so what." Do you see the difference? The "so what" isn't really all that critical; it implies that someone's decisions were wrong, bad, inappropriate, thoughtless, or selfish. By contrast, the "what's so" observation simply points out that a decision made or action taken didn't serve a person as intended. There is no judgment associated with it whatsoever. And that is the kind of mature business leadership that keeps executives objective and aligned with their team members' success.

When in doubt, err on the side of compassion. Assume good intentions until proven otherwise.

When in doubt, err on the side of compassion. Assume good intentions until proven otherwise. And remember the axiom taught by Neale Donald Walsch: "Life begins at the end of your comfort zone."[9] Even if people leadership doesn't come all that naturally to you, and even if the rules and norms in the private sector strike you as odd and illogical at first, just keep in mind that this transition into corporate America offers you all sorts of opportunities to redefine and reinvent yourself in light of a new set of challenges.

You have so much to offer, and there are many organizations out there that will benefit greatly from your knowledge and expertise. Careers are meant to be explored, practiced, and reinvented over time. That's how we grow and evolve. So play with this! Explore your natural leadership style, focus on how it applies to the world of corporate business, give yourself some breathing room, and don't put too much pressure on yourself. Now let's talk about your role in motivating others and increasing their sense of engagement and job satisfaction.

JP's Rules of Engagement

When you and Adam talk, I hear you say "Why?" Always "Why?" You see things; and you say "Why?" But I dream things that never were; and I say "Why not?"

—*The Serpent in* Back to Methuselah,
a play by George Bernard Shaw

Whenever a military unit deploys to a training exercise or downrange for the real thing, soldiers live and breathe by the approved rules of engagement.

These dictate what can and cannot be done on the battlefield. Transferring the same concept into whatever role you land outside the gate will help you and your team operate more efficiently. My personal rules of engagement are handed out to every employee who reports to me so that we start off on the right foot from the beginning. No one ever likes learning what pisses off the boss by actually pissing off the boss—that's not healthy or smart. Setting and leveling expectations across the organizations I have led has paid big dividends for me. Your new "troops" will better understand who you are and where you are coming from if you take some time to develop your own personal rules of engagement. These will help you focus on what you are about to embark on—your next great deployment in finding your new true north!

To help in the development of your own rules of engagement, let me share my personal list with you.

JP's Rules of Engagement

1. **There are a specific set of values that I deem critical to the success of a team.** These values stem from my faith, my parents, and from serving this great nation in uniform. Understanding no one is perfect, I try to follow them to the best of my ability and will share them, as they are a proven guide to success:

    a. **Integrity.** The ultimate core value! Being honest is the best policy, whether you are at work, school, home, or any place throughout your life. Do not make the mistake of compromising your integrity; you will never recover from the loss of it. I always take the high moral ground...the harder right. I honor my commitments. With my words and actions, I build and enhance your trust in me.

    b. **Trust.** You must trust each other to do the right thing. Without trust, you will spend more time looking over your shoulder than getting the job done. In the military, trusting the person on your right and left is paramount to your survival. If you cannot be trusted, don't be on my team.

    c. **Keeping Me Informed.** I am not a micro-manager; however, I need to know when there is a problem that I need to be aware of or that I could get a call on. I need to know the good, the bad and the ugly—in reverse order. Let me help you succeed.

d. **People.** I have a fundamental belief in people and their innate goodness. I desire to improve myself and to help others do likewise. The Golden Rule is in effect at all times in my world. When you succeed, I automatically succeed.

e. **Accountability.** I place a premium on acting in an accountable fashion in all facets of my life and I expect you to do the same: strive to overcome obstacles, ensure high standards are met, produce first-class quality, listen and respond to needs. Step up when you have made a mistake and have a solution ready to fix it. Learn from it and move on.

f. **Teamwork.** I role-model teamwork in every interaction. I support people for the larger win and believe we will not win if our clients are not successful. It is true that there is no "I" in team.

g. **Excellence.** I pursue excellence in all my endeavors. I exceed my client's expectations in every aspect of my work and I expect nothing less from you.

h. **Be Proactive.** To be successful in providing first-class quality service to your clients, you must be proactive. You must strive to anticipate and truly understand the needs of your clients. With time and with my help, this trait in you will improve. (Note that being proactive does not translate to creating unnecessary work. I do not believe, nor do I advocate, "busy work." We all have enough on our collective plates; we will not practice being busy.)

2. My door is open to you all the time. There is no need to set up an appointment or to knock—come on in. If I'm cranking on something, you'll hear the music and my door will be almost closed.

3. I like to interact with people and find out what is going on. Please do not think I'm checking up on you. I'm interested and want to understand what everyone is doing! Remember, I'm always learning! My intent is not to disrupt you. I don't want to conduct business via e-mail and voice mail all the time—I prefer personal interaction. Unfortunately, due to time constraints and our busy schedules, e-mails and voice mails are common practice.

4. Do not ignore my e-mails or invites for meetings. I use the 24-8-and-Up rule: If I don't hear back from you in 24 hours, I will circle back to you

again. I will wait 8 more hours and then, if I do not hear back from you, I will elevate the issue or task to your direct manager/supervisor.

5. When you come to me with a problem, please have a recommendation for a solution regarding how to fix the problem. If you can't come up with a solution, tell me and we'll figure it out together. This is a part of professional development; we will all learn and grow.

6. I do not like being blindsided by my supervisor or senior management. Afford me the common courtesy of dealing with an issue or problem before it escalates—the old good news, bad news in reverse order. Good news always stays good news; bad news needs to be dealt with and resolved.

7. Stand-up meetings, or team meetings, are conducted monthly. Each of you should be prepared to give me a very quick update on what you're doing. Specifically, address any areas that may be problems or hot issues. I'll send invites.

8. I would like a copy of your resume for my files. I will also be setting up one-on-one conversations with each of you in the next couple of weeks. Please be prepared to discuss what you have done at the company, where you see yourself in three to five years, and how you expect to get there.

Bottom-line: I want *you* to get credit for your hard work. If you succeed, we all succeed. As your leader, I want to be a buffer between you and the bureaucrats.

Enablers: Detail time-action planning; being thorough with references; following rules and procedures; working step by step; being concise (getting to the point); getting it in writing in advance; contingency planning; no digressing; freedom to explore; using metaphors and visuals; seeing the big picture; coming up with something new or fun; using imagination; being innovative or conceptual; taking the initiative and driving results; being a long-term planner and strategic thinker.

Derailers: Being volatile; not heading off surprises; being disloyal; holding a grudge; wasting time; being disrespectful; procrastinating; having an agenda (leads to trust issues later on).

Motivation and Employee Engagement

Many of you have been leading and motivating your men and women under very adverse conditions while deployed. A lot of what you are reading here is almost second nature to you, I'm sure. That said, motivating men and women outside the gate is a bit different than you are accustomed to doing. You are moving into an environment where people's feelings actually matter, and when someone gets upset at something you say or do, it can land you in significant trouble. So, read ahead, keep an open mind, and learn. Better that you learn from me than violate a company rule and get yourself in trouble.

So far, we have discussed many of the defensive measures you can take in the workplace—from dealing with difficult conversations to steering clear of some of the legal snares that await unsuspecting leaders in corporate America. However, focusing solely on defensive measures tells only half the story. The fun, the sense of satisfaction, the challenge, the healthy competition, and the psychic income that comes from work often stems from offensive strategies that benefit both the company and the employee.

The key to developing people in light of corporate America's changing needs lies in making them feel that they are making a positive contribution at work (company benefit) while they develop their own skills and build their resumes (individual benefit). Both elements must be present to have a truly balanced and healthy workplace.

Beingness Trumps Doing-ness. Now think of the best boss you have ever had. This individual probably did most of the following:

- Listened to you and really cared about what you had to say.
- Helped you find your own solutions to questions that challenged you at the time.
- Cared about you personally and helped you plot your course for career growth and development.
- Made you feel welcome and created an inclusive work experience.
- Held you to very high standards, but was fair and consistent in the application of company rules.
- At times, expected more of you than you expected of yourself or believed you were capable of.

If nothing else, it is probably safe to say that this individual knew you and took a personal interest in you. Congratulations—you have just learned what motivation is all about by being on the receiving end of its benefits.

The most effective leaders know their people personally; they practice "Management by Walking Around." They spend more time outside their offices than in them—being present, offering advice and counsel, helping, demonstrating, and modeling behaviors that make others want to go out of their way to please them. A common expression that great leaders tend to adhere to is, "Put others' needs ahead of your own, and expect them to respond in kind." Leadership and motivating is about giving, not about getting, and when you, as an employee, see this type of leadership demonstrated, it is nearly impossible for you not to respond in kind.

Think about General Waverly in the movie *White Christmas* with Bing Crosby and Danny Kaye. When the army retired him in 1944 and he opened a bed and breakfast in Vermont, Bing and Bob arranged for all members of their regiment who lived in the New England area after the war to attend a stage show to help the general make money in his retirement and still feel connected to his troops. A key leadership lesson that General Waverly taught us all was simply this: beingness trumps doing-ness. In other words, what attracted people to the general, what made them want to go out of their way to help him, especially now that he appeared vulnerable in retirement, was a function of who he *was*, rather than what he *did*.

It sounds like a fine distinction, but it's actually an important one. Look again at the list above of qualities respected leaders share. All of those descriptions stem more from the kind of person that boss was—not necessarily what she did. If you are a leader who takes time to get to know your team, if you put others' needs ahead of your own, and if you practice selfless leadership, you will be demonstrating your beingness and will usually find that a happy, healthy, and motivated workforce will result.

When it comes to motivating people, you are not really responsible for *doing* anything—you are simply responsible for *being* a certain way, and from that state of beingness, you will naturally *do* things that follow suit. Looking at this another way, you don't have to worry about bringing cheerleader pompoms into the office. No one is going to refer to you as the best boss he has ever had in his career because you brought in donuts every morning or created a tip jar every time someone paid a member of your team a compliment.

We seem to be so preoccupied with doing things in our society that we often forget a much simpler solution exists. *What are you doing to motivate your*

Motivation, dedication, initiative, esprit de corps, and cohesion are all outcomes of this kind of climate.

employees? How engaged do they feel? Quick, let's issue a climate survey to find out how they're really feeling. Oh, and someone better go out and buy one of those books on a-million-and-one ways to motivate your workers. I want a copy for every member of the management team! This type of thinking is an overreaction that many companies cling to whenever an unforeseen challenge comes their way (for example, when their key players are recruited to competitors or when rumors surface that the employees may be considering unionizing).

Life is actually a lot simpler than that. People respect character. Employees want to work for leaders who lead from their hearts as well as their minds. They want to know they are making a positive difference at work, and learning and acquiring new skills and areas of expertise. Allow your team to have the appropriate freedom of action to permit innovative thought and creativity. As you did while you were in uniform, you will need to set the pace with your team and prioritize work, as well as set degrees of acceptable risk and establish control measures that permit an appropriate level of latitude to your team. You will still spend time developing your team and focusing on the human dimension that builds trust and confidence, and that motivates the organization to accomplish their tasks. This requires a climate conducive to teaching, educated risk-taking, integrity, and discipline. Motivation, dedication, initiative, esprit de corps, and cohesion are all outcomes of this kind of climate. None of this is new to you, however, it needs to be reinforced, as it applies outside the gate as well.

Motivation Is Internal. This leads us to the second rule of employee motivation: motivation is internal. Said another way, I can't motivate you, and you can't motivate me. However, even though you cannot motivate others directly, you are indeed responsible for creating an environment in which people can motivate themselves. The question is, how do you do that? How do you create a work environment where team members can find opportunities to motivate themselves? This question is answerable with a few additional guidelines.

- **First**, the key to enlightened leadership lies in setting up people for success and then getting out of the way, allowing them the freedom to gain traction and excel in their own personal way and individualized style.

- **Second**, follow a less-is-more approach to leadership, understand the value of creating a culture where workers can do their very best work every day, and become a best-in-class organization that invites your people to fall in love with your company.

- **Third**, remember that in exit poll after exit poll, the number one reason why workers leave companies in corporate America is lack of praise, recognition, and appreciation. There are additional key reasons as well: little opportunity for career growth or development, lack of communication, and a desire for more money. But money typically ranks third or fourth on most exiting employees' priority lists, so don't give yourself an easy out and simply attribute turnover to lack of competitive pay.

> The ideas that beingness trumps doing-ness and that you are not responsible for motivating others since motivation is internal still hold true.

"But isn't there anything I can do to motivate my team and help them feel more engaged?" you may ask. Okay, I know you're itching for ideas on how to increase employee morale and engagement. The ideas that beingness trumps doing-ness and that you are not responsible for motivating others since motivation is internal still hold true. That being said, there are certain focus areas that could help you in achieving your goal of getting your team feeling more motivated and engaged by their work.

- **Getting to know your team members personally** is the first step in opening the lines of communication with your staff while increasing the feeling of recognition for a job well done. Nothing is more important than this in the motivation game. "Management by Walking Around" and getting to know your people personally does not mean blurring the lines between business and personal matters. It is simply a matter of getting around, smiling, asking people how they are and how their families are doing, and making them feel like they are special because you care. Knowing people's first names goes a long way in making people feel welcome and creating an inclusive work environment.

- **Engage in what are known as "stay interviews"** to gauge your team's level of interest and engagement *before* they leave or start looking for a new job. You don't have to wait until people leave the organization to generate an exit interview survey to find out how they are feeling and why they are thinking of leaving. Consider this as an approach:

Meet with each of your direct reports individually, and ask which of the following six categories holds the most significance for each one career-wise:

1. Career progression through the ranks and opportunities for promotion and advancement.
2. Lateral assumption of increased responsibilities and skill building (via cross training, for example).
3. Acquisition of new technical skills (for example, via external training and certification).
4. Development of stronger leadership, management, or administrative skills.
5. Work/life balance (i.e., "living to work" versus "working to live").
6. Money and other forms of compensation.

Explain that the purpose of your conversation is to not only gauge how the individual is feeling about the organization—a mini climate survey, of sorts—but to remind her of how much you value her and appreciate her contributions. Confirm that you want to encourage her to develop a realistic and customized development plan that will help her prepare for her next move in career progression—at your organization or elsewhere (talk about selfless leadership!). Likewise, ask for her input regarding what can be improved, made more efficient, reinvented, or recreated. Finally, ask how you can provide more support, structure, and direction to increase the team's overall confidence level and willingness to take smart risks. You will be amazed at the amount of goodwill that comes from good faith meetings like this.

- **Create an ambassador program or buddy system for new hires** in their first ninety days so that they can be paired up with more experienced employees who will keep an eye out for them. Likewise, build a structure of thirty-, sixty-, and ninety-day check-ins to gauge the pulse of how new hires are fitting in and feeling about their roles and the company.
- **Catch people being good.** Schools have adopted this model with excellent results. Rather than calling attention to mistakes and errant

behavior, focus on celebrating successes and acknowledging good deeds and achievements.

- **Allow your employees to get to know one another.** Celebrate birthdays, create an employee of the month award, and develop a system of on-the-spot awards or special-recognition award programs that reinforce your corporate values. Take time to allow your employees to get to know one another.

- **Make career guidance a part of your employee communication program.** And unlike performance reviews that only occur once a year, invite your employees to schedule time with their supervisors on a quarterly basis for guidance on how to build their resumes, add new skills, and prepare for greater responsibilities.

- **Consider enlisting the services of training organizations** like the American Management Association and others to develop your high-potential workers and reinvigorate them. One or two seminars per employee per year may add very little to your overhead budget but will give employees a one-day sabbatical and allow them to reflect on their careers and on finding unique ways of applying the theories learned in the classroom back to your organization.

- **Create a Quarterly Achievement Calendar.** Get everyone on your team on the same page in terms of developing an achievement mentality with the help of an Excel spreadsheet and a departmental share drive. Everyone on the team should have equal access to this spreadsheet that tracks key projects, upcoming events, and completion notes. Once a project is complete, simply move it from the "active" to the "completed" page. This way, very little will fall through the cracks, accomplishments will be easily codified for everyone to see, and achievements can be celebrated. Quantify the results in terms of increased revenue, decreased costs, or saved time in dollars or percentages. Instruct your team members to add these bullets to their resumes and self-evaluation forms when holding their performance review and goal-setting discussions with you later in the year.

- **Practice open-book management.** Instruct your team to research the competition on the Internet. Where does your company stand in terms of revenue, profit, and size relative to its nearest competitors? What needs to be done to move up one place on the competition chart, and how can

your department help the company get there? Research what others are saying about your organization on sites like Glassdoor.com, Zacks.com, Guide Star, Charity Navigator, Better Business Bureau, and the like.
- **Consider implementing an open house event** for families to come and see what their loved ones do, which creates a sense of pride and community.

With the proliferation of social media and Internet websites, it is easy to assign a small team for a few hours to see what is being said about your company and how you can address it. You will be developing a core of corporate futurists who will research trends and patterns in your specific business sector as well as growth projections for your industry. This is classic motivation: delegating fun, interesting, and enlightening work and then getting out of the way.

Remember, in growing and developing people, you are fostering the greatest *gifts* the workplace offers. You are shepherding your company's most critical assets every day when you walk into the office. The less-is-more approach to leadership mapped out above will hopefully go a long way in helping you enjoy this very special opportunity that you have to grow a business and improve people's careers at the same time. When you occasionally put your people's career needs above the needs of your day-to-day production demands, you will likely find that people will respond in kind:

- they will work harder to demonstrate their appreciation of your leadership;
- they will find new ways of reinventing their work in light of your department's or company's changing needs;
- and they will hold themselves accountable for the end result.

It all begins with appreciation and recognition for a job well done. Above all else, teach your employees thankfulness and gratitude, because all good things stem from those two values. You can give your company no greater benefit than the gift of a motivated, energized, and engaged workforce.

Ethics

Standards of conduct on and off the job should be aligned to your personal values, which at a minimum boil down to being responsible and accountable for your actions, respecting others (the old Golden Rule), being fair but firm, and being honest in what you do. These values will form the basis of who you are and how you deal with adversity, ambiguity, your personal actions, and your decision making. Let's take a deep dive into each of these areas:

- **Responsibility and Accountability.** Always stand up and take ownership for your actions and inactions. This is all about having a backbone and being accountable for your actions. Based on what I have observed during more than a decade in the private sector, I can tell you it is rare for a senior manager to stand up and admit he did something wrong. It takes personal courage to be responsible and accountable for your own actions.
- **Respect and Trust.** Respect yourself, the people around you, the resources entrusted to you, and those whom you lead and manage. Respecting others fosters an environment of trust, confidence, and excellence in your team that can be contagious. Coming from the military, the concept of trusting one another is second hand to all of us, and the bond of trust can never be broken. In that world, people die if they don't trust each other; in the corporate world, not trusting one another seems to be a way of life. Learn to deal with this new reality and protect yourself at all times!
- **Fairness.** Be fair in how you make judgment on others and on particular situations. Try to be as impartial and objective as you can. Learn what your superiors expect so that you can color between the lines. In the same respect, share your expectations of your employees with them so there is no confusion. Be fair, but be firm and stand by your convictions.
- **Honesty.** Simple—understand the truth and act in a truthful manner, and you will not have a problem. Would you do these same things if people were not looking? Sometimes the truth will hurt and sometimes people simply cannot handle the truth. My experience in the private sector is that many people cannot deal with cold, hard facts that are truthful. They prefer to hear what I call "corporate speak" that tap dances around an issue, leaving one wondering exactly what the truth actually is. Politicians are masters at this type of communication. It is a sort of art form in a sense, but not one I do well nor appreciate. Keep it honest.

11. THE FINAL TURN: TAKE THE HARDER RIGHT

In the end, it's not the number of years in life—it's the life in those years that counts.

—Unknown

We have come to the place in the road where you take that harder right to find your new true north. It is my hope that I left enough footprints here in *Boots* for you to find your way from life in the military to a joyous and successful life outside the gate.

As you reflect on all the material in this book, begin to pull together a plan for your next steps starting with your decision to leave the military—the transition process. Begin to think about how you will reinvent or rebrand yourself—the transformation process. And, with all the skills and knowledge you already bring to the table, coupled with the information and data gathered from this book, there is little doubt that your integration process back into civilian life will be much easier than you imagined.

To my brothers and sisters who have served or are now serving in the United States Armed Services—you know more than you think you do. Never forget that. Reach out, and I promise to do what I can to coach, teach, or mentor you during your journey outside the gate. Thank you for your service and sacrifice.

I will leave you for now with the same words I started with: when situations are difficult and you encounter rejection, you should take time, reflect, and pray. After more than twenty years in the US Army, I know myself, my capabilities and my gaps—just as you know yours. These words by the Honorable Dean Alfange sums up who we are very nicely:

> *I do not choose to be a common man. It is my right to be uncommon—if I can. I seek opportunity—not security. I do not wish to be a kept citizen, humbled and dulled by having the state look after me. I want to take the calculated risk; to dream and to build, to fail and to succeed. I refuse to barter incentive for a dole. I prefer the challenges of life to the guaranteed existence; the thrill of fulfillment to the stale calm of utopia. I will not trade freedom for beneficence nor my dignity for a handout. I will never cower before any master nor bend to any threat. It is my heritage to stand erect, proud and unafraid; to think and act for myself, enjoy the benefit of my creations, and to face the world boldly and say, this I have done. All this is what it means to be an American.*[10]

Keep the faith, brothers and sisters. It will not fail you.

APPENDICIES

APPENDIX 1: BUSINESS TERMINOLOGY AND ACRONYMS

Business Job Titles

CEO—Chief executive officer.

CFO—Chief financial officer.

CIO—Chief information officer.

CMO—Chief marketing officer (head of marketing).

COO—Chief operations officer.

CTO—Chief technology officer (responsible for the tech side).

General Business Terms

B2B—Business to business (companies that sell to other companies).

B2C—Business to consumer (companies that sell to individuals).

Back office—Refers to behind-the-scenes accounting, clerical functions, and other support areas that do not directly pertain to production of goods sold or sales of goods.

DBA—"Doing business as." A company may have two or more names—the legally incorporated name and a fictitious name. If the company decides to use a name other than the legally incorporated name and files the appropriate fictitious-name legal papers, the fictitious name is the DBA name.

LLC—Limited liability company (a legal entity in which the owners are not liable personally).

LLP—Limited liability partnership (a legal entity forming a professional partnership while protecting the partners from personal liability).

NDA—Non-Disclosure Agreement (a contract between two parties to secure the confidentiality of information).

SOHO—Small office/Home office (refers to small or home office environments).

TQM—Total Quality Management (a management strategy to raise awareness of the whole organization towards quality).

Accounting and Financial Terms

Accounts Receivable—Money owed to the business.

Accruals—Often businesses will divide their debt (money owed) over a period of time and show a debit (subtraction) from their income even though the debt will not actually be paid until sometime in the future.

Assets—All of the things the company owns (property, equipment, furnishings, computers, etc.) and all money owed to the company.

Balance Sheet—Financial statement that shows the company's assets, liabilities, and net worth (assets–liabilities=net worth).

Capital—The dollar amount that would go to the owners or stockholders if the business were to cease functioning, sell its assets, and pay off all debt.

Capital expenses—The cost of major purchases such as equipment, land, or buildings.

Cash flow—A measurement showing how much cash will be on hand at any given time, particularly when bills are due.

Cost of goods sold—The total cost of all raw materials, production, labor, and overhead to make the products sold by the company.

Depreciation—The cost of an item spread over the life of the item. A business may spread the cost of a major piece of equipment over the expected life of that equipment, say for five years, rather than show it as a single expense when it is purchased, even though it may or may not actually be paid for during the five-year period.

EBITDA—Earnings before interest, taxes, depreciation, and amortization (an indicator of a company's financial performance).

EPS—Earnings per share (the ratio between the profits of a company and the common shares).

ERP—Enterprise resource planning (a system that integrates all the data from an organization into a single location).

FIFO—First in, first out (used both in computer programs, accounting, and shipping; specifies that what comes first is handled first).

Fixed costs—The unchanging costs that are generally the same from month to month regardless of how much business the company does.

GAAP—Generally Accepted Accounting Principles (a framework used to carry out financial accounting within companies).

Income statement—A financial statement that provides the detail behind the profit, including all of the income the company had and all of the expenses it paid for a period of time.

IPO—Initial public offering (when a company first introduces its shares on the stock market).

LIFO—Last in, first out (used both in computer programs and accounting; specifies that what comes last is handled first).

NPV—Net present value (a method to valuate long-term investments or projects).

OEM—Original equipment manufacturer (a company that manufacturers equipment that will be rebranded and sold by other companies; sometimes refers to the reseller as well).

Operating expenses—Those expenses pertaining to the physical plant or offices the business owns, rents, or leases. These expenses include maintenance, utilities, and taxes for the land and buildings or other fixed assets.

OTC—Over the counter (trade of stocks or other derivatives directly between two persons).

P&L—Profit and loss (also called income statement; an accounting report used to outline how revenues are transformed into profits).

ROI—Return on investment (ratio of money earned relative to total money invested).

ROS—Return on sales (ratio of money earned relative to total sales).

TCO—Total cost of ownership (a method to estimate all the costs—direct and indirect—related to a project or purchase).

TSR—Total shareholder return (a method of valuation which takes into consideration both dividends and share price gains).

VC—Venture capital (a form of financing in which the owners give up part of the ownership).

Computer and Information Technology Terms

EDI—Electronic Data Interchange (a set of standards used to exchange data between different companies and organizations).

ICT—Information and communications technology (term used to encompass the fields related to IT and electronic communications).

ISV—Independent software vendor (a group of developers or companies specializing in the production of software for a certain niche).

SAAS—Software as a service (software or applications that are developed on the Web, which the users access via the Internet).

Sales Terms

MSRP—Manufacturer's suggested retail price (a recommendation made by a company in order to standardize the price of its products across different retailers).

POS—Point of sale (a checkout point in retail stores, or the hardware behind it).

RFP—Request for proposal (an invitation for suppliers to bid on a specific task or service).

APPENDIX 2: SAMPLE DOCUMENTS

Cover Letter.

Dear Recruiter:

Please accept my resume for the Senior Financial Analyst position posted on Monster.com. I am currently transitioning out of the military and into the private sector and I believe that I can make the same contribution to your organization that I have successfully made to the US Army, both at home and overseas, for the past two decades.

I've held progressively responsible accounting and finance positions in the army and I hold my bachelor's degree in business with a minor in accounting from the University of Denver. In my most recent role at Camp [NAME] in [LOCATION], I reported to the [TITLE] and oversaw a team of [#] [TITLES] who focused on [RESPONSIBITIES]. These areas appear to be a close match to the roles and responsibilities outlined in your job posting, which is why I'm very excited to submit my resume for consideration.

I've taken the liberty of researching your organization and reviewing your website prior to submitting my resume, and a smaller, manufacturing and distribution organization in the [INDUSTRY] field is exactly what I am looking for in terms of criteria for selecting my next employer. I hope that my resume demonstrates that I'm a long-term player and a very dedicated and loyal worker. Returning home again to the Raleigh-Durham area makes me realize how fortunate and proud I am of the place where I grew up.

It would be an honor to be considered for this role and the opportunity to join your team. I look forward to hearing from you and hope to have a chance to explain how my skills and accomplishments in the US Army can transfer into future benefits for XYZ Corporation. Thanks so much for your consideration!

Sincerely,
Paul Falcone

Resume: US Army Officer (courtesy of Bradley-Morris, Inc.).

Mark Guardino

123 Ashburton Grove / Austin, TX 78751 / H: (555) 555-5555 / C: (555) 121-1212
candidate@us.army.mil / candidate@hotmail.com

PROJECT MANAGER

Currently possesses a SECRET Security Clearance

Served as the lead Project Manager for more than $10 million worth of reconstruction efforts in Iraq

EDUCATION & TRAINING

Bachelor of Science in Information Systems Engineering – United States Military Academy, 2009

- NCAA Division I Athletics - Track and Field Letterman (holds school records in discus and javelin)

HIGHLIGHTS OF EXPERIENCE: U.S. Army – Field Artillery Officer

COMPANY EXECUTIVE / MAINTENANCE OFFICER   2013 - Present

2nd Brigade Combat Team, 1st Cavalry Division – Ft. Hood, TX and Baghdad, Iraq

Plan and coordinate operator and organizational level maintenance and services for 41 vehicles. Project Manager for the 2nd Brigade Infrastructure Coordination Element in charge of planning, coordinating and managing sanitation, road and school renovation projects in Baghdad, Iraq. Also serve as the Personal Security Detachment Officer in Charge and led more than 200 combat patrols in Central and South Baghdad.

- Due to the high degree of discipline within the security detachment, hand-selected to train an Infantry Division and Civil Affairs Company on combat patrolling and operations.
- Manage 40 civic reconstruction projects in Baghdad valued at nearly $5 million designed to significantly improve the lives of local Iraqi people.
- Awarded the Bronze Star Medal for meritorious service while assigned as the Infrastructure Coordination Element Project Manager and Combat Patrol Leader during Operation Iraqi Freedom.

PLATOON LEADER   2011 - 2012

2nd Brigade Combat Team, 1st Cavalry Division – Baghdad, Iraq

Led a 20-soldier Security Section for a personal security detail conducting combat missions in Iraq. Managed all aspects of training, readiness, deployment, and mission execution. Accountable for six vehicles and 32 weapons systems worth in excess of $2.5 million. Planned, prepared, and executed sanitation and school projects for the Joint Iraqi Infrastructure Coordination Element and District Governance.

- Developed the Combat Patrol Standard Operating Procedures for the Battalion used to train the other five patrolling elements within the organization.
- Served as the lead Project Manager for $10 million in project efforts that improved education for 22,500 Iraqi children and contributed to the implementation of a solid waste management program in the Karkh District.
- Enabled the reconstruction management and partnering efforts of over 268 projects with a total program value of over $33 million, an accomplishment achieved by no other unit or leader in the Division.
- Led Platoon on 120 combat patrols throughout Central and South Baghdad. Awarded the Combat Action Badge for actively engaging the enemy in Operations Iraqi Freedom (OIF) 6-8

BATTERY FIRE DIRECTION OFFICER   2009 – 2010

3rd Battalion, 82nd Field Artillery, 1st Cavalry Division – Ft. Hood, TX

Managed the training and operations of a 25-soldier Platoon Fire Direction Center to include the accurate and safe computation of firing data for the live firing of 93 lb. high explosive artillery shells and the training of Fire Direction Section.

- Earned the Top Fire Direction Section Award in the Battalion for the quickest and most accurate fire computation during Battalion Gunnery.
- Awarded the Army Achievement Medal for dedication and selfless service that contributed to the ultimate success of the Battalion.

Resume: US Navy Officer (courtesy of Bradley-Morris, Inc.).

Rob Hollocks
44 London Way, Austin Texas 78755
Fabregas@arsenal.com – FrankF10@yahoo.com – 512.333.3333

NAVY NUCLEAR TRAINED ENGINEERING PROFESSIONAL

Process Improvement and Quality Assurance Trained / Qualified Navy Nuclear Engineer

Detail-oriented, military-trained leader with nuclear engineering training and a proven track record in coordinating trades and completing projects on time and within budget. Solid foundation in mechanical, electrical, chemical and nuclear engineering coupled with demonstrated skill in leading large teams to achieve objectives. Experienced in international training and relations.

Education & Training

BS Physics and Astrophysics, University of Colorado at Boulder, Boulder, CO   2008
- 3.02 cumulative GPA. Graduated with Honors, Math & Physics tutor, Peer mentor.

Lean Six Sigma Black Belt Candidate, Acuity Institute, estimated completion: Spring 2011

Franklin Covey "Seven Habits of Highly Effective Leaders", Everett, WA   2012

Navy Prototype School, Charleston, SC   2009
- Hands-on study of design and operations of mechanical and electrical systems, including causality response in a nuclear power plant.

Navy Nuclear Power School, Charleston, SC   2008
- Graduate level training in Math, Thermodynamics, Chemistry, Physics, Electrical Engineering, Material Sciences, Reactor Dynamics, and Nuclear Plant Operations.

Highlights of Experience

Reactor Mechanical and Auxiliaries Division Officer / Quality Assurance Manager   2011 – Present

USS ABRAHAM LINCOLN, CVN 72, Everett, WA

Supervise, lead, train, and manage two divisions of over 60 nuclear trained mechanics and 20 enginemen in operation, maintenance, repair, and quality assurance of reactor support mechanical systems, four diesel generators, and reactor safety systems for two A4W nuclear reactors. As Quality Assurance Manager, create and verify procedures, validate maintenance practices, and provide jobsite supervision and post completion verification.
- Reduced the number of mechanical safety incidents by 50% after taking over Reactor Mechanical Division. Revamped the ship's carbon steel safety/inspection program, developed more effective training, and established a higher sense of ownership throughout the division, resulting in increased overall safety onboard.
- Safely executed over 2,000 maintenance/repair items, from identification through planning, execution and completion, during a seven-month repair cycle, allowing for early project completion.
- Commended by inspection teams for calm response and leadership during complex casualty situations. Selected to stand Propulsion Plant Watch Officer by the ship's Reactor officer during an intense Operational Reactor Safeguards Examination and Post Overhaul Reactor Safety Exam. Selected to stand General Quarters Propulsion Plant Watch Officer during heightened security/tactical situations.
- Qualified Nuclear Engineer by Naval Reactors (Department of Energy). Consistently sought out to run the most complex plant evolutions and train peers on aspects of plant operations.
- Qualified Propulsion Plant Watch Officer. Led teams of 22 nuclear trained mechanics, electricians, electronic technicians, chemists, and conventional mechanics in the safe operation, maintenance, and casualty response of a critical or shutdown nuclear reactor.

Supply Officer / Weapons Officer / Anti-Terrorism Officer   2009 - 2011

MHC CREW CONQUEST, Ingleside, TX

Managed all aspects of supply operations, including parts procurement and budget control. Developed and implemented training for the Weapons department. Coordinator for weapons and ordinance expended.
- Oversaw a $2M annual budget. Saved the U.S. Navy over $200,000 through extensive parts research and procurement.
- Qualified Officer of the Deck. Responsible for the safe navigation, routine operation, and tactical maneuvers of three Coastal Mine Hunters during day to day, mine hunting, and combat operations.
- Developed and executed a force protection training plan to ensure safe protection of U.S. Naval Vessels ship during a six month Arabian Gulf Deployment.
- Over a 5-month span, trained one Greek and two Egyptian crews on handling, operations, maintenance, and fire-fighting/damage control of 3 Costal Mine Hunter class ships while preparing them to be sold under Foreign Military Sales.
- Commended by inspection team and Commanding Officer for being responsible for passing the ship's Supply Management Inspection and Maintenance Management Inspection with zero inventory and zero financial discrepancies.

Personal Information

Rocky Mountain Rescue team member, 2004-2006.
- Participated in over 300 rescue missions per year.

Resume: Junior-Career Level (courtesy of Bradley-Morris, Inc.).

Joe Shelby
123 South Ardmore Street
Fort Smith, AR 75601
(501) 555-0000 Cell
Joe.Shelby33@gmail.com

EDUCATION

Duke University, Durham, North Carolina
Bachelor of Science in Political Science, minor in legal studies
Graduated: 05/11/2013

MILITARY AWARDS
Sea Service Deployment Ribbon (awarded twice); Global War on Terrorism Medal; Iraqi Campaign Medal (2-campaign star cluster); National Defense medal; Naval Unit Citation Ribbon; Marine Good Conduct Medal; Combat Action Ribbon; Letter of Appreciation; Expert Rifleman Badge (3rd Award); Pistol Sharp Shooter Badge.

EMPLOYMENT HISTORY

Public Defenders Office- Legal Intern   01/2013-04/2013
Cumberland County Court House, Fayetteville, NC
      Observed and took part in decision making operations during actual court trials, and participated in pre-trail interviews of clients and helped to maintain and organize court documents
      Conducted all other expected duties in an office environment

Behavioral Health Clinic- Access Coordinator   06/2012-12/2012
Cape Fear Medical Center, Fayetteville NC
      Insured that all patients had correctly filled all proper legal documentation
      Notarized involuntary committed patients
      Worked with little or no supervision and handled sensitive information in a mature and professional manner

United States Marine Corps- 0311, Infantry Rifleman   01/2006-01/2010
1st Battalion 3rd Marines, Bravo Company
MCHB at Kaneohe Bay, HI
      Conducted two combat deployments to Iraq
      Deployed as SAW (M249) gunner, Team Leader, and Acting Squad Leader
      Training NCO for 10 months
      Member of the Company Level Intelligence Team for 6 months

SKILLS & QUALIFICATIONS

      Proficient in Microsoft Office tools (Word, PowerPoint, Outlook, and Excel)
      Effective at academic and legal research
      NC Cumberland County Notary: commission expires 09/10/2017
      Secret Security Clearance expires February 2016
      Limited understanding of French and Arabic
      Trained in CQB, MOUT, Desert Operation, Sensitive Material Gathering

ORGANIZATIONS

Duke University Political Science Association-Founder and President from 01/2012 to 05/2013
Pi Kappa Alpha- Founding Father of Colony, Alumni Chairman, and Interview Captain from 01/2012 to 05/2013
Pi Alpha Delta International Legal Fraternity- Active member from Fall 2011 to Spring 2013

Thank You Note

Dear John,

I wanted to drop you a quick note to thank you for taking time out of your busy schedule to interview me for the customer-service supervisor role at your call center. As I shared with you, our meeting was one of the first interviews I've participated in since transitioning out of the military and into the private sector, and I really appreciate how welcome you made me feel, so thank you again for your kindness.

As we discussed, I have a lot of deep-dive experience in terms of leading teams of eight to twelve people in their daily activities. I pride myself on my open communication style and ability to build teams that feel self-motivated and engaged in their work. I've always found that when a strong sense of teamwork is present, there is a spirit of light-heartedness and fun in the office: no drama or tension or feeling as if people have to walk on eggshells. Likewise, whenever people-related situations became problematic, I have been swift to respond in a firm but gentle and respectful manner. And while I don't have previous experience supervising a unionized team, I believe that people respect competency and appreciate an inclusive work environment. I suspect that my approach to leadership will therefore work just as well in a union shop, despite its being a bit more formal and structured. And no worries—I'll read the collective bargaining agreement from front to back on my first day!

Again, I would consider myself very fortunate to be considered further in the interview and selection process with XYZ Company. I'm very impressed by your organization's success, your future plans for growth, and by the talent at the helm. I'm also feeling very encouraged by our meeting. Thank you again for taking so much time to get to know me better, and I'll look forward to hearing from you again soon.

All the best,
Paul

APPENDIX 3: HELPFUL WEBSITES

Business Publications and Resources

Bloomberg Businessweek magazine—www.Businessweek.com

Business Insider—www.BusinessInsider.com

Fast Company—www.FastCompany.com

Forbes magazine—www.Forbes.com

Fortune magazine—
www.Money.CNN.com/magazines/Fortune

Inc. magazine—www.Inc.com

Standard & Poors—www.StandardandPoors.com

Corporate Culture and Salary Ranges

CafePharma.com (pharmaceutical industry)

GlassDoor.com

Indeed.com

JobStar Central: Salary Information—
JobStar.org/tools/salary/index.cfm

MyPlan.com

Payscale.com

Salary.com

SalaryExpert.com

Yelp.com

Education and Training

The GI Bill—www.GIBill.va.gov

Job Search—General

Career Builder—www.CareerBuilder.com

www.CollegeRecruiter.com

www.GlassDoor.com

Hire Disability Solutions—Hireds.com

www.Hound.com

Indeed—www.Indeed.com

Jobfox—www.JobFox.com

www.Monster.com

Net-Temps—www.Net-Temps.com

O*NET OnLine—ONetOnline.org

Simply Hired—www.SimplyHired.com

us.jobs

Job Search—Specialty

AARP—www.AARP.com

FlexJobs—www.FlexJobs.com

US Customs and Border Protection—www.cbpcareers.com

USAJOBS—www.USAJobs.gov

Working Mother magazine—www.WorkingMother.com

Job Search—Veteran Specific

Bureau of Labor Statistics—www.bls.gov

G.I. Jobs—www.GIJobs.com

Hire a Hero—www.HireAHero.org

www.HireVeterans.com

Military Friendly—www.MilitaryFriendly.com

www.MilitaryHire.com

Military Skills Translators—
www.VetSuccess.va.gov/public/military_skills_translators.html

Military Times—www.MilitaryTimes.com

MilitaryVetJobs—MilitaryVetJobs.jobs.careercast.com

The Mission Continues—MissionContinues.org

Monster Veteran Employment Center—
www.Military.com/veteran-jobs

My Next Move: For Veterans—www.MyNextMove.org/Vets

VetCentral—VetCentral.us.jobs

Resume Writing (including Cover Letters and Thank You Notes)

www.SusanIreland.com

Specialty Recruiters

www.OrionInternational.com

www.LucasGroup.com

www.BradleyMorris.com

Veterans Services

County Veterans Service Officers (CVSOs) by state—
http://www.longtermcarelink.net/ref_list_state_county_veterans_service_officers.htm

Feds Hire Vets—fedshirevets.gov

Joining Forces—www.WhiteHouse.gov/JoiningForces

VA offices by state—http://www.va.gov/statedva.htm

Veterans Opportunity to Work—
www.Benefits.VA.gov/VOW

Veterans Employment and Training Service—
www.DOL.gov/Vets

NOTES

Works by Paul Falcone

A portion of the material presented in this book was previously published in slightly different form and is used in this text by permission of the author.

Paul Falcone, *96 Great Interview Questions to Ask Before You Hire*, 2nd ed. (New York: AMACOM, 2009).

———, "College Grads: Here's a Crystal Ball to Your Future Career," PaulFalconeHR, Accessed August 2013, http://www.paulfalconehr.com/2013/07/28/college-grads-heres-a-crystal-ball-to-your-future-career2/.

———. *The Hiring and Firing Question and Answer Book* (New York: AMACOM, 2002).

Epigraphs

Front Matter

"He Has Achieved Success Who Has Lived Well, Laughed Often and Loved Much," Quote Investigator, posted June 26, 2012, accessed November 12, 2013, http://quoteinvestigator.com/2012/06/26/define-success/.

Transition

"Quotation #1861 from Laura Moncur's Motivational Quotations," The Quotations Page, Accessed September 23, 2013, http://www.quotationspage.com/quote/1861.html.

Transformation

Ziglar, Accessed November 12, 2013, http://www.ziglar.com/quotes/what-you-get-achieving-your-goals-not.

"Alex Haley. Biography," Bio. True Story, Accessed November 12, 2013, http://www.biography.com/people/alex-haley-39420.

Integration

Stephen R. Covey, A. Roger Merrill, and Rebecca R. Merrill, *First Things First* (New York: Simon & Schuster, 1994), 48.

"Respectfully Quoted: A Dictionary of Quotations. 1989," Bartleby.com, Accessed November 12, 2013, http://www.bartleby.com/73/609.html.

George Bernard Shaw, Back to Methuselah: A Metabiological Pentateuch (1921), http://www.gutenberg.org/files/13084/13084-8.txt.

Numbered Notes

1. "Redback One Training Philosophy," Redback One Combat Training Systems, posted May 23, 2013, accessed September 17, 2013, http://www.redbackone.com/article.cfm?newsid=41.

2. Dr. John Sullivan, "Why You Can't Get A Job . . . Recruiting Explained By the Numbers," ERE.net, May 20, 2013, accessed September 23, 2013, http://www.ere.net/2013/05/20/why-you-cant-get-a-job-recruiting-explained-by-the-numbers/.

3. James B. Reed, "GI Jobs," State Legislatures, July/August 2013, 42–45.

4. Jill Gilbert Welytok, JD, CPA, and Daniel S. Welytok, JD, LLM, Nonprofit Law & Governance for Dummies (Hoboken: Wiley, 2007), 9–10.

5. Martin Luther King Jr., "I Have a Dream . . . " (speech, March on Washington, Washington, DC, 1963), http://www.archives.gov/press/exhibits/dream-speech.pdf.

6. "401(k) Resource Guide - Plan Participants - Limitation on Elective Deferrals," IRS, Accessed October 14, 2013, http://www.irs.gov/

Retirement-Plans/Plan-Participant,-Employee/401(k)-Resource-Guide---Plan-Participants---Limitation-on-Elective-Deferrals.

7. Colin Powell, "A Leadership Primer" (presentation), Blaisdell Dot Com, Accessed February 13, 2006, http://www.blaisdell.com/powell/.

8. Donald Knauss, "Leadership Makes the Difference" (lecture, Coca-Cola North America, Atlanta, GA, November 10, 2005).

9. Neal Donald Walsch, The Complete Conversation with God: An Uncommon Dialog (Charlottesville, VA: Hampton Roads Publishing Company, Inc., 2005), 148–153.

10. "Respectfully Quoted: A Dictionary of Quotations. 1989," Bartleby.com, Accessed November 12, 2013, http://www.bartleby.com/73/71.html.

AUTHOR BIOGRAPHIES

JOHN W. PHILLIPS has had a distinguished career in both military and civilian service. John is a retired US Army field artillery officer and comptroller with over twenty years of service in Corps Artillery, Division Artillery, Army Headquarters, and Forces Command—the largest command and the generating force provider for combatant commanders, at home and abroad. He has served in Europe as well as throughout the Middle East and the United States. He has been awarded the Legion of Merit, Meritorious Service Medal, and the Air Assault Badge, among other awards and decorations.

John has worked in corporate finance, program and project management, military sales, and product supply for The Coca-Cola Company and Coca-Cola Refreshments located in Atlanta, Georgia. He spends his spare time fly fishing in the mountains of North Georgia, sailing with his wife in the British Virgin Islands, or camping, rafting, canoeing, and fishing out West. John holds a BS in Finance from the University of Central Florida and a MBA from Syracuse University. He lives in the north Georgia mountains with his wife.

PAUL FALCONE is a human resources executive and has held senior-level positions with Nickelodeon, Paramount Pictures, and Time Warner. He is the author of several best-selling books published by the American Management Association (AMACOM Books) as well as the Society for Human Resource Management (SHRM), including *101 Sample Write-Ups for Documenting Employee Performance Problems*, *101 Tough Conversations to Have with Employees*, *96 Great Interview Questions to Ask Before You Hire*, *2600 Phrases for Effective Performance Reviews*, and *2600 Phrases for Setting Effective Performance Goals*. Paul is a long-term contributor to *HR Magazine* and a faculty member in the UCLA Extension School of Business and Management. His newest book, *The Performance Appraisal Toolkit: Redesigning Your Performance Review Template to Drive Individual and Organizational Change*, was released in 2013. Paul holds bachelors and masters degrees from UCLA.

Notes

Notes

Notes